Tableau Dashboard Cookbook

Over 40 recipes for designing professional dashboards by implementing data visualization principles

Jen Stirrup

BIRMINGHAM - MUMBAI

Tableau Dashboard Cookbook

First published: May 2014

Production reference: 2151215

Published by Packt Publishing Ltd.
Livery Place
35 Livery Street
Birmingham B3 2PB, UK.

ISBN 978-1-78217-790-6

www.packtpub.com

Cover Image by Aniket Sawant (aniket_sawant_photography@hotmail.com)

Credits

Author

Jen Stirrup

Reviewers

Shweta Savale

Darwin Witt

Commissioning Editor

Edward Gordon

Acquisition Editor

Rebecca Youé

Content Development Editor

Arun Nadar

Technical Editor

Pankaj Kadam

Copy Editors

Puja Lalwani

Laxmi Subramanian

Project Coordinator

Neha Bhatnagar

Proofreader

Safis Editing

Indexer

Rekha Nair

Production Coordinator

Manu Joseph

Cover Work

Manu Joseph

About the Author

Jen Stirrup is an award-winning and internationally recognized business intelligence and data visualization expert, author, data strategist, and technical community advocate. She has been honored repeatedly, along with receiving peer recognition, as a Microsoft Most Valuable Professional (MVP) in SQL Server. She is one of the top 100 most globally influential tweeters on big data topics. Jen has nearly 20 years of experience in delivering business intelligence and data visualization projects for companies of various sizes across the world.

Acknowledgments

I want to thank the most important person in my life—my son, Matthew. I love him to the moon and back... a million times! I dedicate this book to him.

I have been inspired by the genius of other people. In the words of Sir Isaac Newton, "I stand on the shoulders of giants." My gratitude to Stephen Few, Edward Tufte, Raj M. Ratwani, and Ben Schneiderman. The data communities of Microsoft and Tableau have boundless enthusiasm and a sense of fun, which has helped me keep going. I'd like to thank the great folks at Tableau, especially Andy Cotgreave and Pat Hanrahan.

I would also like to thank the following people for their support and love—I appreciate it more than I can say—Toby, Gill, and Pippa Smith; Charlie and Joe Withey; my parents; my smart brother, Andrew; my wonderful sister-in-law, Karen; and their children, Hannah and Jamie. I am blessed to have them in my life.

I'd also like to remember my grandfather, Sam Hannah, and my great uncle, James Hannah. They inspired me to read books and didn't hesitate to introduce me, a little girl, into the world of technology while I was growing up. They taught me Morse code, gave me my first Sinclair ZX81 computer, and taught me about radio communications, radar, and mathematics. They never said that this wasn't for girls, and most of all, they made it fun. If you're reading this, please be that person for a child in your life, and maybe one day you'll live on through a book that they write too.

I'd also like to thank the "SQLFamily"—those in the global SQL Server and Microsoft Data Platform community—and of course the "softies" themselves. They are simply amazing, amazing people. They brighten my days and nights more than they know. Thank you!

I would like to thank everyone at Packt Publishing for their patience and hard work in helping me make this happen, Arun in particular. I would also like to thank the reviewers for their diligence, careful questions, and help in shaping this book.

About the Reviewers

Shweta Savale is the cofounding partner and head of client engagements at Syvylyze Analytics LLP, an analytic services company that provides business insights using data visualization. An information technology engineering graduate by qualification, Shweta was instrumental in pioneering Tableau's proliferation and success within India during her prior experience of working with a Tableau partner.

Over the years, she has engaged extensively with some of the leading global and Indian multinationals to help them effectively implement visual analytics using Tableau. Additionally, she has trained over 1,200 Tableau practitioners across more than 80 companies over the course of her career.

In 2014, Shweta cofounded Syvylyze Analytics (www.syvylyze.com), where she spearheads a core Tableau-centric team focused on delivering services that provide business insights using the visual analytic capabilities of Tableau. She says, "Tableau allows us to build dynamic visualizations and analytics at the speed of thought, drastically reducing the turnaround time for interactive dashboard development, making insights actionable for our clients when they are still timely and relevant."

Shweta is currently authoring another book about Tableau, which will be published by Packt Publishing. It is aimed at being a ready reckoner for beginners and advanced users alike.

Darwin Witt is a user experience designer and user researcher based in Seattle, Washington, USA. Having earned a bachelor's degree in computer science from the University of Alabama and a master's degree in human-centered design and engineering from the University of Washington, he works on a multitude of projects dealing with medium- and large-scale productivity software. His concerns lie both with understanding the needs of business intelligence and in simplifying and standardizing the process to help make everyone's work a little easier. He has previously worked with Packt Publishing on a webinar series, teaching the basics of Axure as a prototyping tool.

www.PacktPub.com

Support files, eBooks, discount offers, and more

For support files and downloads related to your book, please visit www.PacktPub.com.

Did you know that Packt offers eBook versions of every book published, with PDF and ePub files available? You can upgrade to the eBook version at www.PacktPub.com and as a print book customer, you are entitled to a discount on the eBook copy. Get in touch with us at service@packtpub.com for more details.

At www.PacktPub.com, you can also read a collection of free technical articles, sign up for a range of free newsletters and receive exclusive discounts and offers on Packt books and eBooks.

https://www2.packtpub.com/books/subscription/packtlib

Do you need instant solutions to your IT questions? PacktLib is Packt's online digital book library. Here, you can search, access, and read Packt's entire library of books.

Why subscribe?

- Fully searchable across every book published by Packt
- Copy and paste, print, and bookmark content
- On demand and accessible via a web browser

Free access for Packt account holders

If you have an account with Packt at www.PacktPub.com, you can use this to access PacktLib today and view 9 entirely free books. Simply use your login credentials for immediate access.

Instant updates on new Packt books

Get notified! Find out when new books are published by following @PacktEnterprise on Twitter or the *Packt Enterprise* Facebook page.

Table of Contents

Preface

Tableau Dashboard Cookbook is an introduction to the theory and practice of delivering dashboards using Tableau. The recipes take you through a step-by-step process of creating the building blocks of a dashboard and then proceed towards the design and principles of putting the dashboard items together. This book also covers certain features of Tableau, such as calculations, which are used to drive the dashboard in order to make it relevant to the business user. The book will also teach you how to use key advanced string functions to play with data and images. Finally, this book will help you consider what to do next with your dashboard, whether it's on a server or in collaboration with other tools.

What this book covers

Chapter 1, A Short Dash to Dashboarding!, introduces you to the Tableau interface while ensuring that you are producing dashboards quickly.

Chapter 2, Summarizing Your Data for Dashboards, teaches you how to summarize data as a way of conveying key messages on your dashboards for top-down analysis. It also introduces you to calculations with a particular focus on using dates for analysis and comparison.

Chapter 3, Interacting with Data for Dashboards, guides you through to the next stage after summarizing your data, interacting with your data, and providing more details where appropriate to enhance the story on the dashboard.

Chapter 4, Using Dashboards to Get Results, presents ways to make your dashboards actionable for the dashboard viewer. We will look at a guided analysis in Tableau as a way of facilitating a structured investigation of data. We will also research the ways of enhancing your data via mashups and external data sources, all in your dashboard.

Chapter 5, Putting the Dash into Dashboards, focuses on graphically presenting the data with Tableau dashboards in mind. We will look at sparklines, KPIs, small multiples, and maps, to name a few.

Chapter 6, Making Dashboards Relevant, guides you through the ways in which you can make the dashboards relevant to your organization. We will look at theming and adding more details to the dashboard.

Chapter 7, Visual Best Practices, provides examples of the more advanced features of Tableau, such as calculations. The recipe exercises are underpinned by an explanation of the visual best practices as we proceed through the chapter.

Chapter 8, Tell the World! Share Your Dashboards, shows different ways to share your dashboards with different audiences, both inside and outside your organization.

What you need for this book

You need the following in order to work with Tableau:

- Tableau Version 8.2
- Windows Live login ID and password
- Microsoft Excel
- Internet access

Who this book is for

If you are a business user or a developer who wants to create Tableau dashboards quickly and easily while learning about data visualization theory and techniques as you go along, then this book is for you. It applies the practice and theory of data visualization to dashboards while helping you to deliver effective Tableau dashboards.

Conventions

In this book, you will find a number of styles of text that distinguish between different kinds of information. Here are some examples of these styles, and an explanation of their meaning.

Code words in text, database table names, folder names, filenames, file extensions, pathnames, dummy URLs, user input, and Twitter handles are shown as follows: "On Twitter, `#dataviz` is a well-used hashtag."

A block of code is set as follows:

```
IF ( SUM([SalesAmount]) - WINDOW_AVG(SUM([SalesAmount]), First(),
Last() ) < 0 )
Then 'Below Average'
Else 'Above or Equal To Average'
END
```

New terms and **important words** are shown in bold. Words that you see on the screen, in menus or dialog boxes for example, appear in the text like this: "At the bottom of the entry page, you can see a section called **Sample Workbooks** that contains some examples."

> Warnings or important notes appear in a box like this.

> Tips and tricks appear like this.

Reader feedback

Feedback from our readers is always welcome. Let us know what you think about this book—what you liked or may have disliked. Reader feedback is important for us to develop titles that you really get the most out of.

To send us general feedback, simply send an e-mail to feedback@packtpub.com, and mention the book title via the subject of your message.

If there is a topic that you have expertise in and you are interested in either writing or contributing to a book, see our author guide on www.packtpub.com/authors.

Customer support

Now that you are the proud owner of a Packt book, we have a number of things to help you to get the most from your purchase.

Downloading the example code

You can download the example code files for all Packt books you have purchased from your account at http://www.packtpub.com. If you purchased this book elsewhere, you can visit http://www.packtpub.com/support and register to have the files e-mailed directly to you.

Errata

Although we have taken every care to ensure the accuracy of our content, mistakes do happen. If you find a mistake in one of our books—maybe a mistake in the text or the code—we would be grateful if you would report this to us. By doing so, you can save other readers from frustration and help us improve subsequent versions of this book. If you find any errata, please report them by visiting http://www.packtpub.com/submit-errata, selecting your book, clicking on the **errata submission form** link, and entering the details of your errata. Once your errata are verified, your submission will be accepted and the errata will be uploaded on our website, or added to any list of existing errata, under the Errata section of that title. Any existing errata can be viewed by selecting your title from http://www.packtpub.com/support.

Piracy

Piracy of copyright material on the Internet is an ongoing problem across all media. At Packt, we take the protection of our copyright and licenses very seriously. If you come across any illegal copies of our works, in any form, on the Internet, please provide us with the location address or website name immediately so that we can pursue a remedy.

Please contact us at copyright@packtpub.com with a link to the suspected pirated material.

We appreciate your help in protecting our authors, and our ability to bring you valuable content.

Questions

You can contact us at questions@packtpub.com if you are having a problem with any aspect of the book, and we will do our best to address it.

1
A Short Dash to Dashboarding!

In this chapter, we will cover the following recipes:

- ▸ Preparing for your first dashboard
- ▸ Showing the power of data visualization
- ▸ Connecting to data sources
- ▸ Introducing the Tableau interface
- ▸ Interacting with your first data visualization
- ▸ Sharing your visualization with the world

Introduction

This chapter starts with you being a Tableau beginner, then quickly takes you forward to creating your own visualizations, and explains how to interact with the Tableau sample dashboards—how to find, open, and interact with them.

We can create visualizations by using Tableau in order to produce meaningful dashboards that communicate clearly.

Tableau has a suite of products, which are briefly described here.

Tableau Desktop is an application, which is used by individual data artists, analysts, and people who create data visualizations. It resides on the desktop, and is aimed at individual use. It can use public data, or data that is specific to the enterprise or the individual.

For more collaborative use, organizations may use Tableau Desktop along with Tableau Server, which is an enterprise solution aimed at collaboration of data visualizations. The data can be taken from anywhere, and shared within the organization via desktop or mobile browsers. Tableau Server is an on-premise solution.

Tableau Online is a hosted version of Tableau Server. It is scalable and secure, and suitable for a range of use cases, from start-ups who need to share data fast, to large global organizations who need the ability to scale.

Tableau Public is a free, online version of tableau, which is aimed at community bloggers and people who create data visualizations to share online. The data and workbooks are completely public and available.

In this book, we will focus on Tableau Desktop, because it is a very common usage of Tableau. Smaller organizations may not have Tableau Server, and organizations who cannot place their data in the cloud will not be able to use Tableau Online. Tableau Desktop is the lowest common denominator, and the book is aimed at this particular part of the suite of Tableau's family of software.

The six recipes in this chapter will explain how we can get up to speed with Tableau very quickly in order to produce dashboards that facilitate and expedite the decision making process for strategic decision makers and operational team members within your organization.

[For this book, we will be using version 8.2 to work with Tableau.]

Preparing for your first dashboard

Take a look at the following definition of dashboard, taken from the *Intelligent Enterprise* magazine's March 2004 issue:

> *A dashboard is a visual display of the most important information needed to achieve one or more objectives; consolidated and arranged on a single screen so the information can be monitored at a glance.*
>
> – Stephen Few

For an enterprise, a dashboard is a visual tool to help team members throughout the ranks of the organization to track, monitor, and analyze the information about the organization in order to make decisions to support its current and future prosperity. In this recipe, we will interact with Tableau's sample dashboards, which are constructed from worksheets. People often learn by example, and this is a straightforward way of inspiring you with dashboard samples while also learning about Tableau.

What do dashboards help you to do?

- ▶ **Evaluate**: Dashboards answer questions such as, "Have the goals and objectives been met?", "Are we on track?", and so on
- ▶ **Reveal**: Dashboards help you view and digest information very quickly, which means you have more time for strategic planning.
- ▶ **Communicate**: Using a visual tool can help to get the message across in a common format and create an impact.
- ▶ **Certainty**: Dashboards help you to have confidence in your insights.

Dashboards help key team members to gain insights and discern the health of the organization very quickly. Tracking, monitoring, and analyzing the organization's data is an essential part of making accurate decisions.

Tableau provides a number of example dashboards, both online and as part of the Tableau Desktop installation. We will find, open, and interact with sample Tableau dashboards.

We can also use the example dashboards as a basis to make our own dashboards. They can form a source of inspiration to make your own compelling visualizations. For the purpose of this recipe, we will focus on the sample Sales workbook.

A key feature of dashboards is their interactivity. There are different types of dashboards, and some references are included at the end of this recipe. Dashboards are not simply a set of reports on a page; they should tell a story about the business when they are put together. They should answer a clear business question. In order to facilitate the decision-making process, interactivity is an important part of assisting the decision-maker to get to the heart of the analysis as quickly as possible.

Fortunately, it is straightforward to interact with a dashboard that has been implemented in Tableau. This dashboard looks at sales commission models, based on quota, commission models, and base salary.

How to do it...

We will perform the following steps to see how we can interact with a dashboard:

1. Open up the Tableau Desktop, and you can see the **Getting Started** page. The following screenshot is an example:

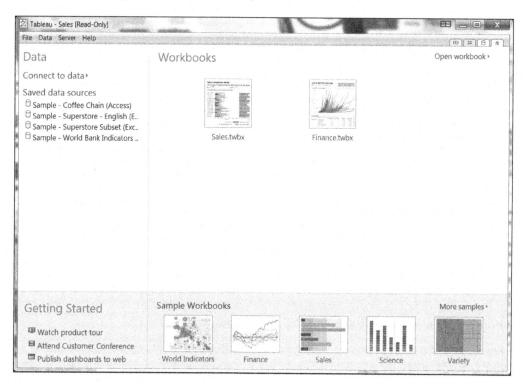

2. At the bottom of the entry page, you can see a section called **Sample Workbooks** that contains some examples. Let's take a look at the **Sales** dashboard. If you double-click on the **Sales** example, it will open and you will see the sample **Sales** dashboard, as shown in the following screenshot:

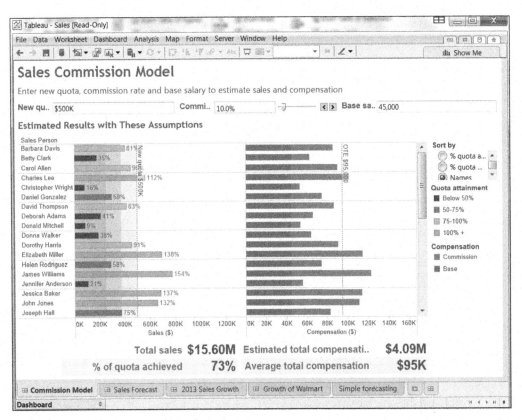

3. A worksheet is like a tab in Excel; it is a data visualization tool on its own. A workbook, on the other hand, is a collection of worksheets. In Tableau, a dashboard allows you to combine and manipulate the worksheets together. Let's interact with this dashboard straightaway using the **Sales** dashboard sample that has been provided by Tableau. On the right-hand side of the dashboard, you can see a box called **Sort by**. You can see an example of this in the following screenshot, where the relevant section has been highlighted with a box:

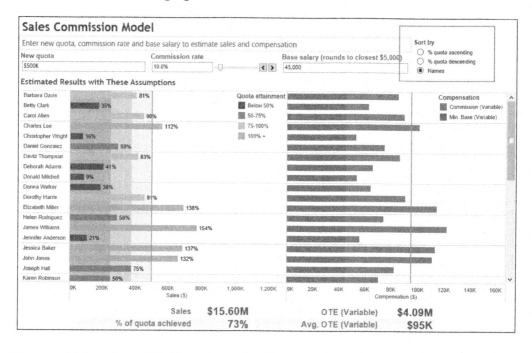

When you click on the middle item, denoted as **% quota descending**, you can see that the horizontal bar charts in the main area of the dashboard change very quickly in response to the user interaction. The dashboard now looks quite different from the previous Tableau example, where the bars were sorted by **Names**. The rapidity of the change means that decision makers can *think as they click* in order to focus on their analysis.

There are a number of different ways in which Tableau can offer useful interactivity for dashboards. For example, we can include sliders, filtering by color, moving from dashboard to dashboard, radio buttons, drop-down lists, and timelines. For example, another interesting feature is that users can enter values into parameters in order to see the impact of their activity. A parameter is a dynamic value that responds to user input. In this example, we use it to filter the data by replacing constant values in calculations.

We use the following steps to view the interactivity:

1. Let's see the impact of interactivity on the performance information given by the dashboard. In the **Sales** dashboard, increase the **New quota** level to $1,000,000.

2. Next, increase the value in the **Commission rate** textbox to **15.0%** by moving the slider to the right.

3. Decrease the base salary to $40,000 by inserting this value in the **Base salary** textbox. Note that the estimated results are now quite different. You can see from the following screenshot that the number of people making the sales target decreases, and the chart now shows a significant increase in the number of people nearing their target or missing it altogether:

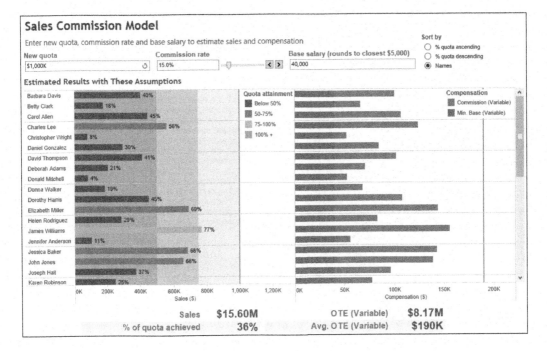

4. In the previous screenshot, note that the colors of the **Estimated Results with These Assumptions** bars have changed so that most of them now show red or yellow. All but two of the green bars have disappeared. This gives a visual cue that the estimated results have changed considerably for the worse after we made changes to the filter. We can also see this due to the presence of the target line, which shows whether the individual met his/her target or not. The following screenshot depicts this, with the target line identified by the tooltip quota reading **New Quote = $1,000K** and highlighted in the box:

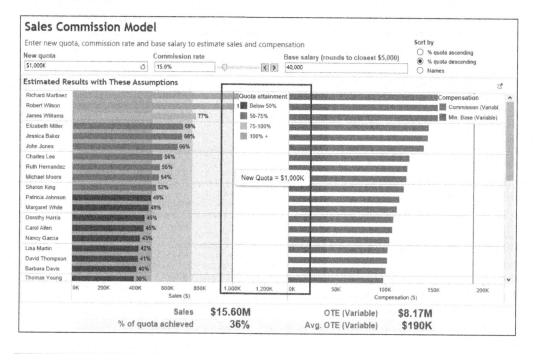

How it works...

Tableau gives you a series of sample dashboards as part of the installation. You can also see more samples online. Some samples are provided by Tableau team members, and you can also visit the Tableau website for samples submitted by keen data visualization fans from around the world. These samples can help to inspire your own work.

In this topic, we compared the changes on a dashboard in order to see how Tableau responded to changes. We noted that the color has changed along with the values. The dashboard provides quick feedback that the values do not change favorably for the new quotes, commissions, and base salary. When decision makers are interacting with dashboards, they are expecting quick-as-a-flash responsiveness from the dashboard, and the sample Tableau dashboards meet this expectation well.

See also

Tableau offers a number of sample dashboards on its website, and it is worthwhile to check the site for ideas and brainstorming for your own dashboards. Take a look at `www.tableausoftware.com` for examples. If you are interested in the dashboard theory in general, then you can look at the following references:

- *Dashboard Confusion, Stephen Few, Intelligent Enterprise, 2004*
- *5 Best Practices for Creating Effective Dashboards* by *Tableau Software* (`http://www.tableausoftware.com/learn/whitepapers/5-best-practices-for-effective-dashboards`)

Showing the power of data visualization

Dashboards rely on the power of visualization in order to let people see the message of the data, in order to make effective decisions. How can you show the power of a dashboard when compared to a crosstab table?

In this recipe, we will see how data visualization can have more impact than a straightforward crosstab. We will make a crosstab table in Tableau, and then turn it into a data visualization to see the impact in action. Understanding your data is an essential part of data visualization, regardless of the technology you are using. Tableau can help you to understand your data by automatically distinguishing between measures and dimensions. How do you know the difference? Look at the title of a report or dashboard. For example, if a dashboard is called `Sales by Country`, then anything that comes after the word `by` is a dimension and the item being counted is a measure. Dimensions and measures are explained as follows:

- **Dimensions**: This describes the data. For example, these may include business constructs such as customer, geography, date, and product.
- **Measures**: These are usually numbers. They may also be known as metrics. For example, %quota, sales amount, commission rate, tax amount, and product cost.

You can usually tell the dimensions and measures in the title of the report. For example, if you take a title, such as Sales by Region, then the measure comes before the word `by`, and the dimension comes after the word `by`.

In this recipe, we will look at the difference between a plain table and a graphical representation of the data. While tables are data visualizations in themselves, Tableau's power lies in its ability to visualize data graphically and quickly. This recipe will demonstrate the ease of going from a table to a picture of the data. We will create a map, and the color intensity of the map coloring reflects the value. To do this, we introduce the Show Me button, which is Tableau's way of making data visualization simple and quick, so that the emphasis is on producing insights rather than focusing on creating the Tableau visualization.

Tableau distinguishes between worksheets and dashboards. Worksheets are analogous to worksheets in Excel, and they contain a single data visualization. Implemented in Tableau, dashboards are a canvas that contain one or more worksheets, which means they can display more than one visualization at a time.

In Tableau, there are many different ways to connect data. In this topic, we will just look at the simplest method, which is to copy and paste the data directly into the Tableau workbook.

Getting ready

Let's start by opening up Tableau to get ready for your first visualization.

We will need to get some data. To obtain some sample, download the `UNICEF Report Card` spreadsheet from the following link: `http://bit.ly/ JenStirrupOfficialTableauBookCode`.

It will have the following columns:

- `Country`
- `Average ranking position (for all 6 dimensions)`
- `Material well-being`
- `Health and Safety`
- `Educational well-being`
- `Family and peer relationships`
- `Behaviours and risks`
- `Subjective well-being`

How to do it...

1. In Tableau, click on **File** in the top left-hand corner and click on **New**. You can see this in the following screenshot:

2. When you've clicked on **New**, you will get a blank Tableau workbook. This is shown in the following screenshot:

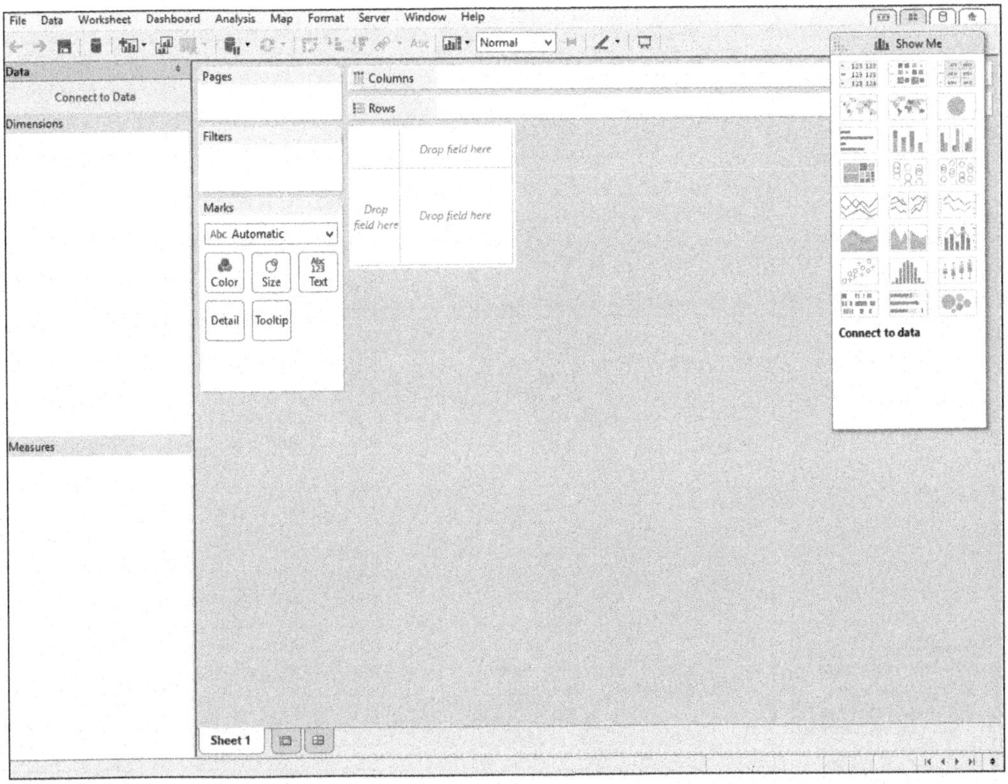

3. Let's insert our downloaded data. To do this, go to the Excel spreadsheet and select all of the data by pressing *Ctrl + A*.

4. Next, copy the data by pressing *Ctrl + C*.

5. Once you have done this, go to Tableau and press *Ctrl + V* to paste it. Here is an example of the data when it is pasted into Tableau:

The following points describe the different panels in Tableau:

▸ **Data**: This holds the measures, dimensions, and calculations in the data. You can see this panel, which is situated under the **File** menu option; it is the long vertical panel found on the left-hand side of Tableau.

- ▸ **Shelf**: This is a place where you drag fields. There are a number of shelves: the **Column** and **Row** shelves, the **Pages** shelf, the **Filters** shelf and the **Marks** shelf.

- ▸ **The Tableau canvas view**: This shows the items held in the **Rows**, **Columns**, **Marks**, **Pages**, or **Filters** shelf. This is the large middle pane, where you can see your data and your visualizations. In the preceding screenshot, it shows you the data that you copied and pasted into Tableau.

The following steps can be performed to create a quick visualization:

1. When you paste the data, it appears as a crosstab. We can see the data, but it is quite difficult to see any patterns in the data.

2. Using the preceding list as a basis, it is very simple to create a quick visualization.

3. Let's take a copy of our work so that we can compare before and after. To do this, click on the **Sheet 1** tab at the bottom of the worksheet. Right-click on the worksheet tab at the bottom of the Tableau interface, and a pop-up menu appears.

4. Select the **Rename Sheet** option and rename the worksheet as Before.

5. Then, choose the option **Duplicate Sheet**, as shown in the following screenshot, to take a copy of the worksheet, and rename the new copy as After:

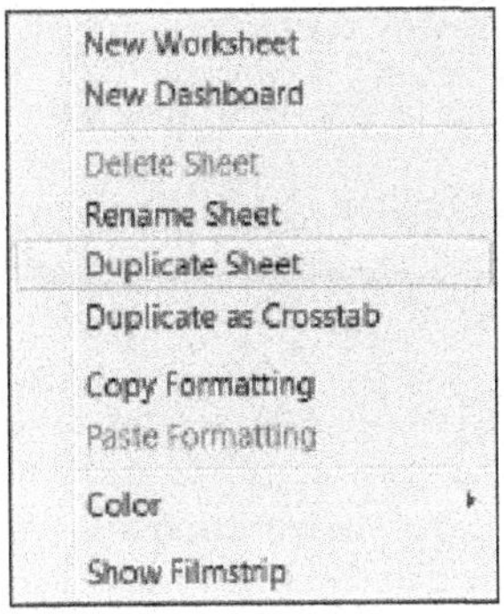

6. In the `After` worksheet, look for Tableau's **Show Me** feature. This is a key feature of Tableau, and you can see the **Show Me** toolkit in the right-hand side of the Tableau interface, as shown in the following screenshot:

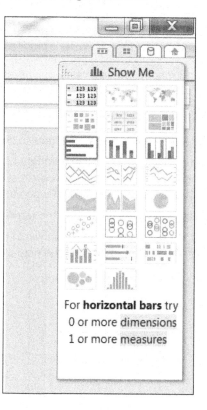

For the purposes of this recipe, we will choose a map visualization.

7. Using the `After` worksheet, click on the first **Measures** column called **Average ranking position_(for all 6 dimensions)** to select it. Right-click on the column and choose **Keep Only**. This excludes the rest of our measures, retaining only this column. The result can be seen in the following screenshot:

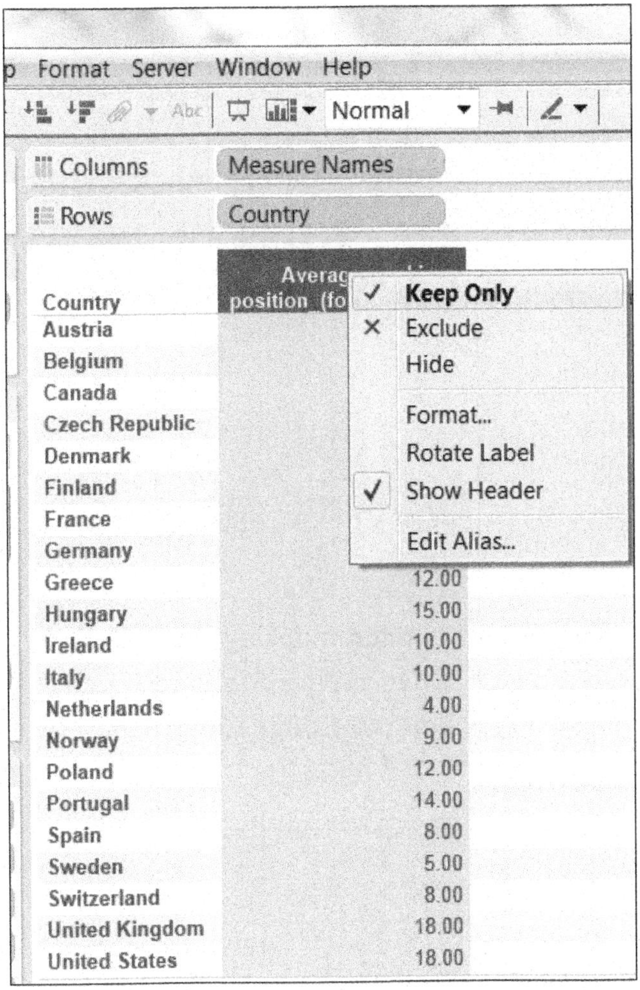

8. When we exclude the other options, the **Show Me** toolkit changes in response to the amendments that have been made in the data table. Now, the map options are available to us. The changes in the **Show Me** toolkit can be seen in the following screenshot:

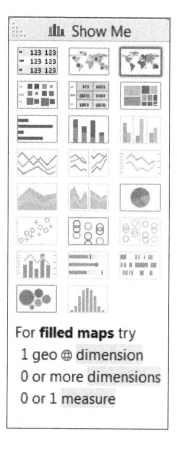

When we select the **filled maps** option, which is bordered with a heavy line at the top right-hand side row, our screen now changes to look like a filled map, in which each color corresponds to the average rank of each country. An example is shown in the following screenshot:

We have Denmark ranked at 7 and the United Kingdom ranked at 18. Denmark is considered as having a higher ranking, even though it has a lower number.

9. To change the color settings, we right-click on the colors item that is located on the left-hand side of the screen, centered vertically. We can see an example in the next screenshot:

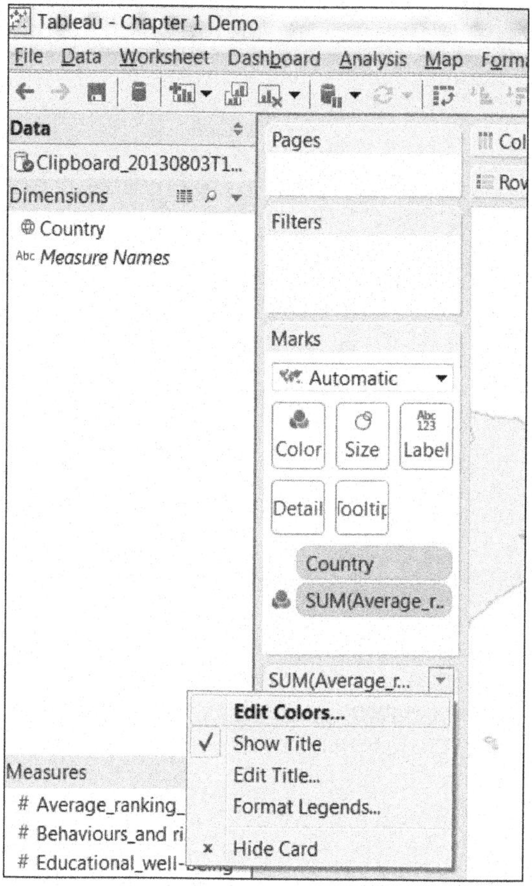

The **Edit Colors** dialog box appears. An example can be found in the next screenshot:

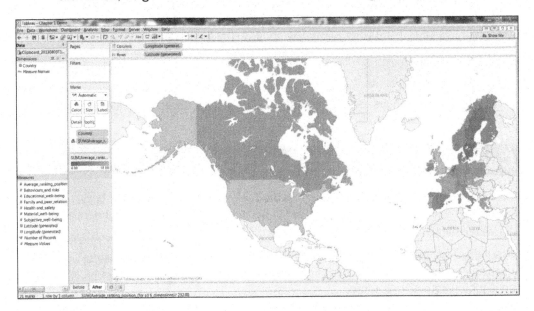

Edit Colors [Average_ranking_position_(for all 6_dimensions)]

Palette:

Custom Sequential

4.00   18.00

☐ Stepped Color   5   ▲▼ Steps

☑ Reversed

☐ Use Full Color Range   Advanced >>

Reset   OK   Cancel   Apply

10. Using the square box, you can change the color. Here, it has been changed to blue. The important item to note here is the **Reversed** option. This option allows us to reverse the color so that the lower numeric values are represented by higher intensities. When we click on **OK**, we get the final result as shown in the following screenshot:

How it works...

The **Show Me** button helps you to choose the data visualization that is most suited to your data. The **Show Me** toolkit takes the guesswork out of what data visualization tool to choose, by offering you a selection of visualizations that are based on your datatypes.

It does this using an in-built, intelligent, knowledge-based system that is part of Tableau. This helps to take the guesswork out of selecting a data visualization, which can often be a contentious issue among data consumers and business intelligence professionals alike.

Data visualization is telling a story; the value is depicted by a corresponding color intensity. This example topic involved ranking data. Therefore, the higher the number, the lower the value actually is. Here, the value refers to the country rank.

How can we make the message clearer to the users? When we visualize the data in a map, we can still use color in order to convey the message. Generally speaking, we assume that the brighter or more intense a color is, the higher the value. In this case, we need to adapt the visualization so that the color is brighter in accordance with the rank, not the perceived integer.

There's more...

Color theory is a topic in itself, and you will see practical applications as we proceed throughout this book. For further references, refer to the *See also* section.

See also

> ▶ Data visualizations can also be known as dataviz for short. On Twitter, `#dataviz` is a well-used hashtag

Connecting to data sources

In the previous recipe, we inserted data into the Tableau workbook by simply copying and pasting. In the real world, however, we need to be able to connect to different data sources that may contain large amounts of data.

We will now look at connecting to multiple data sources at a time. This is a useful way of enriching our data. We have access to multiple data sources. We can open up Tableau and connect numerous data sources.

First, we will see how we can connect to the Windows Azure DataMarket cloud data source, and then continue to connect to the local Excel file. Windows Azure Marketplace is an online market to buy and sell finished **Software as a Service** (**SaaS**) applications and premium data. Some data on Windows Azure DataMarket is free. We will be using one of the free data samples, which will give us a lot of information about individual countries, such as the country code, population, size, and so on. In data warehousing terminology, this data can be considered as a dimension, which is another way of describing data. In this definition, it is a field that can be considered an independent variable, regardless of the datatype. Tableau has a more specific definition of a dimension. Tableau treats any field containing qualitative, categorical information as a dimension, such as a date or a text field.

To connect the online data and local data, we will connect to Windows Azure DataMarket using OData, which is a standardized protocol to provide **Create, Read, Update, Delete** (**CRUD**) access to a data source via a website. It is the data API for Microsoft Azure, but other organizations use it as well, such as eBay, SAP, and IBM.

Getting ready

Before you start, you need to create a folder where you can download data to run through the examples. You should pick a folder name that is meaningful for you. Also, be sure to select a location that has plenty of space. In this example, we will store data at `D:\Data\TableauCookbook`. For the example in this chapter, we will create a folder called `Chapter 1`.

If you are experiencing problems in accessing the Windows Azure DataMarket, you can download a copy of the `Country Codes-CountryCodes.csv` file at `http://bit.ly/JenStirrupOfficialTableauBookCode`.

How to do it...

1. To connect to Windows Azure DataMarket, sign up for a free account using a Windows Live ID. To do this, visit `https://datamarket.azure.com/` and follow the instructions. This may involve activating your account via a link, so follow the instructions carefully.

2. Sign in to Windows Azure DataMarket and navigate to the URL `https://datamarket.azure.com/dataset/oh22is/countrycodes#schema`.

3. Look for the **Sign In** button and click on it. You will need a Windows Live ID.

4. This will take you to a terms and conditions page. After you've read the terms and conditions, and, if you agree with them, tick the box to specify that you agree and click on **Sign Up**.

5. This will take you to a **Thank You** page. Look for the **EXPLORE THIS DATASET** link on this page and click on it, as shown in the following screenshot:

6. When you click on **EXPLORE THIS DATASET**, you will be able to see the data appear in the browser, which you can slice and dice. Here is an example screenshot:

Country Codes

Country Codes contains codes to nearly all countries of the world like ISO2, ISO3 or FIPS. In Addition to the English name the dataset contains country names in 9 different languages like German, Spain, Chinese or Russian.

Primary Account Key Show

URL for current expressed query:

`https://api.datamarket.azure.com/oh22is/CountryCodes/v1/CountryCodes`

Displaying 100 of 252 rows   Page 1 ▸

CountryID	CountryName	ISO2	ISO3	ISONumeric	FIPS	Continent	TLD	CurrencyCode	CountryCallingCode
1	Afghanistan	AF	AF	4	AF	AS	.af	AFN	93
2	Albania	AL	AL	8	AL	EU	.al	ALL	355
3	Algeria	DZ	DZ	12	AG	AF	.dz	DZD	213
4	American Samoa	AS	AS	16	AQ	OC	.as	USD	-683

7. In this example, we will load the data in Tableau rather than in the Data Explorer URL. To do this, we need the primary account key. In Windows Azure DataMarket, this is easy to obtain. From the previous example, we can see a feature called **Primary Account Key**. If you click on the **Show** link next to **Primary Account Key**, then your primary account key will appear.

8. Copy the primary account key to your clipboard by selecting it and pressing the *Ctrl + C* keys. You will need the primary account key to access the data using Tableau.

9. You will also need to get the OData feed for the `Country Codes` data of the Windows Azure DataMarket `Country Codes` store. To get the OData feed, you can see it under the sentence **URL for current expressed query**, and you should copy this information.

10. Before you proceed, you should note the OData URL and the primary account key. Select them and press the *Ctrl + C* keys simultaneously. The following table shows an example of how your data might look:

OData URL	`https://api.datamarket.azure.com/oh22is/ CountryCodes/v1/CountryCodes`
Primary account key	**Aaa0aaAa0aAa00AAaAAA0aaA0AaaOa0aAaeAaA1AAA**

11. To connect to Windows Azure DataMarket, let's open up Tableau, and open the `Chapter 1 Demo` workbook that we started in the *Getting ready* section of the *Showing the power of data visualization* recipe.

12. Go to the **Data** menu item and choose **Connect to Data...**.

13. This action takes you to the **Connect to Data** window, and you can see that there are a variety of data sources for you to choose from! A sample of the list can be seen in the next screenshot:

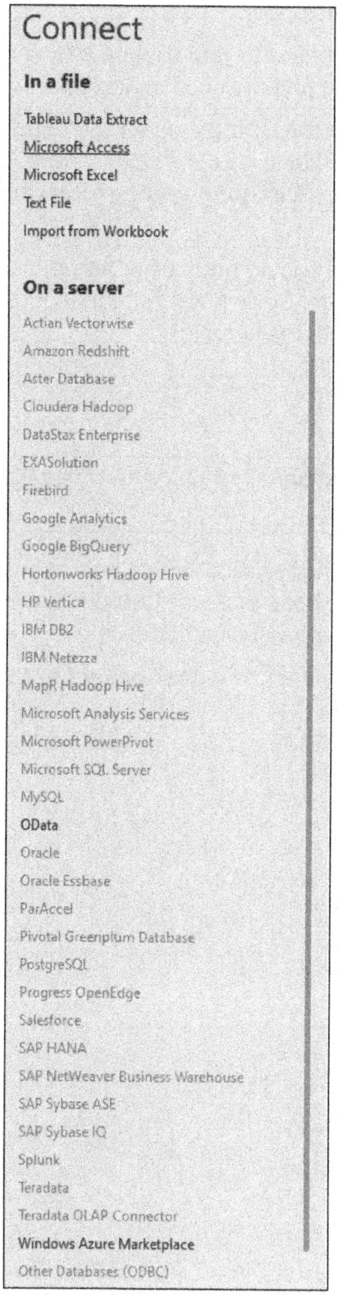

Connect

In a file

Tableau Data Extract
Microsoft Access
Microsoft Excel
Text File
Import from Workbook

On a server

Actian Vectorwise
Amazon Redshift
Aster Database
Cloudera Hadoop
DataStax Enterprise
EXASolution
Firebird
Google Analytics
Google BigQuery
Hortonworks Hadoop Hive
HP Vertica
IBM DB2
IBM Netezza
MapR Hadoop Hive
Microsoft Analysis Services
Microsoft PowerPivot
Microsoft SQL Server
MySQL
OData
Oracle
Oracle Essbase
ParAccel
Pivotal Greenplum Database
PostgreSQL
Progress OpenEdge
Salesforce
SAP HANA
SAP NetWeaver Business Warehouse
SAP Sybase ASE
SAP Sybase IQ
Splunk
Teradata
Teradata OLAP Connector
Windows Azure Marketplace
Other Databases (ODBC)

14. In this example, we are interested in connecting to Windows Azure DataMarket. Here, we will use the information that we saved earlier in this section. You will need the **OData** connection link. The connection panel only needs a few items in order to connect to the `Country Codes` data in Windows Azure, and an example can be seen in the next screenshot:

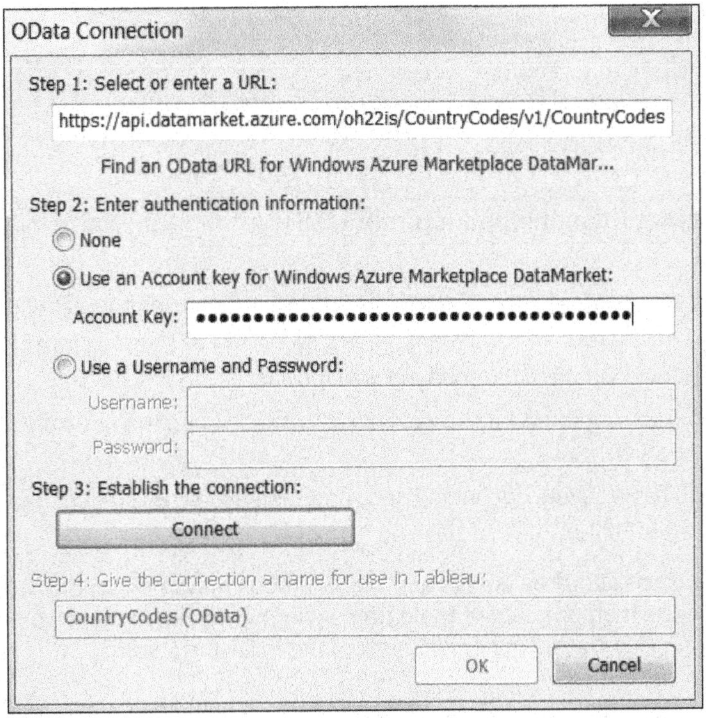

15. Insert the OData URL into the textbox labeled **Step 1: Select or enter a URL**.

16. Next, take a look at the step labeled **Step 2: Enter authentication information**, select the radio button next to the **Use an Account key for Windows Azure Marketplace DataMarket** option, and insert the account key into the textbox. Then, click on the **Connect** button.

17. If all goes well, the data connection will be successful and we can save the Tableau workbook before proceeding to connect to the Excel data source.

18. We will download the GNI data from the World Bank. The URL is `http://data.worldbank.org/indicator/NY.GNP.PCAP.CD?page=1`.

19. To do this, open an Internet browser and navigate to the URL. You can see the web page in the following screenshot:

20. You will see a button called **DOWNLOAD DATA**, which is on the right-hand side.

21. Click on this button and you will be presented with two options: **EXCEL** and **XML**. We will download all of the data in Excel format.

22. Before accessing the data source, let's save the file into the directory that you created earlier.

23. Once the file is saved, open it in Excel, and take a look. If you don't see any data, don't be alarmed.

You will see that there are three sheets and the workbook may open on the wrong sheet. This will only provide metadata about the data held in the worksheet, and we need to look at the worksheet called **Data**. Then, we'll perform the following steps:

1. Let's rename Sheet 1 to something more meaningful. Right-click on the sheet tab name and rename it as GNI.

2. Remove the first two rows of the file. They will only add noise to the import.

3. Once you've done this, save the workbook. Now, you can exit Excel. We will go back to Tableau to connect to the data.

4. To connect to the Excel file, go to the **Data** menu item. Select **Connect to Data....** Look under the heading **In a File** and select **Microsoft Excel**. Then, a file browser will appear.

5. Navigate to the location where the files are stored.

6. Select the worksheet called GNI to import and drag it to the canvas on the right-hand side of the screen.

7. To save the data, make sure that the **Live** radio button is selected. You can see this above the canvas. Then, click on the **Go To Worksheet** button in the center of the screen.

8. Now, we can see the Tableau workbook in the following screenshot. In the **Data** view at the top, we can see two connections: our Windows Azure DataMarket connection and our Excel file connection.

9. If we want to flip between each data source, we can click on each connection and see that the dimensions and measures change in response.

How it works...

Tableau connects to each data source and talks to it using drivers that are specific to each datatype. For example, Tableau has some connectors to popular programs, such as R, Google Analytics, and Salesforce.

You can find more information about drivers on the Tableau website at the link `http://www.tableausoftware.com/support/drivers`.

There's more...

Tableau will connect to each data source independently. Even though they are different types of data sources, they appear to look the same in Tableau. From the user perspective, this is very useful since they should not be distracted by the differences in the underlying data source technologies. This means that the user can focus on the data rather than trying to put the data into one data source. Furthermore, it means that the sources of data can be refreshed easily because the Tableau visualization designer is able to connect directly to the source, which means that the data visualization will always be up to date.

See also

 ▸ Tableau can import data into its own in-memory engine. We will look at this in *Chapter 4, Using Dashboards to Get Results*, in the *Enriching data with mashups* section.

Introducing the Tableau interface

In this recipe, we will look at the components of the Tableau interface and use these features in order to create a simple Tableau visualization. In the previous recipe, we connected to data in Windows Azure DataMarket and a local Excel spreadsheet. We will use these data sources in our example here in order to produce a quick and easy data visualization.

Getting ready

Make sure that you have a copy of the Chapter 1 Tableau data visualization open. You should be able to access both data sources. To do this, click on the Tableau **Data** connection that you will see in the top left-hand corner of the Tableau interface, as shown in the following screenshot:

You should be able to click on the **CountryCodes** and the **GNI** connections alternately, and see the differences in the dimensions and metrics contained in the two data sources.

How to do it...

1. In the `Chapter 1` Tableau data visualization, click on the **GNI** data source. This will change the dimensions and measures, which you can see in the left-hand side column of the Tableau interface. An example is shown in the next screenshot:

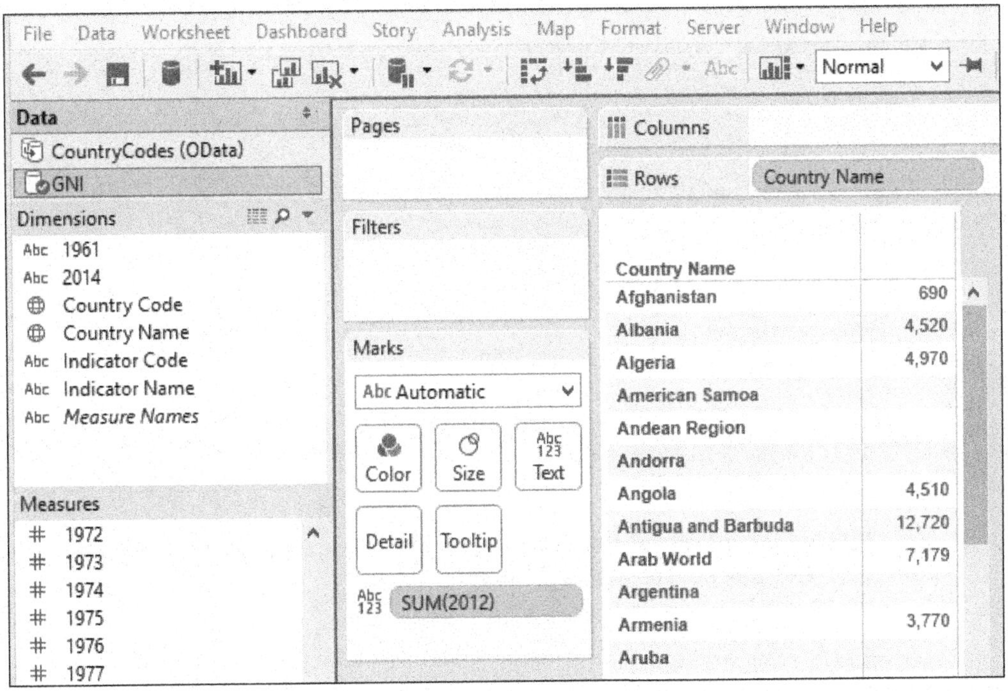

2. You might notice that some of the dimensions are years, but the rest are considered to be metrics. Fortunately, this is very easy to change. You can simply drag the 2014 and 1961 dimensions down to the **Measures** area. The Tableau interface now looks like the following screenshot:

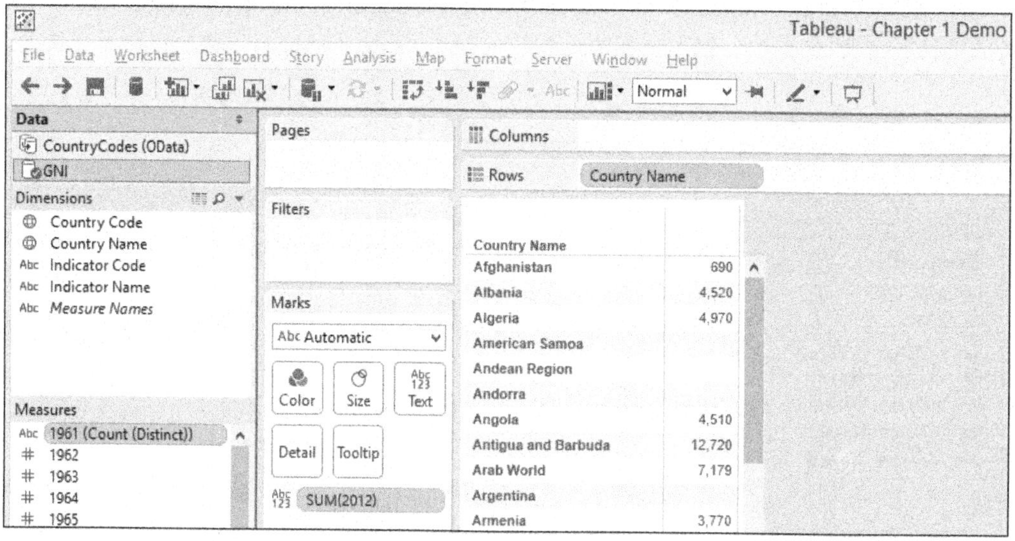

3. Now that we see the measures, you can see that they are still specified as a string datatype, and they are specified as **Count**.

4. Fortunately, this is also very easy to change. If you right-click on the measure 1960, a pop-up menu will appear. You can see an example of the pop-up menu in the next screenshot:

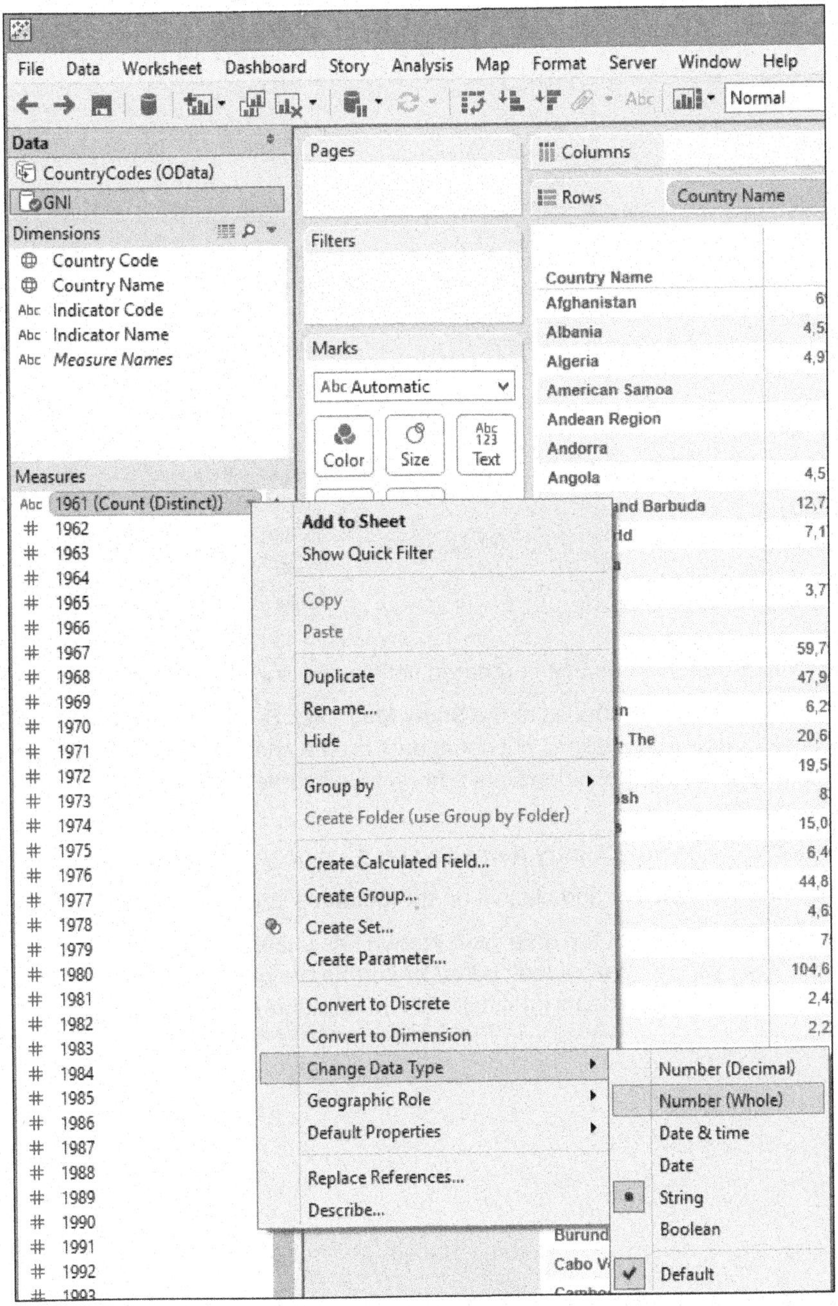

5. If you do this for both `1960` and `1961`, you can change both the datatypes to number. The result can be seen in the next screenshot:

6. Now that the data has been prepared, let's move to visualizing the data.

7. Earlier, we were introduced to the **Show Me** panel. Before we use the **Show Me** panel, however, we need to put some data on the shelves. This is a location where we drag-and-drop the dimensions and metrics in order to make them part of the data visualization.

8. Pick the dimension **Country Name** and drag it onto the **Rows** shelf.

9. Pick the metric `2012` and place it on the **Columns** shelf.

10. You can now see that the data visualization has changed from a table to a horizontal bar chart. We can make it look better by sorting the bars in descending order. This allows us to quickly identify the highest GNI amounts for the top *n* countries.

11. To sort in descending order, look for the button that shows a downward arrow next to a horizontal bar chart. When you hover the mouse over it, you will see that it sorts by the metric. An example is shown in the following screenshot:

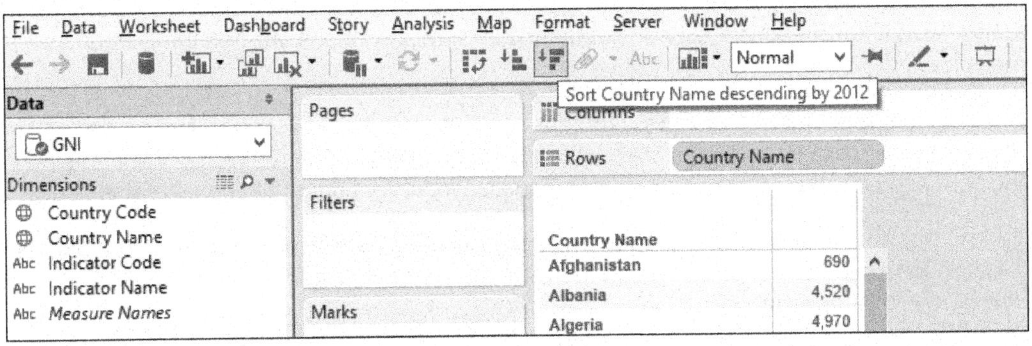

Once you've sorted the data, it will look neater and easier to understand. We can see this in the following screenshot:

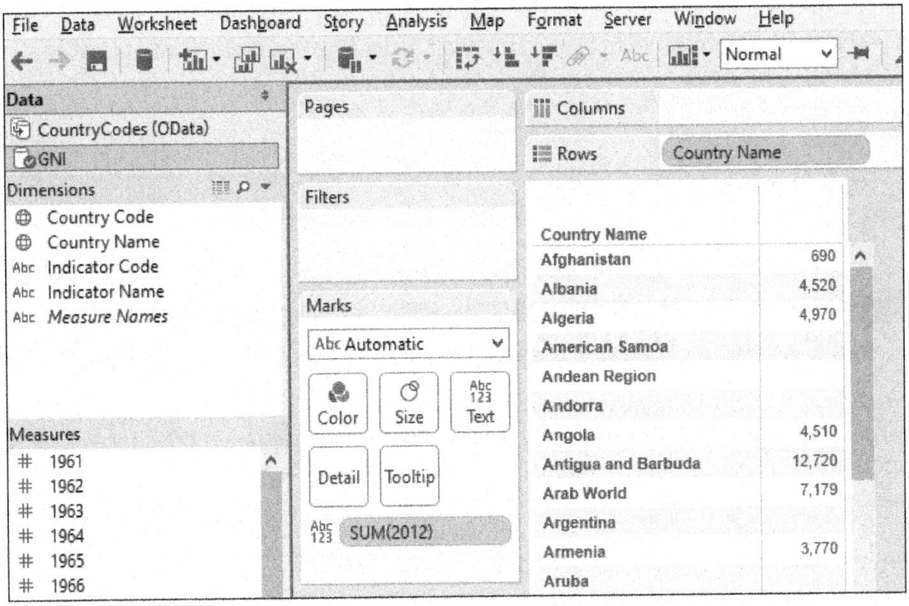

How it works...

One of Tableau's features is that it works out automatically whether the data is a dimension or a measure. Tableau does this by looking at the datatype in the columns. So, for example, in this case, it has identified text and geographical types as dimensions and integers as measures.

You may be wondering why we have data that has a year for each column rather than a column **Year**. This is a good question to ask, and we will look at different ways of shaping the data and how that affects the resulting visualization throughout the course of this book.

Tableau has an internal knowledge base that it uses in order to determine the most appropriate visualization for the data it sees. Initially, in this case, it has suggested a horizontal bar chart in blue. Why is this the case?

We have a horizontal bar chart rather than vertical because we can read more easily along rather than up and down. For people in the West, we tend to read left to right, so we see the country name on the left followed by the bar and the value on the right.

By having horizontal bars, it is easy to see how the bars compare within the chart itself. We have the visual information from the bar itself as well as the metrics labeled at the end of the bar.

See also

> ▸ A book list will be provided at the end of the book for people who are interested in research on data visualization

Interacting with your first data visualization

In this recipe, we will learn about interacting with your first visualization and look at different visualizations that are available to you in Tableau. The **Show Me** panel provides you with a range of options to create data visualizations. Some of these can be adapted so that they pack a lot of information into a very small space, which is ideal for dashboarding. In this recipe, we will look at creating a bullet chart, which has been designed to retain a balance between packing the maximum amount of information into the minimum amount of space while also retaining clarity.

The bullet chart was devised by a data visualization expert and thought leader, Stephen Few. It is designed to replace charts and graphs that show a lot of ink or take up a lot of space on the page but do not show a lot of data. The bullet graph is effective because it takes up little space and allows the viewer to see whether the actual data is comparable to the target by reading from left to right along the bar. Playing with the colors on the bullet chart is a useful way to understand this useful chart better.

We are using a very simple dataset as a starting point, and we will move towards more complexity in terms of data and visualizations for dashboarding as we proceed throughout the book.

Getting ready

Before we open Tableau, let's download the data from a Google Docs spreadsheet provided by the Guardian Datastore, which is provided by *The Guardian* newspaper that is published in the UK. You can visit the link to get the data from here: `http://bit.ly/ JenStirrupOfficialTableauBookCode`. Alternatively, if you are experiencing difficulties in getting the file, you can download a copy of the Excel file called `EU COUNTRIES SHARE OF RENEWABLE ENERGY.xls` from data files that accompany the book at this link: `http://bit.ly/JenStirrupOfficialTableauBookCode`.

If you have obtained the data from the Guardian website, you will need a Google account to open the spreadsheet. Once you have opened the spreadsheet, you copy the data that you can see highlighted in the following screenshot:

Country	2006	2007	2008	2009	2010	2020 target
EU27*	9.0	9.9	10.5	11.7	12.4	20.0
Belgium	2.7	3.0	3.3	4.6		13.0
Bulgaria	9.6	9.3	9.8	11.9	13.8	16.0
Czech Republic	6.5	7.4	7.6	8.5	9.2	13.0
Denmark	16.5	18.0	18.8	20.2	22.2	30.0
Germany	6.9	9.0	9.1	9.5	11.0	18.0
Estonia	16.1	17.1	18.9	23.0	24.3	25.0
Ireland	2.9	3.3	3.9	5.1	5.5	16.0
Greece	7.0	8.1	8.0	8.1	9.2	18.0
Spain	9.0	9.5	10.6	12.8	13.8	20.0
France**	9.6	10.2	11.1	11.9		23.0
Italy	5.8	5.7	7.1	8.9	10.1	17.0
Cyprus	2.5	3.1	4.1	4.6	4.8	13.0
Latvia	31.1	29.6	29.8	34.3	32.6	40.0
Lithuania	16.9	16.6	17.9	20.0	19.7	23.0
Luxembourg	1.4	2.7	2.8	2.8	2.8	11.0
Hungary	5.1	5.9	6.6	8.1		13.0
Malta	0.2	0.2	0.2	0.2	0.4	10.0
Netherlands	2.7	3.1	3.4	4.1	3.8	14.0
Austria	26.6	28.9	29.2	31.0	30.1	34.0
Poland	7.0	7.0	7.9	8.9	9.4	15.0
Portugal	20.8	22.0	23.0	24.6	24.6	31.0
Romania	17.1	18.3	20.3	22.4	23.4	24.0
Slovenia	15.5	15.6	15.1	18.9	19.8	25.0
Slovakia	6.6	8.2	8.4	10.4	9.8	14.0
Finland	29.9	29.5	31.1	31.1	32.2	38.0
Sweden	42.7	44.2	45.2	48.1	47.9	49.0
United Kingdom	1.5	1.8	2.3	2.9	3.2	15.0
Croatia	13.8	12.4	12.2	13.2	14.6	20.0
Norway	60.6	60.5	62.0	65.1	61.1	67.5

Select the table of data as in the preceding screenshot, copy it using *Ctrl + C*, and then paste it into Tableau. This will import the copied data into the model contained in the Tableau worksheet. Alternatively, you could download the Google spreadsheet as an Excel spreadsheet by navigating to **File | Download as | Microsoft Excel (.xlsx)**. Since we will be changing the original visualization in the `Chapter 1` workbook, it is good practice to take a copy of your current visualization and work on the copy. When you work in Tableau, it is very easy to keep clicking around and changing visualizations. However, if you want to roll back to an earlier point, you might find that you've easily clicked away quite far from your preferred point.

In this example, we will work on a copy of the `Chapter 1` workbook, so we can compare our progress from start to finish quite easily. We will use data from the Guardian Datastore, which shows whether countries are on target to meet their environmental targets according to the Kyoto agreement. This is a good preliminary example of dashboard data, because we are displaying the actual versus target data, and this is a common dashboarding scenario.

How to do it...

1. Once the data is copied into Tableau, the workbook will appear as follows:

2. If the years appear as dimensions, then drag them to the **Measures** pane on the left-hand side.

3. Our starting point is a table. In our duplicate sheet, go to the **Show Me** panel on the right-hand side. Select the **horizontal bars** option. You can see a sample of the **Show Me** panel in the next screenshot:

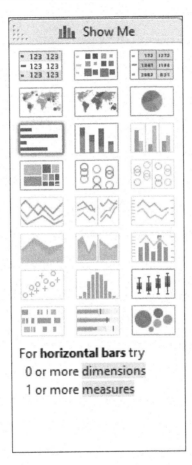

4. Once you have selected the **horizontal bars** option, your screen will look like the following screenshot:

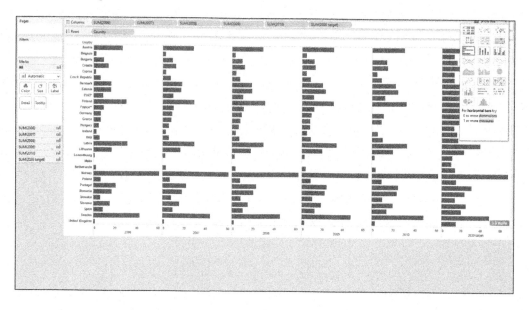

5. We are interested in the target data. To show the scenario of comparing actual data with target data, remove all of the green pills from the **Columns** shelf, except **SUM(2010)** and **SUM(2020 Target)**.

6. Once these columns have been removed, the **Show Me** panel will show more options. We will choose the **bullet graphs** option, which is highlighted with a blue box in the following screenshot:

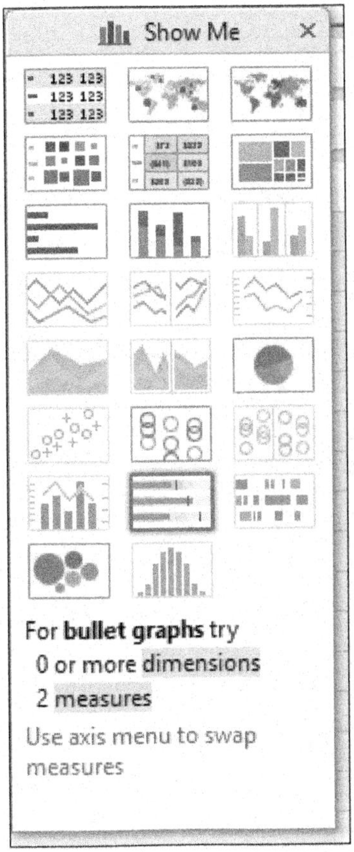

7. Once the **bullet graphs** option has been clicked on, look for the small icon that looks like a horizontal bar chart on the taskbar. You will find it below the menu items. When you wave the mouse over it, you will see that it is a tooltip that says **Sort Country Descending by 2010**. It is circled in the following screenshot:

8. Once you click on the icon, you will see the result shown in the next screenshot, which shows rows of bullet charts:

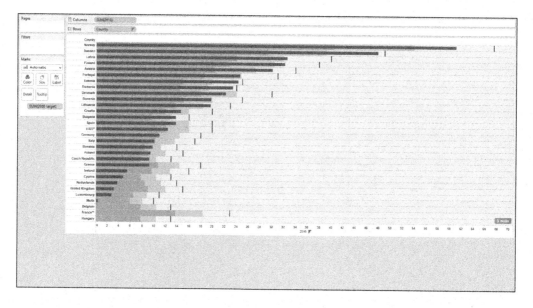

9. This is still a lot of data to show on a dashboard, and still be sure that the data consumer is able to remember and understand it quickly. The idea is that the thick horizontal line displays the actual data and the vertical line on each row displays the target. We can resize it so that the rows are smaller in height. To do this, you can resize by grabbing the bottom of the white canvas and pulling it upwards. This will make the data visualization smaller.

10. We could filter this further in order to show the top five countries who have the greatest share of renewable energy sources in 2010. To do this, drag the **Country** dimension from the left-hand side of the Tableau workbook to the **Filter** panel located just above the **Marks** panel. The following wizard will appear:

11. Select the **Top** tab and select the **By Field** radio button.

12. Then, put the number 5 into the textbox and select the **2010** column from the drop-down list.

13. Click on **OK** to clear the **Filter** wizard.

14. Then, right-click on **Country** in the visualization and select the **Hide Field Labels for Rows** option, as shown in the following screenshot. This will remove unnecessary ink from the screen, which means that there are fewer unnecessary items to distract the viewer.

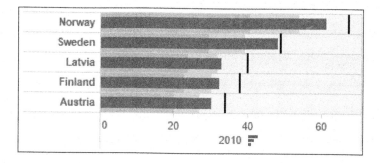

	Sort Ascending
	Sort Descending
	Filter...
	Show Quick Filter
☰	Sort...
	Format...
	Rotate Labels
	Hide Field Labels for Rows

15. Once this is done, resize the visualization so that it is only a few inches in length.

    To do this, go to the right-hand side of the visualization and drag the end along to the desired size. The data visualization now looks like the following screenshot:

Norway				
Sweden				
Latvia				
Finland				
Austria				
	0	20	40	60
			2010	

How it works...

Copying and pasting the data into Tableau is a great way of importing data quickly. Note, however, that this data is static and will not change with any changes in the data source.

There's more...

Removing unnecessary ink from the screen is a useful way of cutting down the items displayed on the dashboard. In this example, the label was redundant and its removal made the graphic neater.

If you require more information on the bullet chart, visit the link `http://bit.ly/BulletGraphbyStephenFew`.

Sharing your visualization with the world

In the first recipe, we specified communication as one of the key features of a dashboard. We need to be able to share the information to the right audience, at the right time, and in the right format.

Tableau offers a number of different ways to share the dashboard in order to help team members throughout the organization to track, monitor, and analyze the metrics about their organization, and we will look at these in the current section.

Given that Tableau offers a number of ways to share a dashboard, what is the best way to do this? The best way to decide which method to use to share your information fundamentally rests on the user requirements. These are listed in the following table:

Objective	Method
For other Tableau users who don't have access to the data	Exporting a Tableau packaged workbook
To view data online and share the data	Sharing your workbook with Tableau Public
For Tableau users who do have access to the data	Sharing your workbook with Tableau Server

In this recipe, we will look at the first two methods of sharing data: exporting a Tableau packaged workbook and sharing your workbook with Tableau Public. When we export a workbook as a packaged workbook, it wraps up the data as part of the Tableau workbook. Why would you want to do this? The following are some reasons:

▶ You might want to send the workbook to someone who does not have access to the data source

▶ You might be prototyping a workbook with some sample data

▶ You will find it quicker to develop offline

When we save a file as a packaged workbook, the workbook points at its own internal copy of the data via the data source connection. If it is a packaged workbook with a data extract, then it no longer references the data from the original data source. Instead, all of the references point to the workbook's internal version of the data via the data source connection, not the original source. Logo images, for example, that are part of the dashboard, are stored as part of the packaged workbook rather than externally referenced.

The workbook is now insulated from changes in the data source, and it won't be impacted by changes in the data source. Individuals who do not have access to the original data source can still see the workbook and manipulate the data, but cannot impact the data source in any way.

If you want to save a workbook to Tableau Public, then you must use a workbook that has a packaged data source. There is a list of criteria that need to be met in order to publish the dashboard to Tableau Public. The data extract may not include more than 1 million rows. Only workbooks with a data extract will be published to Tableau Public. Finally, if the workbook has multiple data connections, then you will need an extract for each data connection.

We will look at this issue first, and then at uploading this workbook to Tableau Public.

Getting ready

Check that your workbook has less than 1 million rows. In this example, it does. So, we can proceed. However, for your own work, you may find that this is not always the case.

Check whether you have a login for Tableau Public. If not, visit the Tableau website in order to set up a login and a password (`www.tableausoftware.com`).

How to do it...

1. To save a workbook in order to upload it to Tableau Public, you need to save it as a packaged workbook. To do this, go to the **File** menu item and choose the **Save As...** option.

2. Enter the filename in the **File Name** textbox.

3. Go to the **Save As** option from the drop-down list, choose **Tableau Packaged Workbook**, and then click on **Save**.

4. Now, go to the **Server** menu item and you will see one option called **Tableau Public**. From here, you can get to a small menu, which is called **Save to Web As...**. You can see an example of this in the following screenshot:

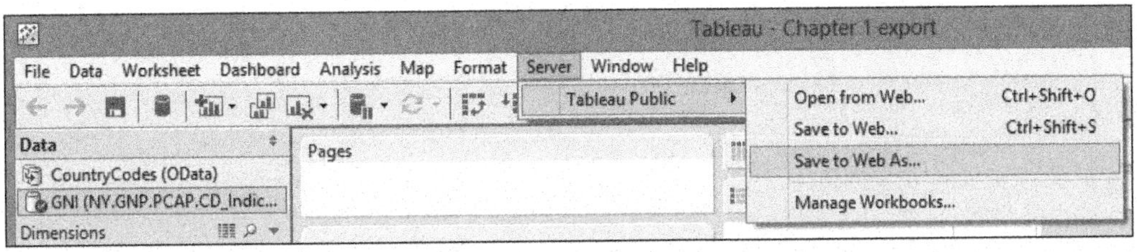

5. Click on the **Save to Web As...** option, and you will get the following dialog box:

6. You will get a message asking you to log in to Tableau Public with your login ID and password. When you have entered these details, click on **OK**.

Next, you will get the message shown in the following screenshot:

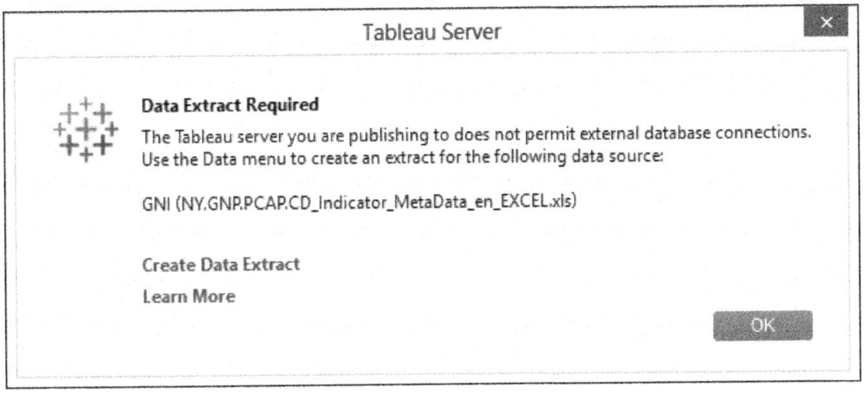

7. Click on the link **Create Data Extract**.

8. You will now get a filter box. We wish to extract all of the data, so click on **Extract**. You can see an example in the next screenshot:

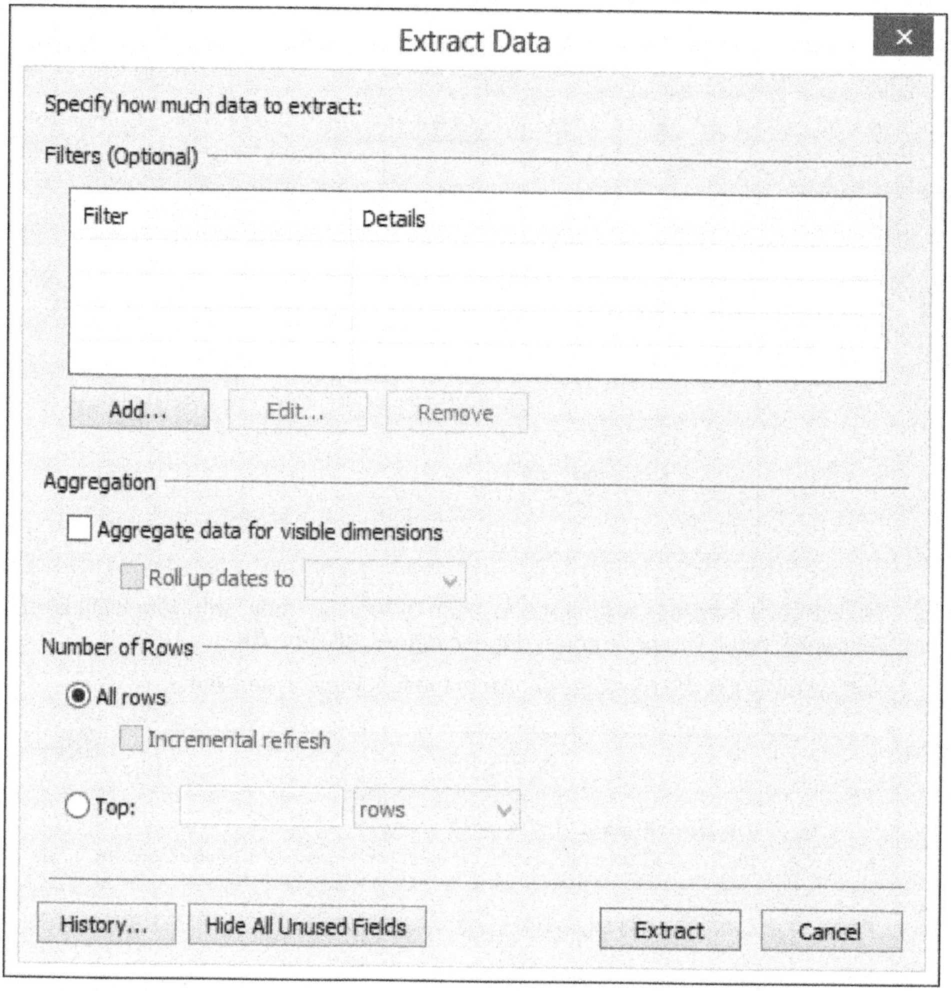

Extract Data ✕

Specify how much data to extract:

Filters (Optional)

Filter	Details

[Add...] [Edit...] [Remove]

Aggregation

☐ Aggregate data for visible dimensions

   ☐ Roll up dates to [▾]

Number of Rows

◉ All rows

   ☐ Incremental refresh

◯ Top: [   ] [rows   ▾]

[History...] [Hide All Unused Fields]   [Extract] [Cancel]

9. Now, you will see your results in an Internet browser, as shown in the following screenshot:

Save To Web Results				⊟ – ▢ ✕

Chapter 1 successfully saved to Tableau Public

Views
This workbook contains the following **2** views

Sheet 1

Interactions

Preview

Copy and Paste link into your email message

http://public.tableausoftware.com/views/C `Copy`

Copy and Paste html code to embed the Viz in your website

<script type='text/javascript' src='http://pu `Copy`

Sheet 1	Interactions

2012			Country Name	
220		98,860	Norway	98,860
			Switzerland	82,730
			Luxembourg	76,960
			Denmark	59,770
			Australia	59,570
			Sweden	56,210
			Canada	50,970
			North America	50,216
			United States	50,120
			Netherlands	48,250
			Austria	48,160
			Japan	47,870
			Singapore	47,210
			Finland	46,940
			Belgium	44,990

↱ Share 📘 ⅀ ✉ ∞   ⬆ ↺

Open in browser window   See more by this author   ⁘ +ableau

Learn how to share   ‹   ›

10. If you want to share your visualization, you can use the links at the bottom-left corner of the browser to share your work. For example, you could share it on Facebook, Twitter, or send it by an e-mail.

> Tableau-packaged workbooks have the file extension *.twbx.
> Tableau workbooks have the extension *.twb.

11. If you are using Microsoft Windows and Tableau Desktop, it is possible to unpack the file. This is not possible in Tableau Reader or in the Mac version of Tableau. Once the file is saved, it is possible to unpack the original data source by unpacking the original workbook. To do this, navigate to the file in Windows Explorer and right-click on it. In the resulting menu, you will see an option to **Unpackage** the workbook. You can see an example of this in the following screenshot:

Name		Da
🔲 Chapter 1 expo		06

Open
Print
Unpackage
Open with...

Share with ▶
Send to ▶

Cut
Copy

Create shortcut
Delete
Rename

Properties

Then, you will be asked where you would like to unpackage the workbook. Select a location on your computer to unpackage the workbook; for example, you could use the location that we created at the beginning of this chapter: `D:\Data\TableauCookbook\Chapter 1`. We will keep the filename as it is.

How it works...

You can publish your workbook to the whole world using Tableau Public. The data is saved to Tableau's data centers, and you can access the workbook from anywhere in the world via the Internet.

Tableau allows you to publish easily from your desktop. However, there are a few restrictions on using Tableau Public. Also, be careful about sharing your work; once the Tableau workbook is published to Tableau Public, anybody can download the data.

2
Summarizing Your Data for Dashboards

In this chapter, we will cover the following recipes:

- ▶ Arithmetic – the queen of mathematics!
- ▶ Dashboards and dates
- ▶ Grouping your data with calculations
- ▶ Correlation with calculations
- ▶ Using cross-tabs flexibly
- ▶ Simplifying your business rules with custom calculations

Introduction

It isn't enough just to make data look beautiful; we know that we can do it with Tableau. The data has to be accurate as well in terms of the business rules of an organization.

Calculations make things easier for the business user. The idea of "intelligent laziness" is often ascribed to Napoleon Bonaparte. The core idea is that people put effort where it is most needed rather than wasting time and resources. Calculations can help you in many ways, such as removing the implementation of repeatable calculations through automation. They also allow you to implement your business calculations so that they are consistently used in your dashboards.

Arithmetic – the queen of mathematics!

This recipe explains how to use simple descriptive statistics and arithmetic as the first step toward analyzing your data. We will also look at ways to import data into Tableau. When we import data, Tableau will create a **Tableau Data Extract** file behind the scenes. This is also known as a TDE file for short.

Descriptive statistics are a great starting point when analyzing data. They are very helpful in delivering an initial overview of the data to help you interpret it. We can glean information about the spread of the distribution of the data, measures of variability around the mean, and measures of deviation from the normal curve. Descriptive statistics have a variety of uses, for example, to help you identify outliers, which are unusual cases in the data that may warrant further investigation. Missing data points are important as well because missing data can mislead our analysis, and data visualization can help us to profile the data to check for potential instances of missing data.

How do we calculate descriptive statistics? Once the `FactInternetSales` data has been imported, we will calculate its mean, median, and mode. These are measures of central tendency that allow us to see the shape of the data. Many business questions are quite simple: What are my average sales? What are my total costs? How well can a dataset be summarized by one number?

We can look at the data in order to see how well it can be described by a single number; this is called the **measure of central tendency**. Often, when we talk about business questions, people listening to us would want to know the average of something. However, when we look at the average, things become more complex. The average may be skewed, for example, by an outlier. We need to know whether our average is representative of a dataset.

The average, median, and mode tell us about the symmetry of our data in terms of its distribution. They give us an initial picture of the data, a simple summary. Further, knowing about the symmetry of the data can help us look at important factors such as probability, which may form part of your analysis.

As you might expect, there are many ways to perform descriptive statistics in Tableau. This recipe will show you how to perform simple and quick descriptive statistics that will help you begin analyzing your data; this will be useful in understanding whether the average is effective in describing the overall data.

In this recipe, we will import some data and look at using some descriptive statistics to describe our data. Firstly, we will calculate the average, which is the most well-known measure of central tendency. Then, we will look at the median and mode.

Getting ready

For this and the future recipes, you will need to download a mix of Excel and CSV files. Perform the following steps:

1. Set up a folder on your computer where you can store the files. As an example, you could call it `TableauCookbookData` and locate it on `D:`. The path for the folder would be `D:\TableauCookbookData`.

2. Go to `http://bit.ly/JenStirrupOfficialTableauBookCode` and download the ZIP file.

3. Right-click on the ZIP file and select **Extract To**.

4. Extract the files to your folder. So, in our example, you would extract the files to `D:\TableauCookbookData`.

How to do it...

1. Open up Tableau and navigate to **File | New**.

2. Save the file as `Chapter 2`.

3. We will connect to the data and import it into Tableau's internal data store mechanism. To do this, click on **Connect to Data**, which is in the **Data** pane on the left-hand side.

4. We are going to connect to a text file. To do this, select the link **Text File** which appears under the heading **In a file** on the left-hand side. Then, a file browser will appear. Navigate to the folder where you stored the CSV files.

5. Navigate to the `FactInternetSales.csv` file. Select the file and click on **Open**.

6. Now, Tableau will open up a data connection canvas. Here is an example of the canvas:

7. Now, let's include date information to our dataset. To do this, drag across the `DimDate` file from the left-hand side to the white canvas in the middle.

8. A table will appear. From the left-hand column under **DataSource**, select **Order Date Key**.

9. From the right-hand column under **DimDate.csv**, select **Date Key**.

Here is how your canvas will look:

10. Next, let's add in some customer data. To do this, drag `DimCustomer.csv` from the left-hand side of the Canvas under **Files**, and drag it to the white canvas. This time, Tableau will know to use **CustomerKey** for the join, since it is present in both the **FactInternetSales** table and the **DimCustomer** data.

    Your canvas will now appear as follows:

11. Finally, let's add in some geographical data. To do this, drag `DimGeography.csv` from the left-hand side under **Files** and drop it onto the white canvas.

12. Tableau will automatically identify that the tables are related through **SalesTerritoryKey**. However, the join is actually via the **GeographyKey** column. Click on the **SalesTerritoryKey** cell under **Data Source**, and from the drop-down list, select **GeographyKey**.

13. Under the heading `DimGeography.csv`, select the **GeographyKey** column. The screen will look like this:

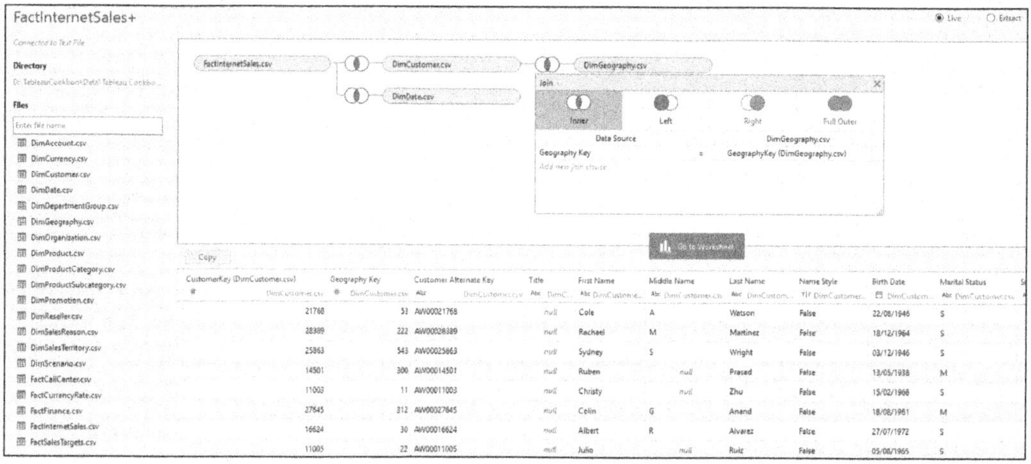

14. Once you have done this, select the **Go to Worksheet** button in the middle of the canvas. You will now be returned to the main Tableau canvas.

15. Let's play with some data! Firstly, we will calculate the average of the sales amount. Take **SalesAmount** and drag it to the **Rows** shelf. You will see that Tableau immediately visualizes the data and turns it into a bar chart with one vertical bar. You can see this in the following screenshot:

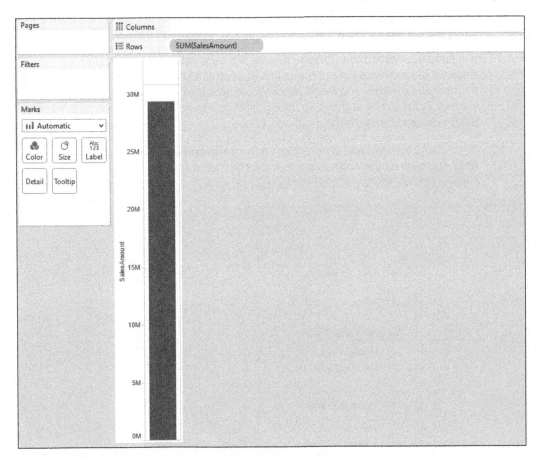

16. We would like to see the actual figure, so we will turn the data into a table. To do this, click on the **Show Me** panel at the top-right corner, and select the **Text Table** option, which is on the top row at the left-hand side of the **Show Me** panel.

17. The **SalesAmount** pill will disappear from the **Rows** shelf and will reappear in the textbox in the **Marks** shelf, since Tableau is now showing a number.

    The first visualization that Tableau selects is a sum of **SalesAmount**. However, since we are interested in the measures of central tendency, we are interested in the average, median, and mode. We will calculate these values to perform a quick summary of the data and also to understand how much we can rely on one number, the mean, to summarize the data.

18. To calculate the average, simply click on the **SalesAmount** pill in the **Marks** shelf and click on the down arrow to show the menu. You can see this in the following screenshot:

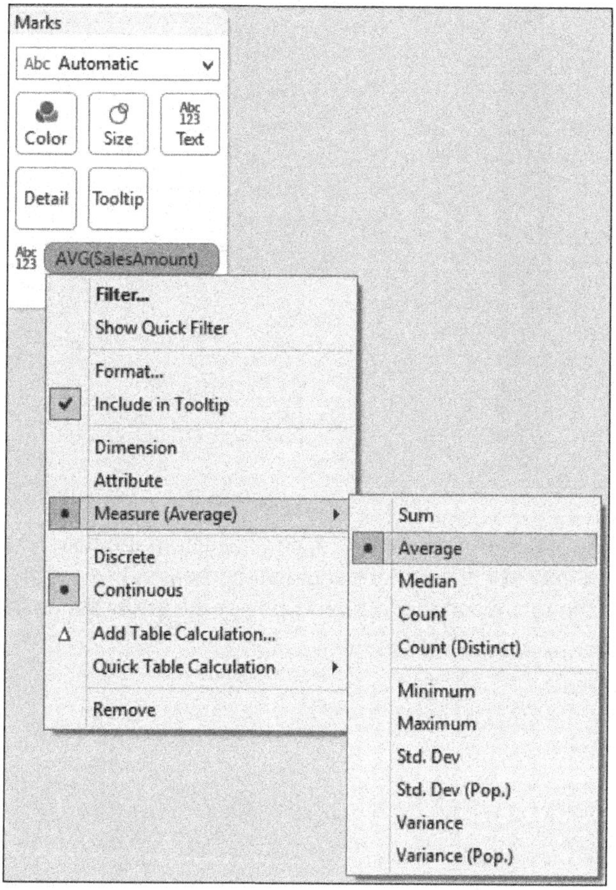

19. The average sales amount is $486.09.

20. The average is calculated and visualized in a table. However, we would like to see the median as well.

21. Right-click on the **SalesAmount** pill on the **Marks** shelf and navigate to the **Measure** option, and slide the mouse along to the right-hand arrow. In the drop-down list, select **Median**. The median **SalesAmount** is given as 29.99.

22. Next, remove **SalesAmount** from the **Marks** shelf so that we have a clean canvas again.

23. Then, we need to calculate the mode, which can be defined as the number that occurs most frequently. To calculate the mode, we need to make a copy of **SalesAmount** and make it a dimension. This is a workaround to help the Tableau user to work out how many times each price occurred. To do this, right-click on the **SalesAmount** column in the **Measures** window and select **Duplicate**. You can see the menu item in the following screenshot:

| **Add to Sheet** |
| Show Quick Filter |
| Copy |
| Paste |
| Duplicate |
| Rename... |
| Hide |
| Create Calculated Field... |
| Create Group... |
| Create Bins... |
| Create Parameter... |
| Convert to Discrete |
| Convert to Dimension |
| Change Data Type ▶ |
| Geographic Role ▶ |
| Default Properties ▶ |
| Replace References... |
| Describe... |

24. Once you have duplicated the **SalesAmount** figure, you will see that the duplicate is called **SalesAmount (copy)**.

25. Next, drag **SalesAmount (copy)** to the **Dimensions** shelf in the **Data** sidebar so that the table works properly.

26. Drag the **SalesAmount (copy)** item to the **Rows** shelf.

27. Next, you can go back to the **Measures** pane and move the **Number of Records** pill to the canvas area, next to the **SalesAmount (copy)** column.

28. This will give us the number of records for each sales amount. However, it is quite difficult to work out the most commonly-occurring sales amount from the table simply by looking at it. What we can do instead is sort the data so that the maximum is at the top, and the top item provides us with the mean.

29. To sort the data, go to the top of the Tableau interface, and look for the horizontal bar chart symbol with the downward arrow. This will sort the data by the number of records in descending order. You can see this under the **Format** menu item, as highlighted in the following screenshot:

30. Once you've done this, drag the **Number of Records** item from the **Measures** pane on to the **Color** shelf of the **Marks** shelf. Once this is done, your screen should resemble the following screenshot:

31. The mode is actually the topmost number; the highest frequently occurring **SalesAmount** is $4.99.

How it works...

To summarize, in this section, we learned the following:

- ▸ Basic calculations
- ▸ Changing the color
- ▸ Basic sorting

We can see that the average and median values are quite different. The mode is $4.99, but the median is $29.99. Since the average is much higher than the median and the mode is different from the other two numbers, the data is not symmetrical. Often, when business analysts look at data, they try to find out whether the data is close to a normal curve or not. The average, median, and mode help us to determine whether the data is close to a normal distribution or whether the data is shaped. Therefore, we can't just simply use the average to summarize the data; we need to know about the other items too. This helps us understand the skewedness of the data, or how far it is from the central measures.

There's more...

If you are interested in learning more about analyzing data and the normal curve, then you can take a look at `http://en.wikipedia.org/wiki/Normal_curve`.

If statistics interests you, why not look at doing a Khan Academy course? This is a free facility for learning statistics yourself online; refer to `https://www.khanacademy.org/`.

Dashboards and dates

In Business Intelligence, dates are an essential part of analysis, and they are an important part of Business Intelligence projects. Data warehouses, for example, have a Date dimension as a way of helping business users to describe their data by date. People's business questions often include a *when* element. Additionally, dashboards will often reference dates.

Comparison is fundamental to analysis. Time is a fundamental part of comparison. Dashboards will often display comparisons between periods of time, so time is an essential part of the dashboard display. It is easy to envisage the following business questions that involve time:

- ▸ What are my numbers compared to last year?
- ▸ How did my sales region perform this month as compared to the last month?
- ▸ When will my department reach its target?

This recipe explains how to use dates in order to analyze your data using the Dates functionality in Tableau.

In the last recipe, we imported the `FactInternetSales` table. Once the `FactInternetSales` data has been imported, we will also do the same for the `DimDate` table. To analyze our data, we will perform the following actions:

- Join data together
- Activate links in relationships
- Date analysis in Tableau

Getting ready

We will continue to use the same Tableau workbook that we set up in the first recipe. It was called `Chapter 2`.

How to do it...

1. Let's create a new sheet by going to the tab at the foot of the worksheet with the worksheet name on it. Right-click to select **Duplicate Sheet**. Let's make the canvas clean again by removing all of the pills from the **Columns**, **Rows**, and **Marks** shelves.

2. Let's use the new worksheet to proceed.

3. Go to **DimDate#csv** under **Dimensions**, and look for **Calendar Year**.

4. Make sure **Calendar Year** is set to the String data type by right-clicking on **Calendar Year** on the **Data** pane, then navigating to **Change Data Type**, and finally selecting **String**.

5. In the **Data** pane, select **Calendar Year** and drag it into the **Rows** shelf.

6. Go to the `FactInternetSales` table on the **Measures** pane. Drag the **SalesAmount** column from the **Measures** pane to the column next to the **Calendar** year on the canvas. You can see this in the following screenshot:

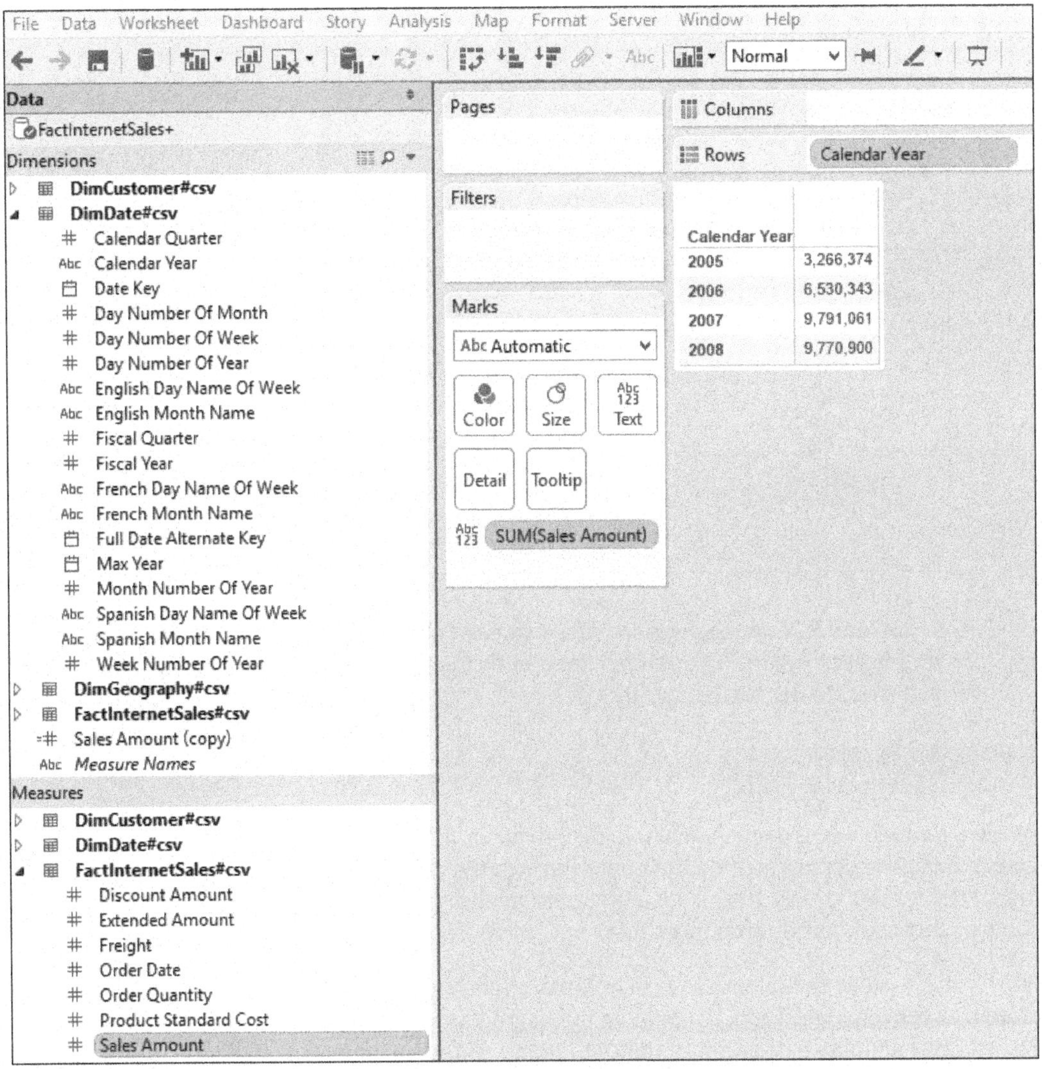

7. Let's look at what happens if we use a different aggregation, **Count Distinct**. This returns a count of the distinct **SalesAmount** values. When we link the `OrderDateKey` column and select **Count Distinct** for the **SalesAmount** figure, Tableau returns the **Count Distinct** value for each calendar year. You can see an example of this in the following screenshot:

Pages		Columns	
		Rows	Calendar Year

Filters

Calendar Year	
2005	4
2006	10
2007	38
2008	33

Marks

Abc Automatic

Color   Size   Abc 123 Text

Detail   Tooltip

Abc 123   CNTD(Sales Amoun..

8. In Tableau 8, if the aggregation is considered not valid, Tableau saves the user from themselves by graying out the screen until it is fixed. You have the facility to undo the last step. To do this, press *Ctrl + Z*.

How it works...

While a formula might be technically valid, it may not make much business sense. Tableau allows business users to enrich their data through the addition of calculations that get stored as part of the workbook. This is useful for data analysis, since we can look and see how simple steps can quickly affect the data.

Why is this the case? Tableau issues separate queries to each data source and joins the two data sources together. Then, it conducts the aggregation on the joined data sources at the lowest level of detail in the view of the data from the Tableau interface. Earlier in the book, we joined all of our sources together in one place, which Tableau then reads. If we pull data in from different sources, we have to consider the granularity.

Unfortunately, if the level of detail in the underlying query is different from the level of detail in the view, then the calculation will not be correct. In this case, they would be said to have different levels of granularity.

The moral of the story is to keep the relevant dimensions in the Tableau view, that is, put their features in the **Columns** and **Rows** shelves or in the **Marks** shelf. By putting more elements in the view, these shelves will move the query towards serving up data that can be used for matching the data sources. Then, the user can try to incorporate the query by including as many dimensions as possible, which in turn will produce as much detail in the query as possible in order to facilitate matching between the tables.

There's more...

Dashboards use a lot of calculations to summarize data. Research by specialists such as Ben Shneiderman shows that people tend to want to see the summary first, followed by zooming and filtering the data, and then finally see the details on demand. This is a very natural way of engaging with data. Shneiderman calls this the "Visual Information Seeking Mantra".

If you are interested in the psychology of how individuals interact with data, then Ben Shneiderman's paper *The Eyes Have It* (1996), which you can find at `http://dl.acm.org/citation.cfm?id=834354`, will be of help.

Grouping your data with calculations

In the first recipe, we specified communication as one of the key features of a dashboard. We need to be able to share the right information with the right audience, at the right time, to the right people, and in the right format.

Sometimes, data needs to be translated so that it matches the business rules and the business understanding of the organization. Tableau offers a number of different ways that help you translate data into something that the business decision makers will understand.

Grouping is one way of making data meaningful to the business. In this recipe, we will look at grouping some dimension members into a single member. Rolling up some of the members in one dimension is a good way of summarizing data for dashboards.

In this recipe, we will look at grouping dimension members; then, we will look at more complex grouping of calculations. The business question is an investigation into the characteristics of customers, for example, those who have children, and those who do not. We will group the **Number Children At Home** dimension members into the group of customers who have children and those who do not.

Then, we will look at a more advanced example of grouping the data by measure rather than dimension. To do this, we can create a calculation that will distinguish the values that are below the average sales amount and above the average. Results that are classified as above average are labeled **Above or Equal to Average**, and below average sales are labeled **Below Average**. We can then use this calculation to convey a visual message to the business user; for example, we could color the above average sales in one color and the below average sales in another in order to make the distinction easily identifiable.

Getting ready

We will need to add in a new data source for this recipe. Note that this recipe has a basic part, and then a more advanced part.

How to do it...

1. Click on *Ctrl + M* to get a new worksheet in Tableau. Alternatively, go to the **Worksheet** menu item and select **New Worksheet**.

2. Go to the **Measures** pane and drag **Number of Records** from the **Measures** pane to the **Rows** shelf.

3. Go to the `DimCustomer#csv` table, which is under the **Measure** part of the **Data** pane on the left-hand side.

4. Drag the **Number Children At Home** measure from the **Measures** pane directly up to the **Dimension** pane in the **Data** pane.

5. Right-click on **Number Children At Home** and change data type to **String**. The next screenshot shows you an example of how your screen will look:

6. Drag the **Number Children At Home** dimension onto the **Rows** shelf and place it to the left of the **NumberOfRecords** column. You can see an example in the next screenshot:

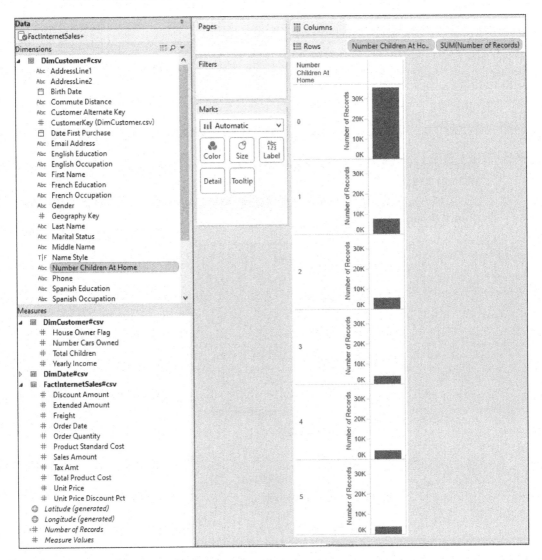

7. Let's change the visualization to a table. Go to the **Show Me** panel and click on the **Text Table** option. When we look at the **Number Children At Home** dimension, we see the following members and the number of customer records associated with each member:

Number Children At Home	
0	35,535
1	7,695
2	5,338
3	4,028
4	4,216
5	3,586

8. We will group the dimension members, so it is easier to see the customers who have children and the ones who do not.

9. Go to the dimension called **Number Children At Home**, right-click on it, and select the **Create Group** option, as shown:

Add to Sheet
Copy
Paste
Duplicate
Rename...
Hide
Create Calculated Field...
Create Group...
Create Set...
Create Parameter...
Create Hierarchy...
Convert to Measure
Change Data Type ▶
Geographic Role ▶
Default Properties ▶
Replace References...
Describe...

10. This produces the **Create Group** dialog box, which you can see in the following screenshot:

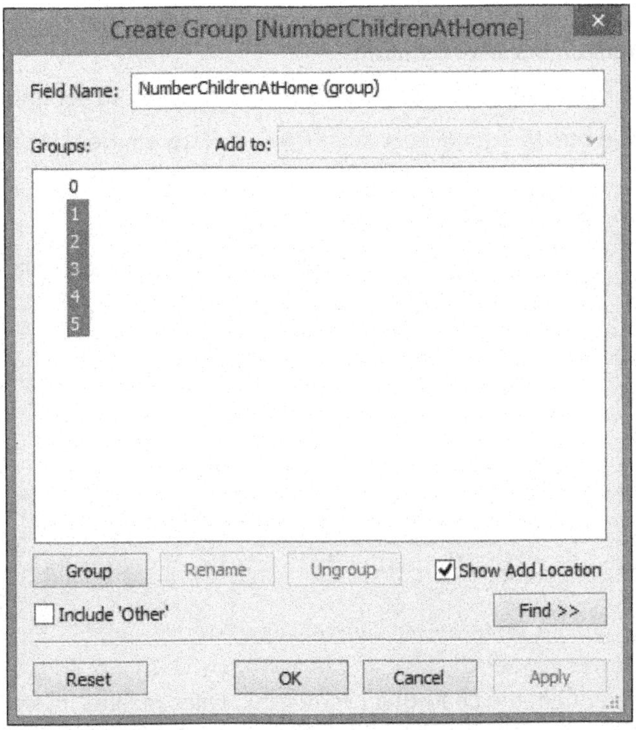

11. In the **Field Name** field, you will see the name of the field.

12. Multiselect the numbers 1 through to 5 by holding the *Shift* key and clicking to select more than one number at a time.

13. Click on **Group**, rename the group to `Customers With Children`, and click on **OK**.

14. You can then see the new group on the left-hand side of the **Dimensions** pane, at the bottom of the list. Drag your new grouping to the **Rows** shelf.

15. Remove the **Number Children At Home** pill that is NOT a group. The **Number Children At Home** group should be on the Rows shelf. Then, choose **Number of Records** from the **Measures** pane and put it into the **Columns** shelf. You can see that the table now only has two rows in it: one that consists of a zero and another that has **Customers With Children**.

16. In order to make things clear, right-click on the zero and select **Edit Alias**.

17. Rename the zero to Customers with No Children. Here is an example:

18. It is now clear from the chart that over 24,000 sales records involve customers who have children, whereas just over 35,000 sales records involve customers who do not have children. We can visualize this information in a better way, and we will do this for the rest of the exercise.

19. To do this, change the visualization to a **Stacked Bar** chart using the **Show Me** panel.

20. Click on the **Swap** button so that the bar appears in a horizontal line. You can see that the **Swap** button is placed under the menu bar. Here is an example:

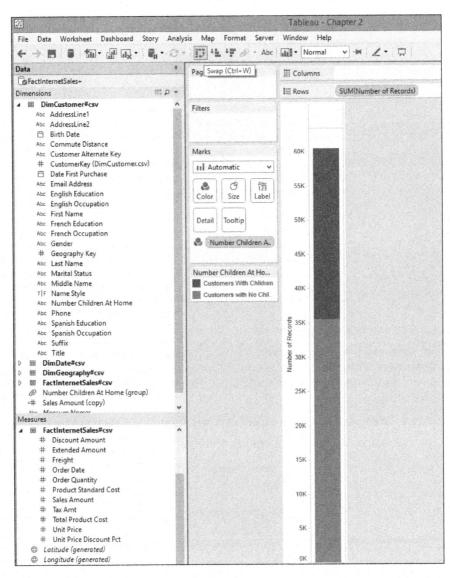

21. We can then change the colors by dragging **Number of Children at Home** to the **Color** panel on the **Marks** shelf.

22. Next, click on the downward arrow on the **SUM(Number of Records)** item under the **Marks** shelf and you will see the following dialog box:

Edit Colors [Number Children At Home (group)]

Select Data Item:

Customers With Children

Customers with No Children

Select Color Palette:

Automatic

Assign Palette

Reset | OK | Cancel | Apply

23. For **Customers With Children**, we will choose blue.

24. For **Customers With No Children**, we will choose orange. Orange is selected for **Customers With No Children** because there is a greater number of customers who do not have children. Brighter and more intense colors are often used in order to denote higher values.

25. Drag the **Number of Children at Home** dimension to the **Label** button.

26. Your Tableau canvas should appear as shown in the following screenshot:

27. Next, we will look at a more advanced example of grouping the data by the measure, rather than the dimension. To do this, we can create a calculation that will distinguish the values that are below the average sales amount and above the average. Results that are classified as above average are labeled as **Above or Equal to Average**, and below average sales are labeled as **Below Average**. We can then use this neat calculation as a label to convey a visual message to the business user; for example, we could color the above average sales in one color and the below average sales in another in order to make the distinction easily identifiable.

28. To do this, stay in the `Chapter 2` workbook and continue to work in the existing worksheet.

29. Right-click on the **SalesAmount** measure.

30. Select the measure **Create Calculated Field** that is illustrated in the following screenshot:

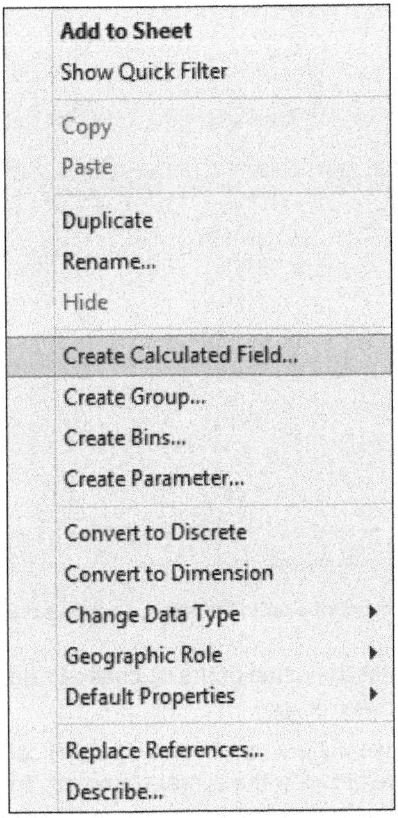

Add to Sheet
Show Quick Filter

Copy
Paste

Duplicate
Rename...
Hide

Create Calculated Field...
Create Group...
Create Bins...
Create Parameter...

Convert to Discrete
Convert to Dimension
Change Data Type   ▶
Geographic Role   ▶
Default Properties   ▶

Replace References...
Describe...

31. When you select this option, you will get the following dialog box:

32. In the **Name** field, enter the name of the calculated field:
    SalesAboveOrBelowAverage.

33. In the **Formula** field, we will put in a formula that will calculate whether or not the sales amount is above or below the average amount. The formula is as follows:

```
IF ( SUM([SalesAmount]) - WINDOW_AVG(SUM([SalesAmount]), First(),
Last() ) < 0 )
Then 'Below Average'
Else 'Above or Equal To Average'
END
```

[
]

34. Once you've placed the formula into the calculation editor and clicked on **OK**, you will be returned to the main Tableau interface. You will see your new calculation on the left-hand side in the **Measures** pane.

35. Remove the **Number Children At Home** label from the **Marks** shelf.

36. Add **SalesAmount** to the **Columns** shelf.

37. On the **Measures** window in the data pane, go to DimCustomer#csv and look for **Number Cars Owned**.

38. Drag the **Number Cars Owned** measure attribute to the **Dimension** pane.

39. Drag **Number Cars Owned** from the **Dimension** pane to the **Rows** shelf.

40. Drag your new calculation **SalesAboveOrBelowAverage** to the **Color** button on the **Marks** shelf.

    Your screen should now look like this:

To summarize, we have created a calculation that is meaningful to a business user. It provides the color display of the measure, which helps the business user understand things more efficiently. To summarize, it is simple and effective to conduct a grouping of dimension members into a binary grouping. This is useful for dashboards in order to provide an "at a glance" metric visualization that shows the organization has more customers who do not have children than those who do.

Essentially, this formula uses the WINDOW_AVG function to work out the average of the values that are in the Tableau view of the data. Basically, this average works out the value of the data that is viewable in the Tableau canvas and does not include data that has been filtered.

It uses `First()` and `Last()` to work out the average of all the data shown in the canvas, from the first row right until the last row. The calculation takes the current **SalesAmount** value and compares it with the average **SalesAmount** value.

How it works...

Tableau allows you to group data together by simply arranging fields of your data source on a Tableau worksheet.

When you group fields in a worksheet, Tableau queries the data using standard drivers and query languages (such as SQL and MDX). It then groups data together wherever necessary. Finally, it presents a visual analysis of the data.

Correlation with calculations

Data visualization is all about communicating a message using data. In the first chapter, we specified communication as one of the key features of a dashboard.

The problem with data visualization is that people don't always like what visualization tells them about their business. It can defy commonly held assumptions about a business that go against the grain of what people believe. This can be particularly uncomfortable if people have been with an organization for a long time and perhaps have not changed their perspective as the business has moved ahead.

In this recipe, we will look at how we can use correlation to test a hypothesis and then display this information so that the message of the data is easy to understand.

Getting ready

We will continue to use the same worksheet as we have used in the previous recipes of this chapter.

How to do it...

In this recipe, we will use a real-life example where a business analyst wants to know if people with more cars spend less on bikes. We will test whether there is a correlation between the number of cars owned by a customer and how much money is spent on bikes. Since the AdventureWorks store is selling bikes, there is an assumption that people who own fewer cars will spend more on bikes. However, this hypothesis would need to be tested, and data visualization can help us "sense-check" the data and see patterns easily.

Perform the following steps to create correlations in Tableau:

1. Open up the `Chapter 2` workbook and create a new worksheet by pressing *Ctrl + M*, or by going to the **Worksheet** menu item and then selecting **New Worksheet**.

2. Rename the `Correlation with Calculations` tab.

3. Take the dimension named **Number Cars Owned** from the `DimCustomer#csv` table and drag it on to the **Rows** shelf. Change the measure to **Count** by right-clicking on **Number Cars Owned** and navigate to **Measure**. In the pop-up menu, select the **Count** option.

4. Take the **SalesAmount** measure from the `FactInternetSales#csv` table and place it on the **Columns** shelf.

5. Take the **Number Cars Owned** member from the **DimCustomer** dimension and place it on the **Color** attribute in the **Marks** shelf.

6. Next, we will add a trend line order to convey the relationship between the sales amount and the number of sales. To do this, navigate to **Analysis | Trend Lines** and select **Show Trend Lines**. You can see this in the following screenshot:

The visualization now appears as follows:

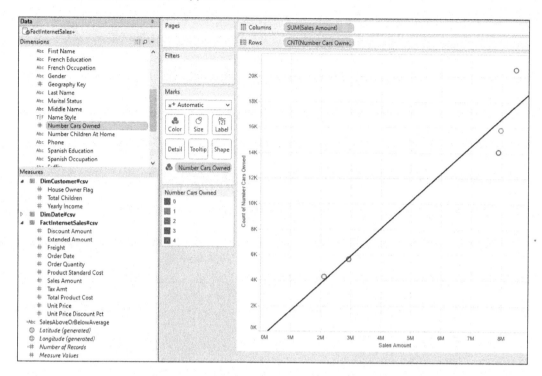

7. The image needs some more detail in order to clarify the message of the data. We can add labels to the data points that will help us identify the data points more clearly. To do this, we can drag the **Number Cars Owned** dimension to the **Label** option in the **Marks** shelf.

8. The black trend line looks quite harsh, and we can soften it by turning it into a light gray color. This would still get the message of the data across, but without attracting too much attention away from other pieces of the image.

9. To change the image, right-click on the trend line and you will get the following menu:

Describe Trend Line...

Format...

✔ Show Trend Lines

Edit Trend Lines...

Describe Trend Model...

10. Select **Format** and the following menu item will appear:

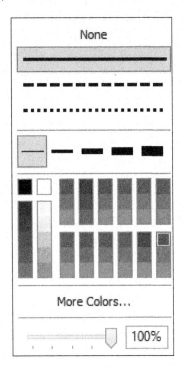

11. We can soften the trend line by changing the width. To do this, click on the arrow and the following panel appears. This allows us to soften the trend line:

The resulting visualization appears, as you can see in the next screenshot:

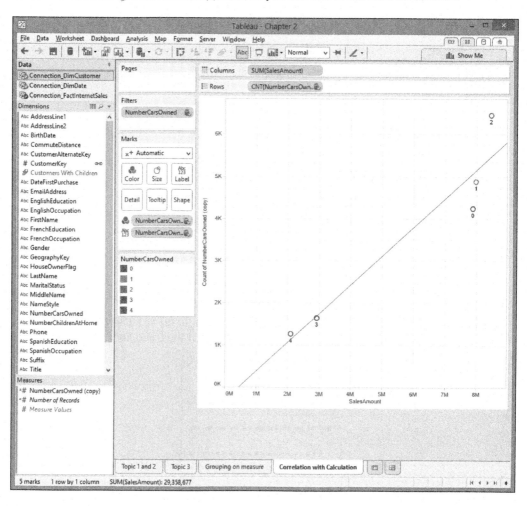

12. We can learn more about the trend line by going to the **Analysis** menu item and selecting **Describe Trend Model** from the **Trend Lines** menu. This provides us with the following information:

We can see the results of the analysis in the resulting window.

How it works...

Tableau provides a way to test hypotheses quickly and help business users to identify the relationships between variables. Tableau does this by simplifying the process of creating visualizations quickly and on the fly.

The visualization shows us that a linear correlation is produced, which shows how the sum of transactions or **Number of Records** is related to the sales amount.

We can see that the R-squared value is 0.92, and when we find the square root of this number, we will find that $R = 0.95$. This shows there is a very strong relationship between the two variables. We could then proceed to do some more analysis, but this would provide us with a great starting point.

There's more...

From a dashboard perspective, Tableau also helps business processes by allowing analysts to test assumptions that are perhaps long-held and subtle. When a visualization like this is placed with other visualizations that tell a similar story, then the dashboard becomes a valuable tool for promoting real business change.

Using cross-tabs flexibly

When we create dashboards, we are conveying a unified message of data that can be made up of moving parts. The context of the data can help to ensure that data pieces *move together* and are consistent with one another. This can mean that showing an aggregated number is not the most meaningful form of data. Instead, percentages or differences can be more meaningful.

In Tableau, we can create very simple calculations using table calculations. What is a table calculation? **Table calculations** are easy calculations that are provided by default as part of the Tableau interface. Table calculations are quick to create and are a powerful tool that can help to enhance your understanding of the data. From a dashboard perspective, we need to maximize the amount of information in a small space, and table calculations will help you to compress the message of the data while helping the data to be meaningful.

In this recipe, we will create a table calculation and see how it adds to the comprehension of the data in a small space. In this recipe, we will create a chart that shows the percentage of sales attributed to each region, rather than the number.

Getting ready

Open up the Tableau Chapter 2 workbook and start a new sheet by selecting *Ctrl + M*.

How to do it...

1. Create a new worksheet, and call it **Using Crosstabs Flexibly**.

2. Go to **FactInternetSales** in the **Measures** pane, select **SalesAmount**, and drag it to the **Columns** shelf.

3. Go to **DimGeography#csv** on the **Dimensions** pane, and drag **Country Region Code** to the **Rows** shelf.

4.   Click on the **Sort** button on the menu bar. The data bars will appear as follows:

5.   For our example, we will change the metric to **Percent of Total**. To do this, click on the downward arrow on the right-hand side of the **SUM(Sales Amount)** pill.

6.   Select **Quick Table Calculation**, and select **Percent of Total** from the drop-down list. Here is an example:

7.   The **SalesAmount** figure will change, and you will see a small triangle appear on the right-hand side. This feature is illustrated as follows:

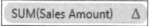

8.   Take the **SalesAboveOrBelowAverage** calculation we created earlier and place it in the **Color** section.

9.   For the visualization, choose a horizontal bar chart from the **Show Me** panel. Your screen should be the same as the following screenshot:

Pages			
	Columns	SUM(Sales Amount) △	
	Rows	Country Region Code F	

Country Regi..
US
AU
GB
DE
FR
CA

0%   5%   10%   15%   20%   25%   30%
% of Total Sales Amount

Filters

Marks

Automatic ▾

Color   Size   Label

Detail   Tooltip

SalesAboveOrBe.. △

AGG(SalesAboveOrBelow...
■ Above or Equal To Aver..
■ Below Average

10. Now, it is important to note that the x axis labeling has changed to show **% of Total SalesAmount**. This is more accurate, but how could we make it more obvious to the data consumer that they are in fact looking at percentages without cluttering the "real estate" on the dashboard? We will look at these steps next.

11. We can set up a variation on a heat map. From the **Show Me** shelf, select the **heatmap** option.

12. We will use a label to convey the percentage. To do this, take **SalesAmount** from the **Measures** pane and drag it to the **Label** option.

13. Make sure that you change the calculation so that it uses the **Percentage of Total** option, as we did previously in this recipe. To do this, click on the downward arrow seen on the right-hand side of **SUM(Sales Amount)**, which is the pill marked as configuring the label. Here is an example:

14. The label will now read the percentage of the total rather than the actual value.

15. Then, go back to the **Marks** shelf and select the drop-down list so that it shows **Shape**; after this, space the heat map so that it looks more even. The following is an example of the resulting chart:

Pages

Columns

Rows　　　Country Region Code

Filters

Country Region Code		
US	◯	31.98%
AU	◯	30.86%
GB	◯	11.55%
DE	◯	9.86%
FR	◯	9.01%
CA	◯	6.74%

Marks

x+ Shape

Color　Size　Label

Detail　Tooltip　Shape

SalesAboveOrBe.. Δ

SUM(Sales Amo.. Δ

SalesAboveOrBe.. Δ

SUM(Sales Amo.. Δ

AGG(SalesAboveOrBelow...
Above or Equal To Aver..
Below Average

To summarize, the data is shown in a very compressed way, which provides details as well as a visual message about the data in question. It's clear that the US and Australia regions have above average sales; if more detail is required, the percentages are also given.

How it works...

Tableau allows us to tell a story simply in a small space! The use of table calculations is a very simple way to enhance the data, both visually and also in terms of details. Sometimes, however, using the default table calculations are not enough to meet the business needs and custom calculations are required. This is the subject of our next recipe.

There's more...

The author of the *Le Petit Prince* books, Antoine de Saint-Exupéry, was once quoted as saying the following:

> *"A designer knows he has achieved perfection not when there is nothing left to add, but when there is nothing left to take away."*

The simplicity of a design is often an asset in data visualization, and is better than adding more detail that deviates from the purpose of data visualization.

Edward Tufte coined the term **chartjunk**, which he defined as follows:

> *"Chartjunk refers to all visual elements in charts and graphs that are not necessary to comprehend the information represented on the graph, or that distract the viewer from this information."*

This is an important aspect of data visualization. When we are creating dashboards, we have to be careful about adding nonessential items. This is particularly important in situations where we have a small screen space, such as a dashboard or a mobile device.

Table calculations are useful because they help us maximize the space on the screen by providing more enhanced information and encoding business rules effectively. They help us get across essential business information, which is the key to the visualization. If you are interested in reading more about chartjunk, it is recommended that you read *The Visual Display of Quantitative Information, Edward Tufte* (1983).

Simplifying your business rules with custom calculations

Dashboarding concentrates on representing data in a small space while still getting across key concepts in the data. It is important to use the space effectively. There should be a balance between representing too much information and representing not enough information.

Some people circumvent the issue altogether by avoiding data visualization or perhaps simply not requiring it for their roles. For example, you might run up against individuals who are not interested in the "pretty pictures" and want to see the numbers. How do you combine this requirement with other people's requirements to have a visual representation of the data?

Fortunately, there are a number of ways in which we can use data visualization techniques to convey the message of the data in a table. In itself, a table is a valid data visualization technique because tables are very good at representing detail. In particular environments, such as finance, it is the minute details within the table that make all the difference.

In data visualization, we also have to cater to the people who just want the numbers as well as those who have a more visual requirement.

In this recipe, we will create a crosstab that has a custom calculation in it, which allows us to enhance the representation of the data for those who prefer a more visual approach; in addition to this, we'll also provision numbers for those who simply want a table.

In this example, we will use the calculation `Index()`. This ranks members depending on their value. We can use the ranking calculation in order to restrict our data visualization so that it only shows the top three best performers. This is a concept that is key to many dashboards, and we will look at implementing this element in this recipe.

Getting ready

We will continue to work on the Tableau `Chapter 2` workbook and start a new sheet by selecting *Ctrl + M*.

How to do it...

1. Open up the Tableau `Chapter 2` workbook and duplicate the worksheet called **Using Crosstabs Flexibly**. Rename it to `Custom Calculations`.

2. Click on the **Connection_FactInternetSales** data view and duplicate the **SalesAmount** measure by right-clicking on it and selecting **Duplicate**.

3. Rename it to `Rank` and then right-click on it to see a pop-up menu. Select the option called **Create Calculated Field**. You can see an example in the following screenshot:

Add to Sheet
Cut
Copy
Paste
Edit...
Duplicate
Rename...
Hide
Delete
Create Calculated Field...
Convert to Discrete
Geographic Role ▶
Default Properties ▶
Replace References...
Describe...

4. Once you have renamed the **Calculated Field** to `Rank`, click on it and choose **Edit**.

5. You will see the **Calculated Field** dialog box; an example of this dialog box is shown in the following screenshot:

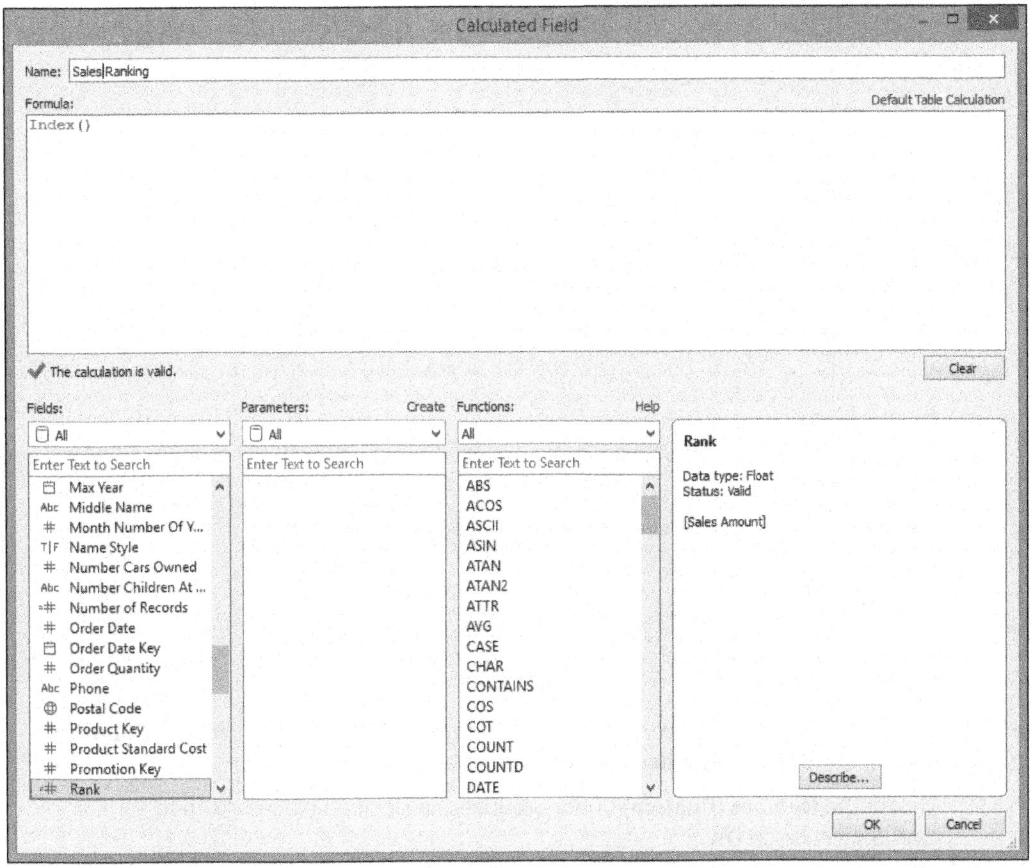

6. To use this calculation as a rank, simply type `Sales Ranking` in the **Name** field.

7. Next, type `Index()` in the **Formula** field.

8. Fortunately, Tableau provides a helpful guide to show you whether the formula is correct. Here, we can see that the calculation is valid. Once you have typed `Index()` in, click on **OK** and you are returned to the main Tableau interface.

9. Next, change the visualization to a table using the **Show Me** panel.

10. Now, drag the **SalesRanking** calculated field to the **Columns** shelf. You will see that **SalesRanking** appears as a number with two decimal points. To change the format, simply go back to the **Measures** pane and right-click on **SalesRanking**. Under the **Default Properties** heading, you will see an option specified as **Number Format**. You can see this in the following screenshot:

11. We will change the number format to an integer. When we select **Number Format**, we get the **Default Number Format** dialog box.

12. Select the **Number (Custom)** option, reduce the decimal places down to zero, and then click on **OK**.

13. The **SalesRanking** number will appear as an integer. Drag **SalesRanking** to the **Columns** shelf.

14. Go to the **Show Me** panel, and choose the **Text Table** option.

15. Go to the **Measure Values** pane, and make sure **Sales Ranking** only appears once, and that it is above **SUM(Sales Amount)**.

16. Our data visualization appears as illustrated in the following screenshot:

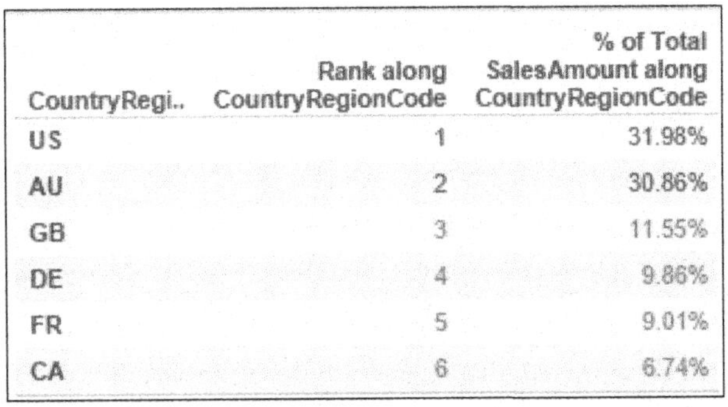

CountryRegi..	Rank along CountryRegionCode	% of Total SalesAmount along CountryRegionCode
US	1	31.98%
AU	2	30.86%
GB	3	11.55%
DE	4	9.86%
FR	5	9.01%
CA	6	6.74%

Now, let's take the scenario in which we want to display only the top three performers by region.

17. Simply drag **Sales Ranking** from the **Measures** pane through to the **Filters** pane. When you do this, you will get the following dialog box:

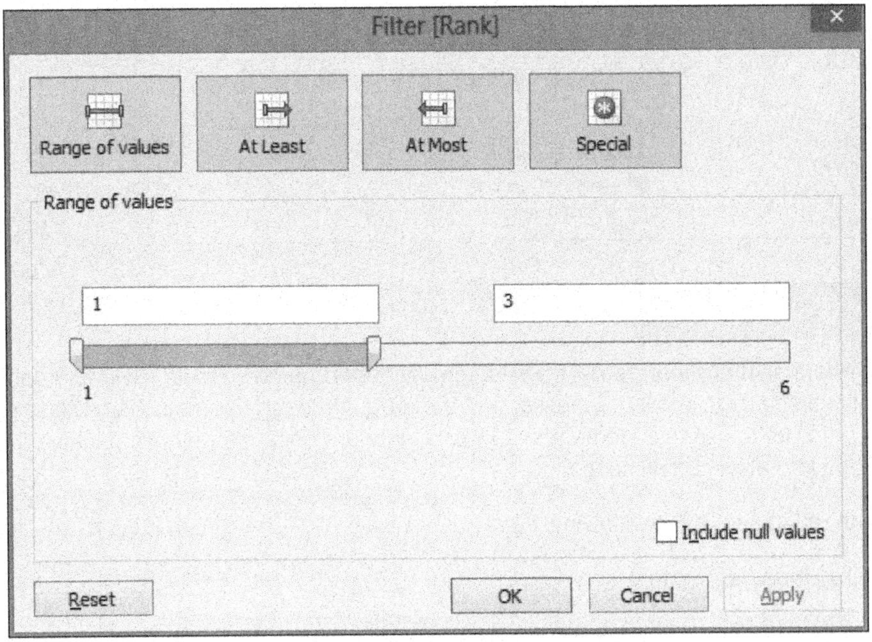

Make sure you enter the number 3 on the right-hand side rather than 6. Although there are six options, this filter means that Tableau will only display the top three best-selling regions.

You can see the final data visualization in the following screenshot:

File	Data	Worksheet	Dashboard	Analysis	Map	Format	Server	Window	Help

Data

🗒 Connection_DimCustomer
🗒 Connection_DimDate
🗒 Connection_DimGeography
🗒 Connection_FactInternetSales

Dimensions

Abc CarrierTrackingNumber
CustomerKey
Abc CustomerPONumber
📷 DueDate
OrderDate
OrderDateKey
SalesOrderLineNumber
Abc SalesOrderNumber
SalesTerritoryKey
📷 ShipDate
Abc *Measure Names*

Measures

CurrencyKey
DiscountAmount
DueDateKey

Pages

Filters

Rank

Measure Names

Marks

Abc Automatic

Color | Size | Text

Detail | Tooltip

Abc Measure Values

SalesAboveOr..

AGG(SalesAboveOrBelow...
■ Above Average
■ Below Average

Columns | Measure Names
Rows | CountryRegionCode

CountryRegion..	Rank along CountryRegionCode	% of Total SalesAmount along CountryRegionCode
US	1	31.98%
AU	2	30.86%
GB	3	11.55%

How it works...

Tableau offers us many interesting ways to compact the data down to its minimum design while still helping us to show the message of the data. Although the main visualization is very small, it helps us to use this element in a later dashboard because we have packaged a lot of information into a very small space.

The visualization shows the following:

▸ Top three performers

▸ The third performer is actually below average

▸ The overall percentage of sales as a number in order to provide numerical detail as well as some ways of visualizing the data so it provides "at a glance" information too

To summarize, making data tell a story is a challenge, particularly when there is not much space to play with. However, making data tell a story is fun with Tableau.

There's more...

Often, the column names in the data source are not meaningful to business users. They may need to be translated into something that is useful. Fortunately, Tableau allows you to use aliases to translate dimension names into something else.

3
Interacting with Data for Dashboards

In this chapter, we will cover the following recipes:

- ▶ Fun with filters – grouping your data with clarity
- ▶ Hierarchies for revealing the dashboard message
- ▶ Classifying your data for dashboards
- ▶ Actions and interactions
- ▶ Drilling into the details
- ▶ Working with input controls

Introduction

A key aspect of dashboarding is that a dashboard should convey its message clearly and simply in order to help team members draw the right conclusions. Dashboards became more interesting to businesses when Kaplan and Norton introduced their *Balanced Scorecard* methodology in the 1990s. This introduced the dashboard as a way of measuring business performance with a particular focus on **Key Performance Indicators** (**KPIs**), which helped to measure the success and direction of the organization. With the Enron scandal in 2001, businesses realized that it was perfectly possible to drown in data and not really understand what is going on at the executive level. Therefore, the dashboard concept gained renewed interest, which continues to date.

Creating dashboards is both a top-down and bottom-up process. It is top-down because we need to be able to summarize and put all of the pieces together. It is also a bottom-up process because the dashboard is made up of its constituent parts.

In this chapter, we will look at making the most of the constituent parts, so this chapter uses the bottom-up approach. Later on in this book, we will look at top-down processes while creating the dashboard.

In order to achieve the objective of conveying the message of the data effectively, users should be able to interact with data to get the information they need. The subject of this chapter is to help you create dashboards that will facilitate team members to get the most out of their dashboards by setting up interactivity, navigation, and an awareness of the underlying data. According to the guidelines, such as *Eight Golden Rules of Interface Design* by Professor Ben Shneiderman, it is vital to allow users to interact with the data by offering the filtering, categorizing, and zooming in functionalities to access the details. Business users gain trust in the data by having a look at the details, which allows them to validate the truth of the data.

Interacting with dashboards is a vital way of allowing business users to understand the data better. It also allows components to tell stories individually as well as provide a coherent story of the data as a whole.

From a practical perspective, it allows us to make the most of the space. Instead of having lots of reports with different dimensions and filters, we can help the user move towards **Self-Service Business Intelligence** (**SSBI**). We do this by furnishing the user with the data that they require in a dashboard format while allowing them to focus on the dimensions and attributes that are most important to them.

Dashboards are different from reports in that users expect to be able to view the data and understand it at a glance. In other words, very little interaction is required as the necessary data should be presented; that said, it is expected that the data is highly integrated and that the various elements of the dashboard are highly coupled together.

This section will help you to see the different ways of facilitating interactions with the data on the dashboard while getting the message of the data across as quickly and effectively as possible. Currently, we are in a bottom-up part of dashboard creation, and not top-down. In Tableau, we create worksheets that then go into the dashboards. This is why we will initially focus on worksheets.

Fun with filters – grouping your data with clarity

Filters are a useful way of helping users focus on particular aspects of the data that they are most interested in. This helps them to investigate and compare data and perhaps look for outliers and exceptions in the data.

Filtering data is an essential part of a dashboard. Users like to interact with data in order to understand it better, and it is natural to filter data so that users can pinpoint the data that particularly interests them.

Tableau allows users to filter measures, calculations, and dimensions, which is extremely useful in a dashboard. For example, take the case where you need to see the sales figures that are less than the given amount over a period of time.

In this recipe, we will import some more data and look at taking some descriptive statistics. We will also look at filters. Users have a lot of flexibility when it comes to combining filters, which means that you can have a lot of creativity in your analyses.

Getting ready

For this recipe, we will need to have Tableau open and ready to create a new workbook. For the exercises in this chapter, we will import multiple tables into our new workbook as the basis for creating calculations.

Let's create a new folder to store the Tableau workbook. For example, in this book, we will use the `Chapter Three` folder under `D:\Data\TableauCookbook\`. Therefore, you will need to have the folder open where you will download the data files. In *Chapter 1, A Short Dash to Dashboarding!*, we specified `D:\Data\TableauCookbook` as an example. We will be importing the following files:

- `DimProductCategory`
- `DimProductSubCategory`
- `DimProduct`
- `FactInternetSales`
- `DimDate`

How to do it...

1. Open up Tableau and navigate to **File | New**. This will start a new workbook in Tableau.

2. Go to **File** and then click on **Save As**.

3. Save the file as `Chapter Three`.

4. Let's rename the worksheet to `Fun with Filters`.

5. We will connect to the data and import it into Tableau's data store. To do this, select **Connect to Data**, which you will see under **Data**.

6. Under the **In a file** heading, select the **Text File** option.

7. Drag the `FactInternetSales.csv` file from the left-hand side onto the canvas.

8. Next, drag `DimProduct.csv` from the left-hand side list, onto the canvas.

9. Then, we will drag `DimProductSubcategory.csv` from the left-hand side, and place it next to `DimProduct.csv`.

10. Next, let's take the `DimProductCategory.csv` file from the left-hand side, and drop it next to **DimProductSubcategory**.

11. Finally, let's take `DimDate.csv` and drag it onto the canvas.

12. We will be asked to specify the join between the `DimDate.csv` table and the **FactInternetSales** file.

13. For the **Data Source** column, select the **Order Date Key** field. For the `DimDate.csv` field, select **Date Key**.

    The join should appear as follows:

Join			✕
Inner	Left	Right	Full Outer

Data Source		DimDate.csv	
Order Date Key	=	Date Key	
Add new join clause			

14. Click on the **Go to Worksheet** button to be taken back to the Tableau main canvas.

15. On the **Data** pane in the Tableau side bar, let's rename the data source to something more meaningful. Right-click on the data source under the **Data** pane. By default, Tableau will have given it a name that is the same as the first table that was selected. Here, it will be called `FactInternetSales+`. Right-click on it and select **Rename**.

16. Enter `CombinedProductsWithFacts` so we know that this data source is a combination of facts and products.

17. We can look at putting in dimensions and metrics in order to make a start and be productive straightaway with Tableau.

18. Let's visualize a table as the starting point. Take the **FullDateAlternateKey** field from the **DimDate** table and drag it onto the **Columns** shelf. Tableau will automatically recognize that this is a date, and it will aggregate the data according to the year level. Therefore, it will appear as **Year(FullDateAlternateKey)**.

19. Next, take the **EnglishProductCategory Name** attribute from the `DimProductCategory` table and place it on the **Rows** shelf.

20. Go to **FactInternetSales** under the **Measures** pane, and drag **SalesAmount** to the canvas.

21. Then, we will add a few table calculations as an exercise to explore this concept more while also adding to our filters in this exercise.

22. On the **Marks** shelf, right-click on the **Sum(Sales Amount)** metric and select the **Add Table Calculation** option, as shown in the following screenshot:

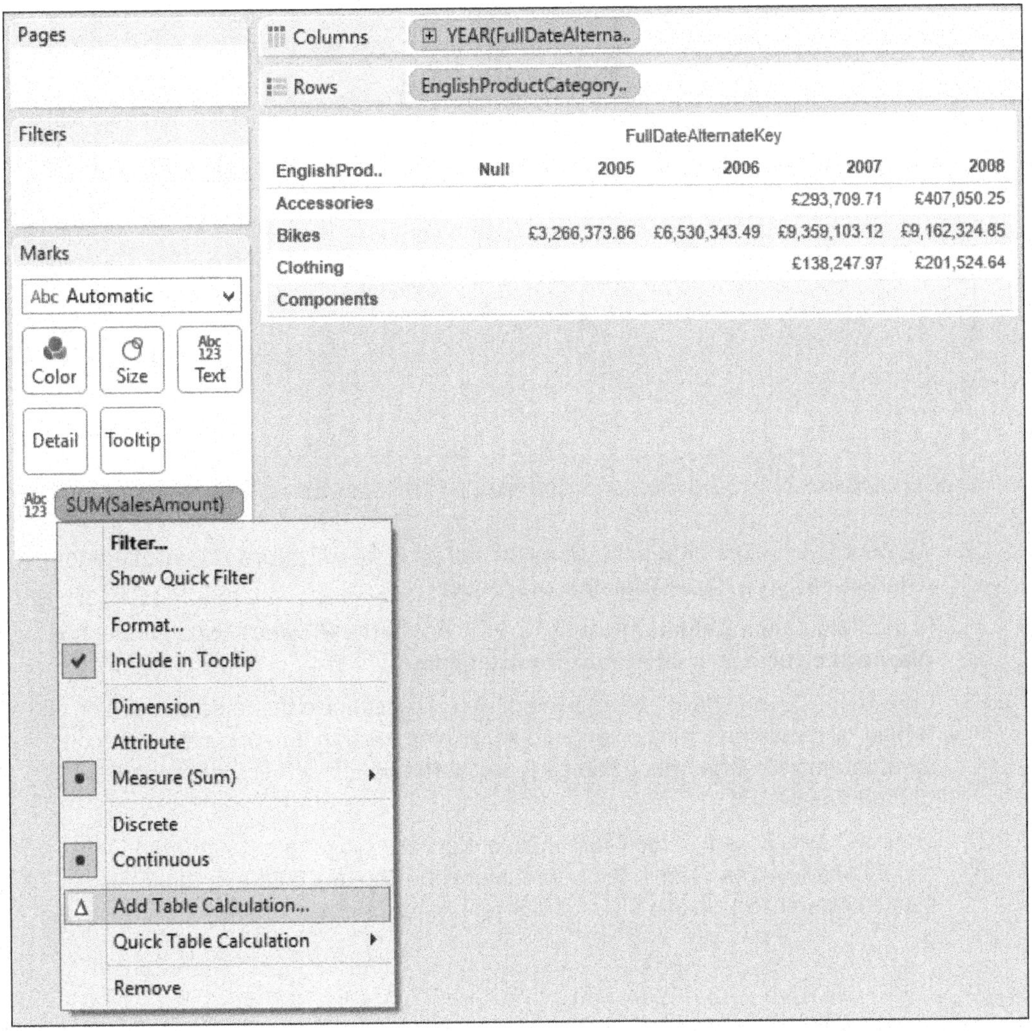

| Pages | Columns | ⊞ YEAR(FullDateAlterna.. |
| | Rows | EnglishProductCategory.. |

		FullDateAlternateKey			
EnglishProd..	Null	2005	2006	2007	2008
Accessories				£293,709.71	£407,050.25
Bikes		£3,266,373.86	£6,530,343.49	£9,359,103.12	£9,162,324.85
Clothing				£138,247.97	£201,524.64
Components					

Filters

Marks

Abc Automatic

Color | Size | Abc 123 Text

Detail | Tooltip

Abc 123 SUM(SalesAmount)

- Filter...
- Show Quick Filter
- Format...
- ✔ Include in Tooltip
- Dimension
- Attribute
- ● Measure (Sum) ▶
- Discrete
- ● Continuous
- △ Add Table Calculation...
- Quick Table Calculation ▶
- Remove

23. When we right-click on the **Sum(Sales Amount)** metric, we get the Add **Table Calculation** window, as shown in the following screenshot. For our purposes, we will choose **Difference From** as the value for **Calculation Type**.

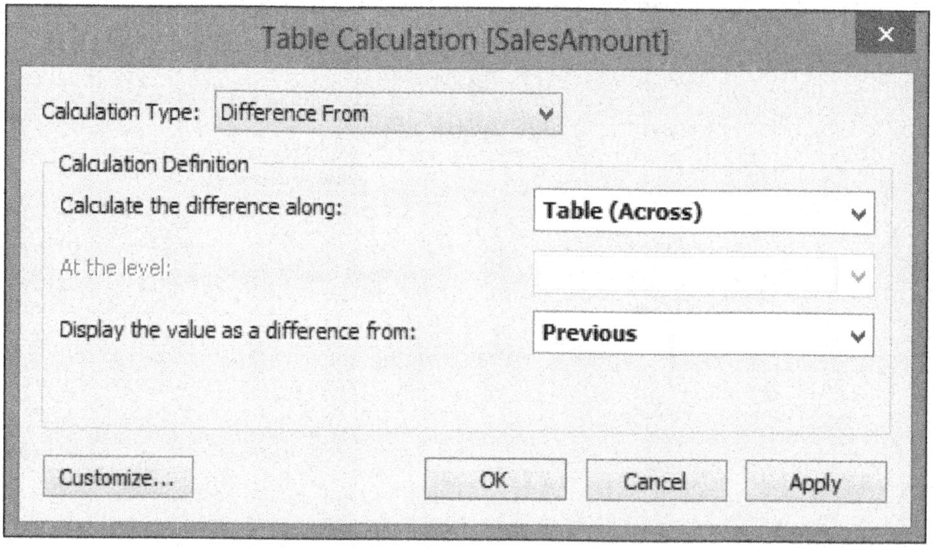

24. We will calculate the difference along the table, so we will choose to calculate the difference along with the **Table(Across)** option.

25. In the **Calculation Definition** panel, we will choose the **Previous** option under the **Display the value as a difference from:** dropdown.

26. Once these options have been selected, we can customize the table calculation further by renaming the calculation to something meaningful. To do this, click on the **Customize** button, which can be found at the bottom-left corner of the **Table Calculation** box.

27. After we have clicked on the **Customize** button, we will get the **Calculated Field** dialog, which you can see in the next screenshot. The text button at the top is labeled **Name:** and we can insert a different name in this textbox.

28. Here, we will rename the table calculation to `YoY Sales Difference`. The formula itself works out the current sales amount and compares it to the previous sales amount. If a null value is found, for example, where there is no previous sales amount available because we are looking at the data for the first year, then a zero is returned; this is the job of the **ZN** expression. Once you have renamed the table calculation, click on **OK**.

Calculated Field [Calculation1]		

Name: YoY Sales Difference

Formula:

```
ZN(SUM([SalesAmount])) - LOOKUP(ZN(SUM([SalesAmount])), -1)
```

✔ The calculation is valid.   Clear

Fields: **Parameters:**   Create   **Functions:**   Help

All   All   All

Enter Text to Search   Enter Text to Search   Enter Text to Search

# CalendarQuarter	VAR
# CalendarSemester	VARP
# CalendarYear	WINDOW_AVG
Abc CarrierTracking...	WINDOW_COUNT
Abc Class	WINDOW_MAX
Abc Color	WINDOW_MEDIAN
# CurrencyKey	WINDOW_MIN
# CustomerKey	WINDOW_STDEV
Abc CustomerPONu...	WINDOW_STDEVP
DateKey	WINDOW_SUM
# DayNumberOf...	WINDOW_VAR
# DayNumberOf...	WINDOW_VARP
# DayNumberOfY...	YEAR
# DaysToManufac...	ZN

ZN(expression)

Returns <expression> if it is not null, otherwise returns zero. Example: ZN(Profit)

OK   Cancel   Apply

29. You are then taken back to the previous window, and you will see a description of the formula in the **Description** window. You will also see the formula in the **Formula** box. When you reach this point, click on **OK**, as shown in the following screenshot:

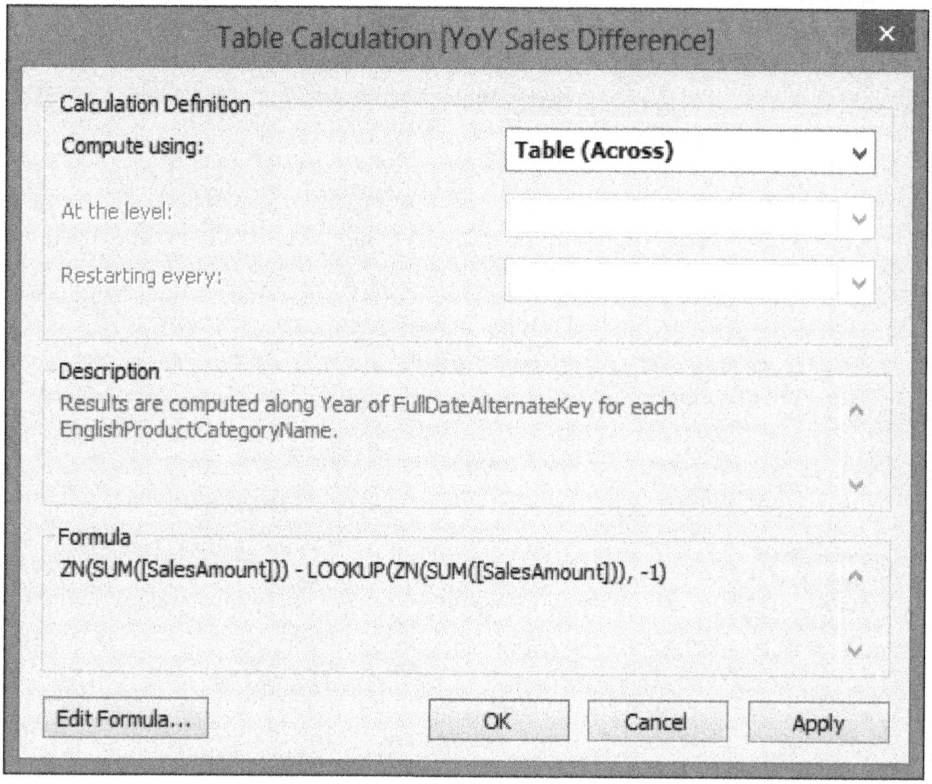

Table Calculation [YoY Sales Difference]   ✕

Calculation Definition

Compute using: Table (Across)   ⌄

At the level: ⌄

Restarting every: ⌄

Description
Results are computed along Year of FullDateAlternateKey for each
EnglishProductCategoryName.   ⌃
                                                                          ⌄

Formula
ZN(SUM([SalesAmount])) - LOOKUP(ZN(SUM([SalesAmount])), -1)   ⌃
                                                                          ⌄

[Edit Formula...]   [OK]   [Cancel]   [Apply]

30. Drag **Sum(Sales Amount)** from the **Measures** part of the side bar over to the **Marks** shelf. Here is an example of how the screen should look, so far:

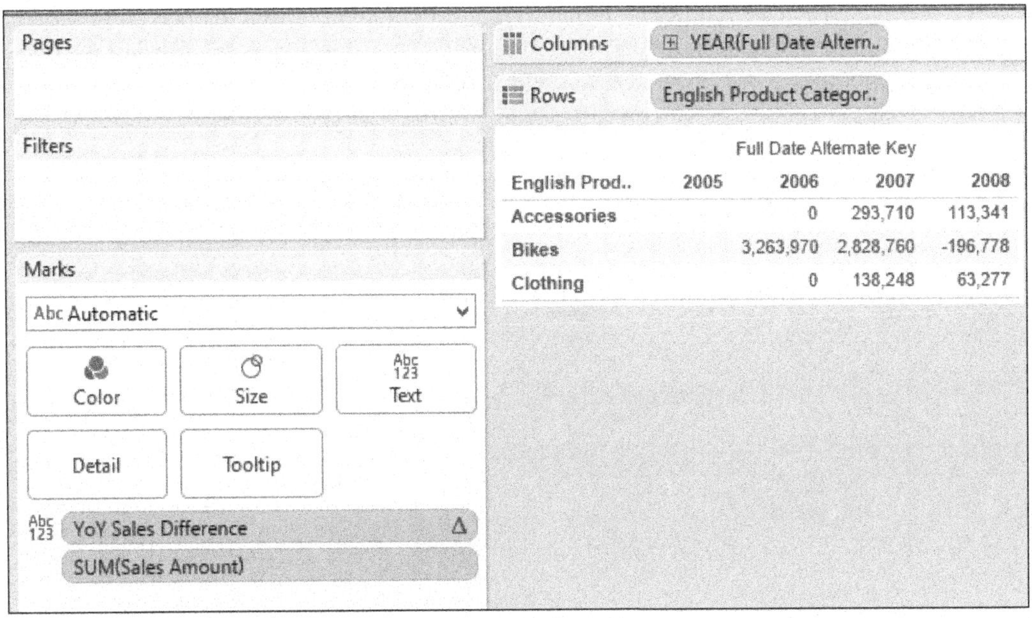

		Columns	⊞ YEAR(Full Date Altern..

Pages

		Rows	English Product Categor..

Filters

		Full Date Alternate Key			
English Prod..		2005	2006	2007	2008
Accessories			0	293,710	113,341
Bikes			3,263,970	2,828,760	-196,778
Clothing			0	138,248	63,277

Marks

Abc Automatic ⌄

Color	Size	Abc 123 Text

Detail	Tooltip

Abc 123 YoY Sales Difference △

SUM(Sales Amount)

31. Drag **Sum(Sales Amount)** from the **Measures** part of the sidebar over to the canvas so that it appears in the table, along with **YoY Sales Difference**.

32. Let's change **Sales Amount** so that it is a currency. To do this, go to **Sales Amount** on the **Marks** shelf and right-click to get the pop-up menu. Select the item **Default Properties**, and then select **Number Format**.

33. On the **Default Number Format** dialog box, select **Currency (Standard)**.

34. In the drop-down list, select your preferred currency, then click on **OK**. In these examples, we will use **English (United States)** and the dollar sign.

35. Let's repeat these steps the same for **YoY Sales Difference** so that it has the same currency format as **Sales Amount**. Right-click on **YoY Sales Difference** on the **Marks** shelf.

36. Click on **Format**, and you will see the **Format** pane appear on the left-hand side of the screen.

37. On the **Pane** tab, go to the **Numbers** drop-down list.

38. Select **Currency (Standard)**.

39. Right-click on the **Sum(Sales Amount)** measure on the **Marks** shelf and choose the **Quick Table Calculation** option from the menu list. Then, select the **Moving Average** option. You can see this in the following screenshot:

40. This will create a new measure that shows the moving average. To rename the new calculated measure, right-click on the **SUM(SalesAmount)** measure in the **Measure Values** shelf and choose the **Edit Table Calculation** option.

41. In the **Table Calculation [Moving Average of SalesAmount]** dialog box, select the **Customize...** option.

42. In the **Name:** box, rename it to `Moving Average` and click on **OK**.

43. To summarize, we will now have two measures: one for **Year on Year** changes and another for the **Moving Average Difference** over time.

44. Our next step is to work out the difference between the two calculations that we have just made. In other words, what is the difference between the year-on-year change and the moving average for the sales amount?

45. Our first step in this process is to create a new calculated field that will work out the difference between the year-on-year change and the moving average. To do this, firstly we will need to go to the **Analysis** tab at the top menu item and select the **Create Calculated Field** option. You can see this in the menu in the following screenshot:

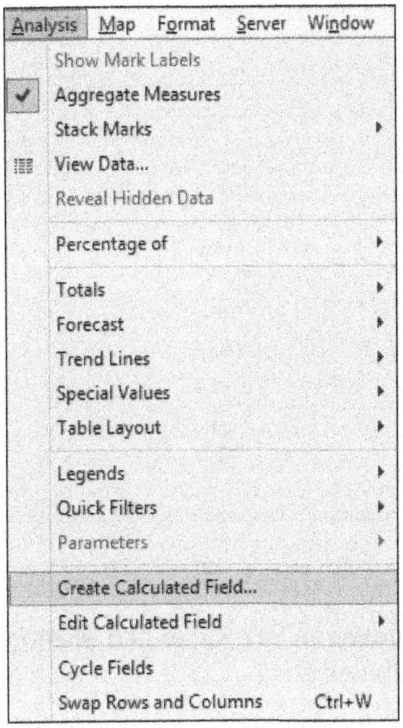

46. We will now get the **Calculated Field** editor box, and we need to subtract **Moving Average** from the **Year on Year** average. We can see this in the following screenshot:

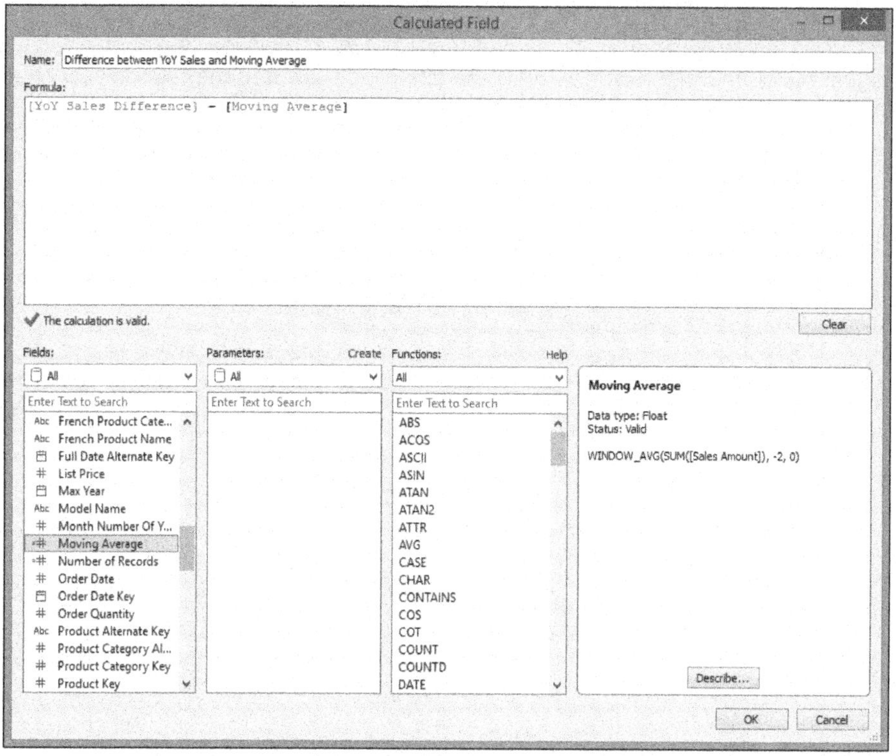

47. Click on **OK** once you have entered in the calculation.

48. Now, drag **Difference between YoY Sales and Moving Average** from the **Measures** pane to the **Measure Values** shelf.

49. When we place all the three calculations on the table, it looks a little confusing with a lot of numbers, and it is hard to differentiate the difference between patterns and outliers contained in the data. The following is an example:

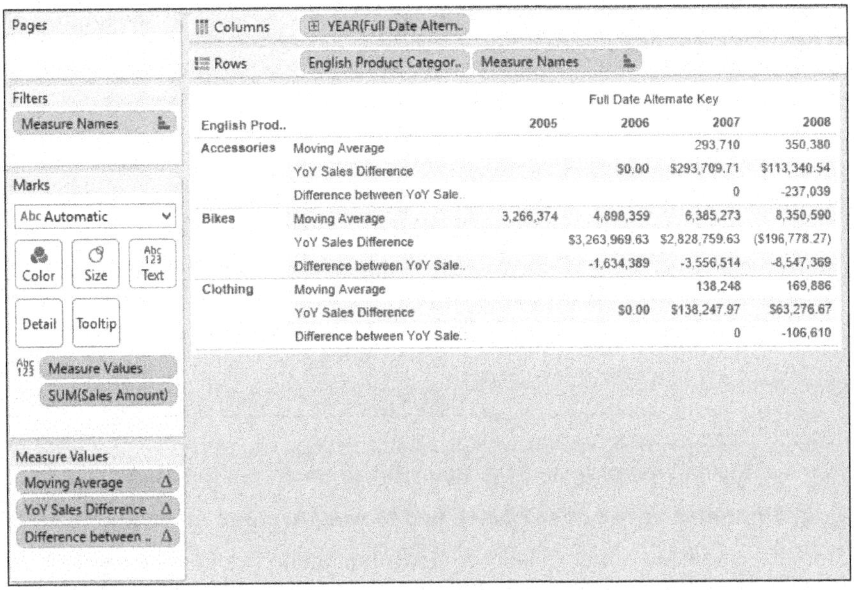

Pages						
	⊞ Columns	⊞ YEAR(Full Date Altern..				
	⊞ Rows	English Product Categor..	Measure Names			

Filters			Full Date Alternate Key			
Measure Names	English Prod..		2005	2006	2007	2008
	Accessories	Moving Average			293,710	350,380
		YoY Sales Difference		$0.00	$293,709.71	$113,340.54
Marks		Difference between YoY Sale..			0	-237,039
Abc Automatic	Bikes	Moving Average	3,266,374	4,898,359	6,385,273	8,350,590
		YoY Sales Difference		$3,263,969.63	$2,828,759.63	($196,778.27)
		Difference between YoY Sale..		-1,634,389	-3,556,514	-8,547,369
Color Size Text	Clothing	Moving Average			138,248	169,886
		YoY Sales Difference		$0.00	$138,247.97	$63,276.67
Detail Tooltip		Difference between YoY Sale..			0	-106,610

Measure Values
SUM(Sales Amount)

Measure Values
Moving Average Δ
YoY Sales Difference Δ
Difference between .. Δ

50. We can use our measures in order to filter the data, and it's very simple to do this. Drag the measure **Difference between YoY Sales and Moving Average** to the **Filters** shelf on the left-hand side.

51. A **Filter** window will appear; then, an example appears, as shown in the following screenshot:

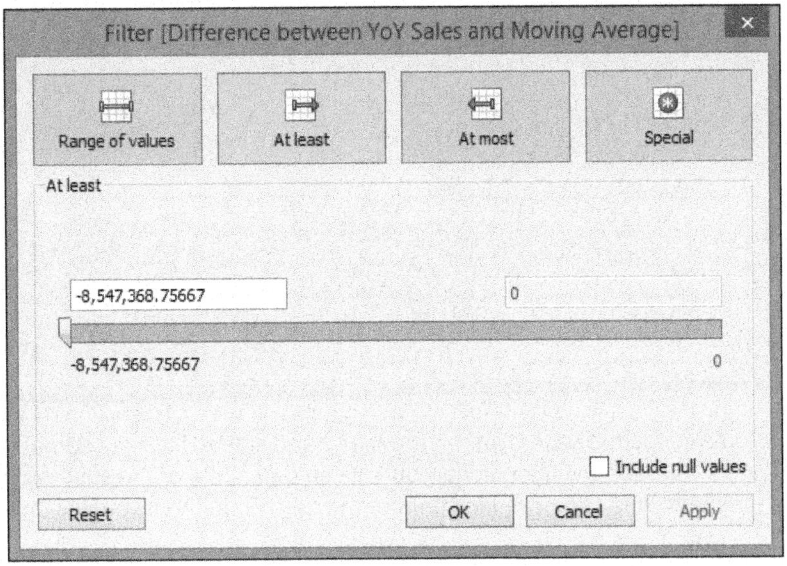

Filter [Difference between YoY Sales and Moving Average]

Range of values   At least   At most   Special

At least

-8,547,368.75667   0

-8,547,368.75667   0

☐ Include null values

Reset   OK   Cancel   Apply

52. Once you have created the filter, right-click on it and select the **Show Filter** option. Here is an example:

53. Remove **Moving Average** and **YoY Sales Difference** from the **Marks** shelf.

54. Drag **Difference between YoY Sales and Moving Average** to the **Filters** area.

55. From the **Show Me** panel, select the **Heatmap** option from the panel. Your visualization now looks like this:

56. Now you can use the slider filter on the right-hand side to filter out some of the data points. As you slide the filter along, you will see that some of the squares disappear and reappear. This allows you to filter out the data points that you don't need.

57. If we click on the data points, we can obtain more details of specific values.

How it works...

To summarize, in this section, we have shown that we can use table calculations and measures in order to filter data to show the information that we would like to see on the dashboard. Here, we filtered using a custom calculation, based on a business rule. This helps to provide the "at a glance" purpose of a dashboard.

Tableau allows you to filter out the data that you don't need, in a way that is intuitively familiar. This means that the important points can jump out at the business user. Further, using tooltips can enhance understanding of individual data points.

See also

▶ *Designing the User Interface: Strategies for Effective Human-Computer Interaction, Ben Shneiderman, Cath Plaisant, Maxine Cohen, Steven Jacobs, Prentice Hall*

Hierarchies for revealing the dashboard message

It can become difficult to manage data, particularly if you have many columns. It can become more difficult if they are similarly named, too. As you'd expect, Tableau helps you to organize your data so that it is easier to navigate and keep track of everything.

From the user perspective, hierarchies improve navigation and use by allowing the users to navigate from a headline down to a detailed level. From a Tableau's perspective, hierarchies are groups of columns that are arranged in increasing levels of granularity. Each deeper level of the hierarchy refers to more specific details of the data.

Some hierarchies are natural hierarchies, such as date. So, say Tableau works out that a column is a date and automatically adds in a hierarchy in this order: year, quarter, month, week, and date. You have seen this already, for example, when you dragged a date across to the **Columns** shelf, Tableau automatically turned the date into a year.

Some hierarchies are not always immediately visible. These hierarchies would need to be set up, and we will look at setting up a product hierarchy that straddles across different tables. This is a nice feature because it means that the hierarchy can reflect the users' understanding of the data and isn't determined only by the underlying data.

Getting ready

In this recipe, we will use the existing workbook that you created for this chapter.

We will use the same data. For this recipe, let's take a copy of the existing **Fun with Filters** worksheet and call it `Hierarchies`. To do this, right-click on the **Worksheet** tab and select the **Duplicate Sheet** option. You can then rename the sheet to `Hierarchies`.

How to do it...

1. Navigate to the `DimProductCategory` dimension and right-click on the **EnglishProductCategoryName** attribute.

2. From the pop-up menu, select the **Create Hierarchy** feature. You can see its location in the following screenshot:

3. When you select the option, you will get a textbox entitled **Create Hierarchy**, which will ask you to specify the name of the hierarchy.

4. We will call our hierarchy `Product Category`. Once you have entered this into the textbox, click on **OK**.

5. Your hierarchy will now be created, and it will appear at the bottom of the **Dimensions** list on the left-hand side of Tableau's interface.

6. Next, go to the **DimProductSubcategory** dimension and look for the **EnglishProductSubCategoryName** attribute. Drag it to the **Product Category** hierarchy under **EnglishProductCategoryName**, which is already part of the **Product Category** hierarchy.

7. Now we will add the **EnglishProductName** attribute, which we will find under the **DimProduct** dimension. Drag-and-drop it under the **EnglishProductSubCategoryName** attribute that is already under the **Product Category** hierarchy. The **Product Category** hierarchy should now look like this:

8. The **Product Category** hierarchy will be easier to understand if we rename the attributes. To do this, right-click on each attribute and choose **Rename**. Change **EnglishProductCategoryName** to Product Category.

9. Rename **EnglishProductSubcategoryName** to Product Subcategory by right-clicking on the attribute and selecting **Rename**.

10. Rename **EnglishProductName** to Product.

11. Once you have done this, the hierarchy should look like this:

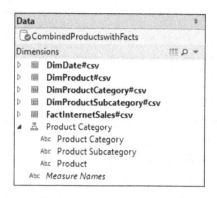

12. You can now use your hierarchy to change the details that you wish to see in the data visualization. Now, we will use **Product Category** of our data visualization rather than **Dimension**.

13. Remove everything from the **Rows** shelf and drag the **Product Category** hierarchy to the **Rows** shelf. Then, click on the plus sign; it will open the hierarchy, and you will see data for the next level under **Product Category**, which are subcategories.

14. Drag **Sales Amount** onto **Size** on the Marks shelf.

15. An example of the Tableau workbook is given in the following screenshot. You can see that the biggest differences occurred in the **Bikes** product category, and they occurred in the years 2006 and 2007 for the **Mountain Bikes** and **Road Bikes** categories.

16. To summarize, we have used the **Hierarchy** feature in Tableau to vary the degree of analysis we see in the dashboard.

How it works...

Tableau saves the additional information as part of the Tableau workbook. When you share the workbook, the hierarchies will be preserved.

The Tableau workbook would need revisions if the hierarchy is changed, or if you add in new dimensions and they need to be maintained. Therefore, they may need some additional maintenance. However, they are very useful features and worth the little extra touch they offer in order to help the dashboard user.

There's more...

Dashboarding data usually involves providing "at a glance" information for team members to clearly see the issues in the data and to make actionable decisions. Often, we don't need to provide further information unless we are asked for it, and it is a very useful feature that will help us answer more detailed questions. It saves us space on the page and is a very useful dashboard feature.

Let's take the example of a business meeting where the CEO wants to know more about the biggest differences or "swings" in the sales amount by category, and then wants more details.

The Tableau analyst can quickly place a hierarchy in order to answer more detailed questions if required, and this is done quite simply as described here. Hierarchies also allow us to encapsulate business rules into the dashboard. In this recipe, we used product hierarchies. We could also add in hierarchies for different calendars, for example, in order to reflect different reporting periods. This will allow the dashboard to be easily reused in order to reflect different reporting calendars, say, you want to show data according to a fiscal year or a calendar year. You could have two different hierarchies: one for fiscal and the other for the calendar year. The dashboard could contain the same measures but sliced by different calendars according to user requirements.

The hierarchies feature fits nicely with the Golden Mantra of Information Visualization, since it allows us to summarize the data and then drill down into it as the next step.

See also

▸ http://www.tableausoftware.com/about/blog/2013/4/lets-talk-about-sets-23043

Classifying your data for dashboards

Bins are a simple way of categorizing and bucketing values, depending on the measure value. So, for example, you could "bin" customers depending on their age group or the number of cars that they own. Bins are useful for dashboards because they offer a summary view of the data, which is essential for the "at a glance" function of dashboards.

Tableau can create bins automatically, or we can also set up bins manually using calculated fields. This recipe will show both versions in order to meet the business needs.

Getting ready

In this recipe, we will use the existing workbook that you created for this chapter.

We will use the same data. For this recipe, let's take a copy of the **Hierarchies** worksheet and by right-clicking on the **Worksheet** tab, select the **Duplicate Sheet** option. You can then rename the sheet to Bins.

How to do it...

1. Once you have your **Bins** worksheet in place, right-click on the **SalesAmount** measure and select the **Create Bins...** option. You can see an example of this in the following screenshot:

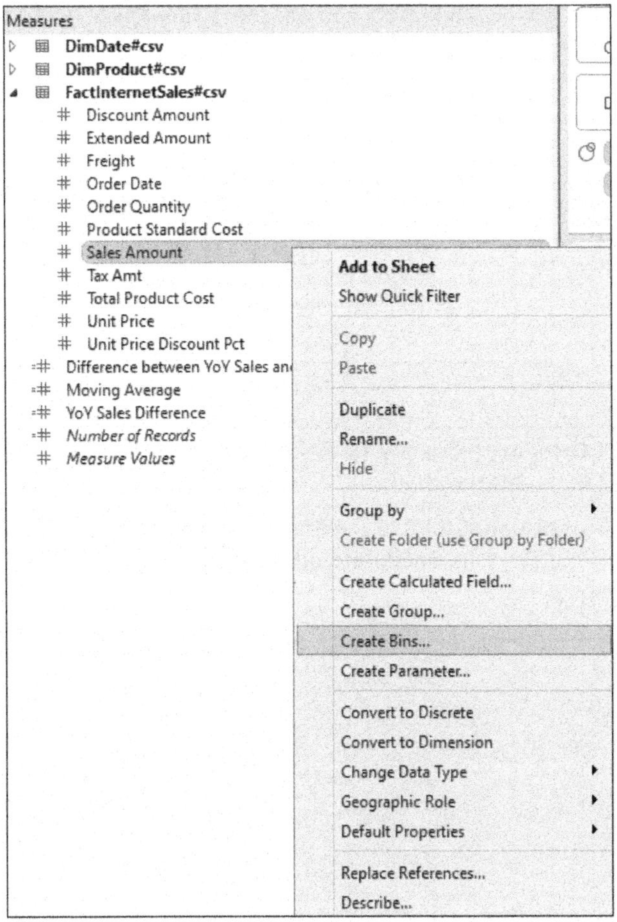

2. We will change the value to 5. Once you've done this, press the **Load** button to reveal the **Min**, **Max**, and **Diff** values of the data, as shown in the following screenshot:

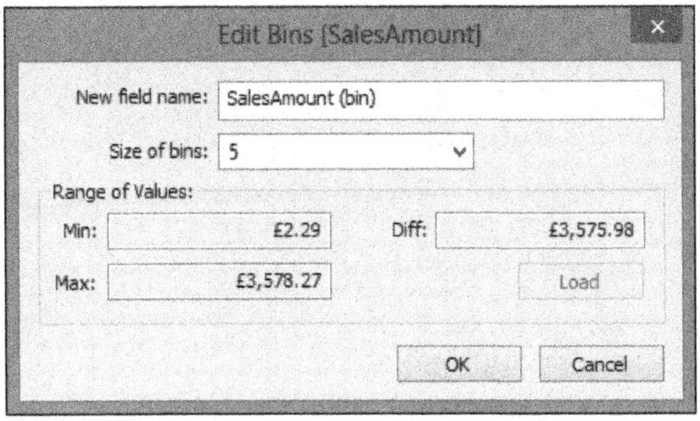

3. When you click on the **OK** button, you will see a bin appear under the **Dimensions** area. The following is an example of this:

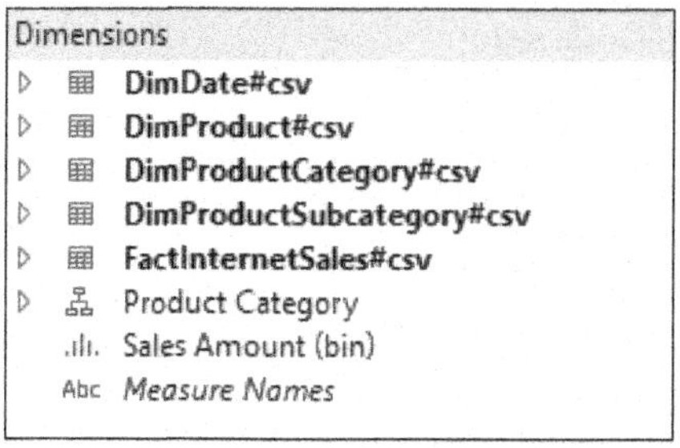
Dimensions
DimDate#csv
DimProduct#csv
DimProductCategory#csv
DimProductSubcategory#csv
FactInternetSales#csv
Product Category
Sales Amount (bin)
Abc
Measure Names

4. Let's test out our bins! To do this, remove everything from the **Rows** shelf, leaving only the **Product Category** hierarchy. Remove any filters from the worksheet and all of the calculations in the **Marks** shelf.
5. Next, drag **SalesAmount (bin)** to the **Marks** area under the **Detail** and **Tooltip** buttons. Once again, take **SalesAmount (bin)** and drag it to the **Color** button on the **Marks** shelf.

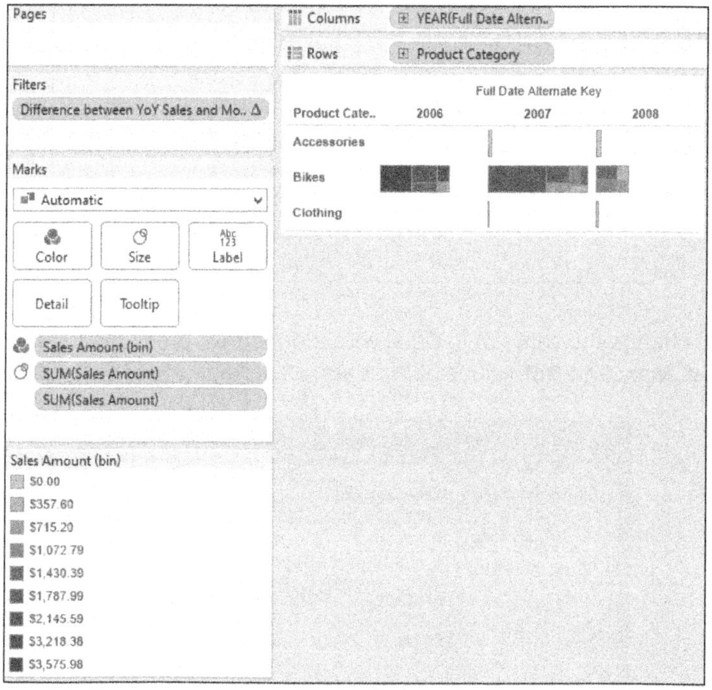
Pages
Columns
YEAR(Full Date Altern..
Rows
Product Category
Filters
Difference between YoY Sales and Mo..
Marks
Automatic
Color
Size
Label
Detail
Tooltip
Sales Amount (bin)
SUM(Sales Amount)
SUM(Sales Amount)
Full Date Alternate Key
Product Cate..
2006
2007
2008
Accessories
Bikes
Clothing
Sales Amount (bin)
$0.00
$357.60
$715.20
$1,072.79
$1,430.39
$1,787.99
$2,145.59
$3,218.38
$3,575.98

6. Now, we will change the size of the data points to reflect the size of the elements. To do this, drag **SalesAmount (bin)** to the **Size** button.

7. You can vary the overall size of the elements by clicking on the **Size** button and moving the slider horizontally so that you get your preferred size.

8. To neaten the image, right-click on the **Full Date Alternate Key** column heading and select **Hide Field Names for Columns** from the list.

    The Tableau worksheet should now look like this:

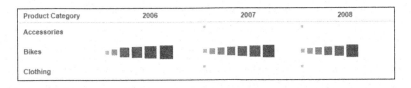

9. This allows us to see some patterns in the data. We can also see more details if we click on the data points; you can see an illustration of the details in the data in the following screenshot:

10. However, we might find that the automated bins are not very clear to business users. We can see in the previous screenshot that the **SalesAmount (bin)** value is **#610,298.76**. This may not be meaningful to business users.

    How can we set the bins so that they are meaningful to business users, rather than being automated by Tableau? For example, what if the business team wants to know about the proportion of their sales that fell into well-defined buckets, sliced by years?

    Fortunately, we can emulate the same behavior as in bins by simply using a calculated field. We can create a very simple IF... THEN... ELSEIF formula that will place the sales amounts into buckets, depending on the value of the sales amount. These buckets are manually defined using a calculated field, and we will see how to do this now.

11. Before we begin, take a copy of the existing worksheet called **Bins** and rename it to Bins Set Manually.

12. To do this, right-click on the **Sales Amount** measure and choose the **Create Calculated Field** option.

13. In the calculated field, enter the following formula:

```
If [SalesAmount] <= 1000 THEN "1000"
ELSEIF [SalesAmount] <= 2000 THEN "2000"
ELSEIF [SalesAmount] <= 3000 THEN "3000"
ELSEIF [SalesAmount] <= 4000 THEN "4000"
ELSEIF [SalesAmount] <= 5000 THEN "5000"
ELSEIF [SalesAmount] <= 6000 THEN "6000"
ELSE "7000"
END
```

14. When this formula is entered into the **Calculated Field** window, it looks like what the following screenshot shows. Rename the calculated field to **SalesAmount Buckets**.

![Calculated Field dialog box titled "Calculated Field [SalesAmount Buckets]". Name field contains "SalesAmount Buckets". The Formula box contains the If/ELSEIF formula. The calculation is valid. Below are Fields, Parameters, Functions lists with CalendarQuarter highlighted (Data type: Integer).]

15. Now that we have our calculated field in place, we can use it in our Tableau worksheet to create a dashboard component.

16. On the **Columns** shelf, place the **SalesAmount Buckets** calculated field and the **Year(Date)** dimension attribute.

17. On the **Rows** shelf, place **Sum(SalesAmount)** from the **Measures** section.

18. Place the **Product Category** hierarchy on the **Color** button.

19. Drag **SalesAmount Buckets** from the **Dimensions** pane to the **Size** button on the **Marks** shelf.

20. Go to the **Show Me** panel and select the **Circle View** option. This will provide a dot plot feel to data visualization. You can resize the chart by hovering the mouse over the foot of the *y* axis where the £0.00 value is located.

21. Remove **Sales Amount (bin)** from the **Marks** shelf.

22. Drag **SalesAmount Buckets** to the **Size** button.

23. Once you're done with these activities, the Tableau worksheet will look as it appears in the following screenshot:

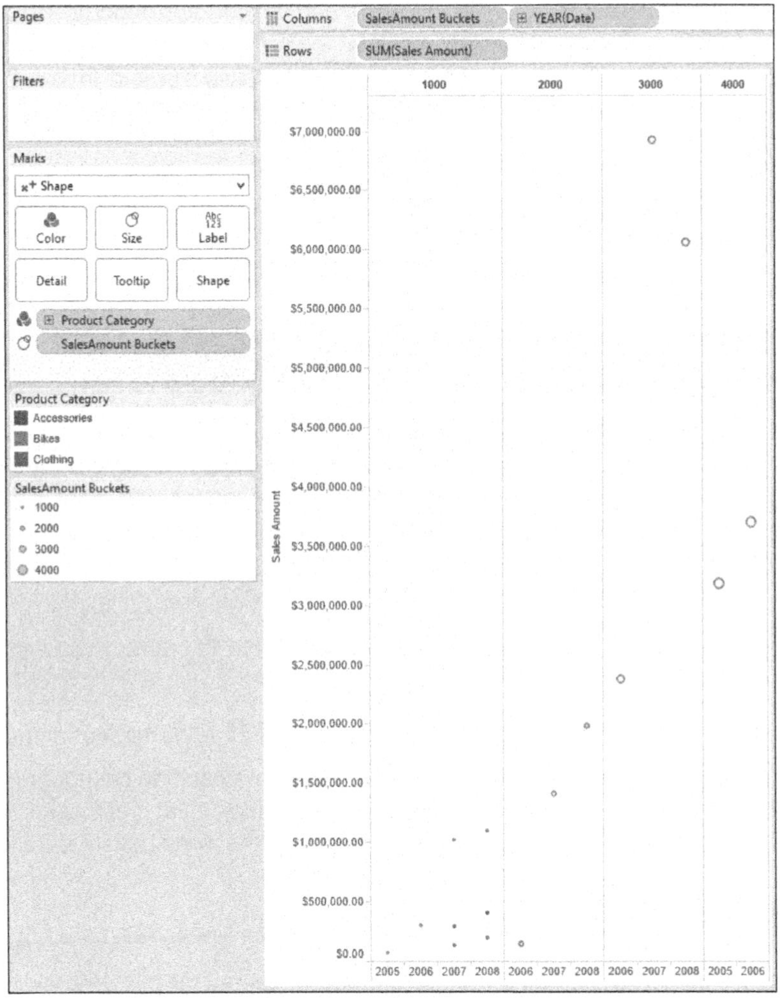

To summarize, we have created bins using Tableau's automatic bin feature. We have also looked at ways of manually creating bins using the **Calculated Field** feature.

How it works...

Bins are constructed using a default **Bins** feature in Tableau, and we can use **Calculated Fields** in order to make them more useful and complex. They are stored in the Tableau workbook, so you will be able to preserve your work if you send it to someone else.

In this recipe, we have also looked at dot plot visualization, which is a very simple way of representing data that does not use a lot of "ink". The data/ink ratio is useful to simplify a data visualization in order to get the message of the data across very clearly. Dot plots might be considered old fashioned, but they are very effective and are perhaps underused. We can see from the screenshot that the **3000** bucket contained the highest number of sales amount. We can also see that this figure peaks in the year 2007 and then falls in 2008. This is a dashboard element that could be used as a start for further analysis. For example, business users will want to know the reason for the fall in sales for the highest occurring "bin".

See also

▸ *The Visual Display of Quantitative Information, Edward R. Tufte, Graphics Press USA*

Actions and interactions

We can make the dashboard more effective by highlighting certain aspects of data visualization. Basically, when the user hovers over the data point, it will highlight the column and row where the data point is found. Highlighting the data means that other irrelevant data points are grayed out, thereby emphasizing the relevant data points. This is a useful dashboarding tool because the relevant features are made more prominent, thereby enhancing the speed with which the data is understood.

We can create highlights using the **Actions** feature in Tableau. To create a highlight action, use the following options:

▸ For workbooks, we can find an **Actions** option under the **Worksheet** menu item.

▸ When we move towards creating a full dashboard, we can find dashboard actions under the **Dashboard** menu item. For now, we are looking at creating components that will go onto a dashboard, so we will stick with the worksheet feature for now.

Getting ready

In this recipe, we will use the existing workbook that you created for this chapter.

We will use the same data as before. For this recipe, we will take a copy of the **Bins Set Manually** worksheet and select the **Duplicate Sheet** option. You can then rename the sheet to `Actions`.

How to do it...

1. Once you have your worksheet in place, you will need to locate the correct **Actions** item. To do this, go to the **Worksheet** menu and look for **Actions**. You can see an example of this in the following screenshot:

2. This will bring up the **Actions** dialog box. The following is an example:

3. In the **Actions** dialog box, select the **Add Action** button; this will bring up some options. We will choose the **Highlight** option.

4. Once we have selected the **Highlight** option, you will see the **Edit Highlight Action** dialog box appear, which you can see in the next screenshot.

5. We will call this `Bin Highlight Action`, and it will be based on the **Actions** worksheet.

6. We will then choose the **Hover** option, which you can see on the right-hand side of the **Edit Highlight Action** dialog box.

7. For the **Target Highlighting** option, select all the fields. The dialog box will then appear, as shown in the following screenshot:

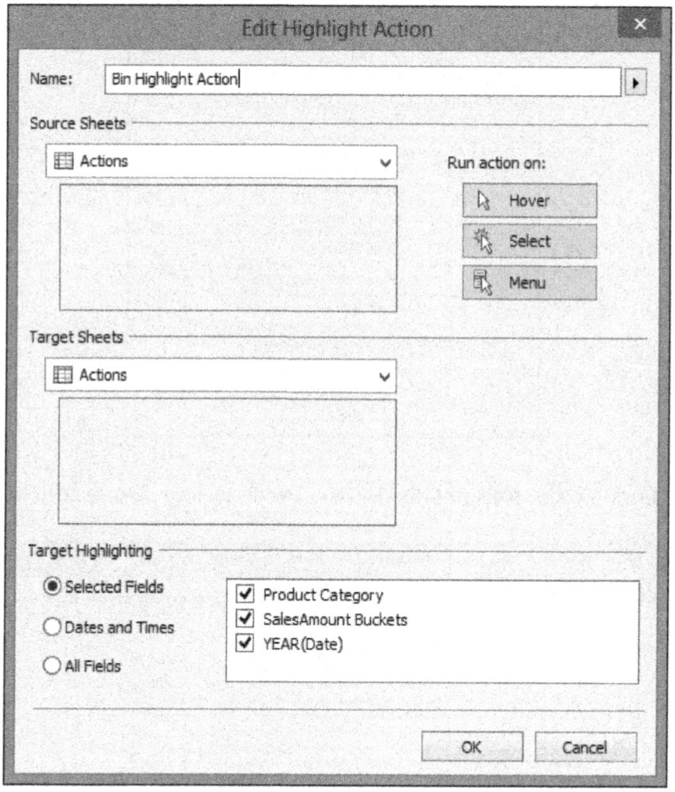

8. Click on **OK**. Now, on the **Actions** dialog box, again click on **OK**.

9. Go back to the Tableau worksheet. We will change the Tableau worksheet so that we can see the result of the action.

10. On the **Columns** shelf, place the **Product Category** hierarchy, the **SalesAmount Buckets**, and the **Year(Date)** dimension attribute.

11. On the **Rows** shelf, select **SUM(SalesAmount)**. We will place **Year(Date)** on the **Color** button.

12. Finally, select **Discrete (Lines)** from the **Show Me** panel in order to show the patterns over the years for each bucket type. Change the mark type to a shape by going to the drop-down list and selecting the shape. You can see this in the following screenshot:

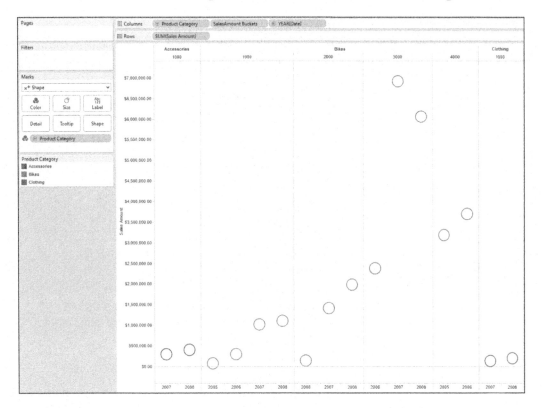

13. If you hover the mouse over one of the bucket names, you will see that the relevant data points are highlighted. In the following example, when we hover the mouse over the **1000** bucket, we can see that it lights up the data points for that bucket; also, the relevant years are highlighted. It's clear that other data points are grayed out.

How it works...

To summarize, we can use **Actions** to highlight data, and this functionality assists with the comparison process. Business users do not have to type in any information to achieve this result; a simple mouse hover will give them the patterns they are looking for.

See also

▶ *Show Me the Numbers: Designing Tables and Graphs to Enlighten, Stephen Few, Analytics Press*

Drilling into the details

Filters are a useful way to help users focus on particular aspects of the data that they are most interested in. This helps them to investigate and compare data and perhaps look for outliers and exceptions in the data.

Filtering data is an essential part of a dashboard. Users like to interact with data in order to understand it better, and it is natural to filter data so that users can pinpoint the data that particularly interests them.

Tableau allows users to filter data based on measures, calculations, and dimensions, which is extremely useful in a dashboard. For example, take the case where you need to see sales that are less than a given amount over a period of time. Users have a lot of flexibility when it comes to combining filters, which means that you can have a lot of creativity in your analyses.

In this recipe, we will look at combining the high level with the detailed view. In dashboards, we tend to stick to the summary data only. However, very occasionally, business users may ask for details as well, and this recipe caters to this particular scenario.

We create a dashboard, make the dashboard appear more appealing to business users, and help to make it read better. Furthermore, we will explore some of the options to deliver detailed data to the business users.

Let's make the current dashboard look better!

Getting ready

For the exercises in this chapter, we will continue to use the `Chapter Three` workbook. In this recipe, we will duplicate the **Bins Set Manually** worksheet and rename the duplicated sheet to `Bins Set Manually Table`.

How to do it...

1. Make sure that **SalesAmount Buckets** is in the **Columns** shelf.

2. Ensure **Year(Date)** is on the **Columns** shelf to the right of **SalesAmount Buckets**.

3. Drag **Product Category** to the **Rows** shelf.

4. Remove everything from the **Marks** shelf.

5. Drag **Sales Amount** to the canvas.

   The visualization should appear as follows:

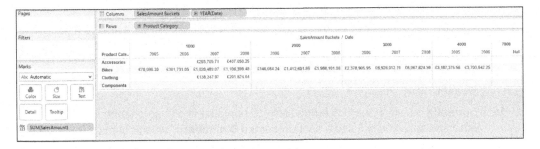

6. We will swap the rows and columns so that the table does not use up as much space on the page. To do this, click on the **Swap** button that is located just under the **Format** menu item. The Tableau workbook will now appear as follows:

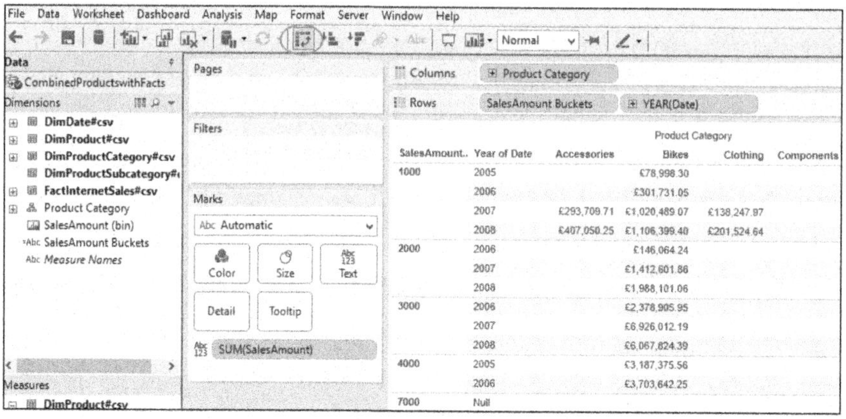

7. Now, we need to show the chart and the table next to each another. To do this, we create a dashboard, which is how Tableau combines different charts and tables together.

8. We create a dashboard by navigating to the **Dashboard** menu item and selecting the **New Dashboard** option. You can see an example of this in the following screenshot:

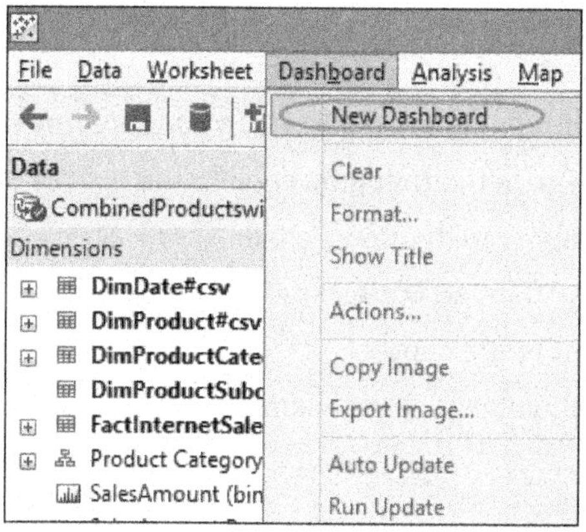

9. A new dashboard will appear, and the tab will simply read **Dashboard 1**. To rename it, right-click and choose the **Rename** option. Here, we will call the dashboard, Bucket Analysis.

10. Currently, our dashboard is empty, so let's populate it with some tables. On the left-hand side, you will see a section named **Dashboard**, which contains the names of other worksheets in the Tableau workbook.

11. In our example, let's drag the workbook named **Bins Set Manually** to the dashboard area on the right-hand side. Then, drag the workbook named **Bins Set Manually Table** so that it sits under the **Bins Set Manually** chart. Your dashboard should now look like this:

12. You will notice in the screenshot that we could make the columns align for each chart. So let's swap the bottom chart back to its original layout. To do this, go to the **Bins Set Manually Table** worksheet and select the Swap button again.

13. Firstly, you will need to resize the bottom table so that it has the same width as the top chart. To resize, hover over the edge until the cursor goes into a double-ended arrow. Then, pull the edge to where you would like it to go.

14. Then, to improve clarity, you will need to resize the columns in the bottom table so that the column lines match the lines in the top table. You may find that resizing has affected the readability of some of the numbers in **Bins Set Manually Table**. Tableau gives us the ability to change the number format plus the appearance of the data in the table. We can make changes in order to make the data more readable.

15. We can easily change the format of the data so that it is much more readable, so let's do that first. To change the format properly, go back to the **Bins Set Manually Table** worksheet.

16. In the first instance, let's change the format of the data in the table by going to the **Format** menu item. You can find it easily by going to the **Marks** shelf, then to the **Sum(SalesAmount)** pill and clicking on the downward-pointing arrow on the right-hand side. You can see this in the following screenshot:

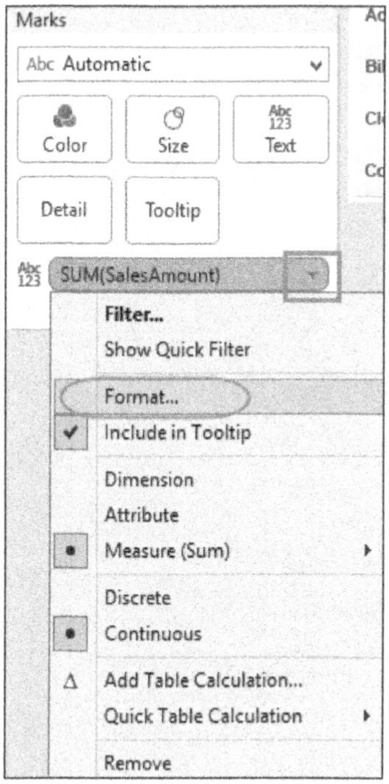

17. When you select the **Format** option, the left-hand side of the Tableau workbook changes to a specific format-based panel. Normally, the left-hand side panel is dedicated to **Data**. However, it changes flexibly in response to the user needs. You can see the **Format** panel in the following screenshot:

18. As the first step, we can remove unnecessary data by changing the number format to remove the pennies. This costs us two extra characters in space, which may not seem very much per cell. However, across the 13 columns, this soon adds up to 26 unnecessary characters.

19. To remove the pence, go to the **Numbers** option in the **Default** part of the **Format** panel and select the **Currency (Custom)** option.

20. Then, under the **Decimal Places** option, reduce it to 0 and then save the file.

    Make sure that the decimal places are set to zero; this will remove the pennies. This gives us more free space for more important data while retaining the width of the table to match the top chart.

21. You can also reduce the font size by selecting the **Font** option under the **Default** heading, as shown in the following screenshot:

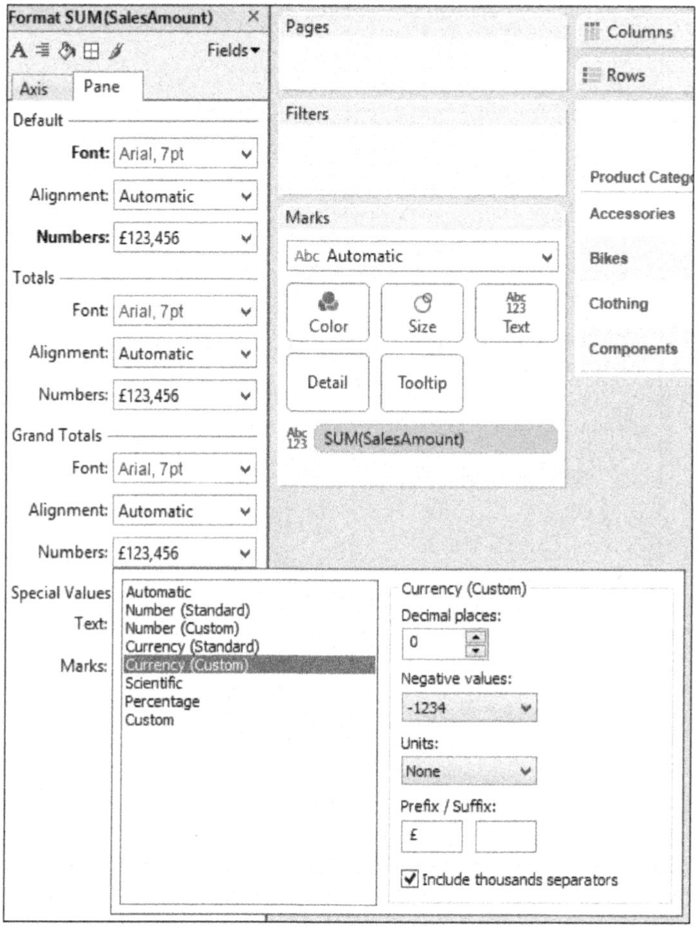

22. Go back to the **Bucket Analysis Dashboard**, which now appears as you can see in the following screenshot:

Bins Set Manually

SalesAmount Buckets / Date

SalesAmount	1000				2000			3000			4000		7000
	2005	2006	2007	2008	2006	2007	2008	2006	2007	2008	2005	2006	Null

(£7,000,000.00 — £0.00 scatter plot)

Product Category
- Accessories
- Bikes
- Clothing
- Components

SalesAmount Buckets
- 1000
- 2000
- 3000
- 4000
- 7000

4 nulls

Bins Set Manually Table

SalesAmount Buckets / Date

Product Catego..	1000				2000			3000			4000		7000
	2005	2006	2007	2008	2006	2007	2008	2006	2007	2008	2005	2006	Null
Accessories			£293,710	£407,050									
Bikes	£78,998	£301,731	£1,020,489	£1,106,399	£146,064	£1,412,602	£1,988,101	£2,378,906	£6,928,012	£6,967,824	£3,187,376	£3,793,642	
Clothing			£138,248	£201,525									
Components													

23. To change the sorting of the table so that the rows are sorted by the value of the data and not the name of the product category, we will need to go back to the **Bins Set Manually Table** worksheet.

24. Go to the **Rows** shelf, and you will find the **Product Hierarchy** dimension attribute. Right-click on it, and you will get a pop-up menu. Click on **Sort**, as shown in the following screenshot:

25. Once you have clicked on **Sort**, you will get a dialog box where you specify what you'd like to sort by. The following is an example of the dialog box:

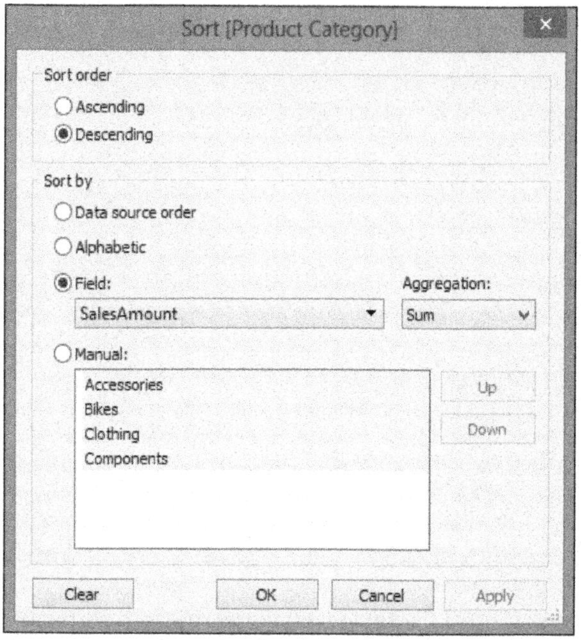

26. If we sort the data in descending order, by value, then it will be clearer for the business users to understand it quickly. As shown in the previous screenshot, you will find a series of options for sorting the data. Here, we have chosen **Descending** as the value of **Sort Order**, and we have sorted by the **SalesAmount** field.

27. Now that the data is sorted, we can go back to our dashboard, and we see that the table corresponds much better with the chart. To make the dashboard flow better, we can remove some unnecessary items, thereby adhering to our earlier discussion on chartjunk as a distraction in dashboards. For example, if we right-click on the title of the **Bins Set Manually** table, we can hide the title so it does not form an interruption between the chart and the table. The option is shown in the following screenshot:

28. Now that we have removed the titles, the image is simpler. Furthermore, the chart and table are consistent with one another.

29. We can also add in text to make the dashboard clearer. To do this, go to the top workbook item and select **Edit Title**. Next, type in What are my Sales Buckets by Category and by Year?.

We can see this from the following final screenshot:

How it works...

Tableau helps you to combine the summary and the detailed data by placing them together on the same page. When you click on a value in the legend, it highlights the appropriate values on the page. We have set up the configuration visually using Tableau so that we don't have to handcraft all of the programming language that occurs behind the scenes. This is stored in the .twb file, and we don't need to know any programming language to create dashboards.

Brushing the data gives us the opportunity to highlight and filter relevant data, which helps the business user to see emerging patterns in the data.

To summarize, we have used a combination of charts and details to create a dashboard. Normally, in dashboards, we focus on the summary of the most important information to help people make decisions. Occasionally, however, users will ask to be provided with the details and this technique allows people to see the pattern of the data alongside the actual detail. Some of you will notice, however, that there is something wrong with the ordering of the data in the table. The rows are ordered by the **Product Category** hierarchy, and these are ordered in alphabetical order. However, this does not match the data that appears in the chart above it. For example, if you take the **1000** bucket, you will see that the data points are accurately representing the value. So, the **Bikes** sales are represented by the values that appear at the highest point of the *y* axis. However, in the table below, the **Bikes** sales appear in the second row with the **Accessories** value above them.

Working with input controls

Removing some of the data can actually reveal more of the message of the data by narrowing the focus. Using filter controls in worksheets and dashboards is a way to pinpoint the data that you would like to show. Filters are very easy to set up, and their "clickiness" can help maintain "stickiness" in interacting with the dashboard itself.

In this recipe, we will create dashboards that provide a summary while adding filters to include an interactive aspect to the dashboard, thereby engaging users further in the data. We will filter by measure and then show how this filter can be used in a dashboard.

Getting ready

For the exercises in this chapter, we will continue to use the `Chapter Three` workbook. In this recipe, we will focus on the **Bins Set Manually** worksheet and rename the dashboard from **Dashboard 1** to `Sales Dashboard`.

How to do it...

1. Take the **SalesAmount** metric from the **Measures** pane and put it in the **Filters** panel.

2. When you release the measure into the panel, you will see the following **Filter Field** dialog box pop up:

3. We will filter on the **Sum** value, so select **Sum** and click on **Next**.

4. Then, you will get the **Filter** dialog box, and an example of this is as follows:

5. In the worksheet, you can get a slider filter by simply clicking on the **OK** button.

6. If you want the filter to appear as a separate slider, then right-click on the **SUM(SalesAmount)** filter and select the **Show Quick Filter** option. You can see this option in the following screenshot:

7. You can now see that the slider is located on the right-hand side of the dashboard. The following screenshot shows a close-up of the slider:

8. The numbers look a little odd, don't they? Let's make it look better. If you click on the downward arrow on the **SUM(Sales Amount)** filter, you will see the option to edit the filter; you can change the values of **MIN** to 0 and **MAX** to £7,000,000. Now it looks cleaner:

9. We need to decide whether or not we should include the NULL values. The option to show nulls is labeled **Show Null Controls**, and you can find it in the pop-up menu, as the following screenshot shows:

10. The slider now has a drop-down list, which you can see in the following example:

11. Now, if you go to the **SalesDashboard** worksheet, you cannot see the **SalesAmount** filter. How do we make it appear? Go to the **Sales Dashboard** worksheet and click on **Bins Set Manually Table.** If you click on the small downward arrow at the end of the dashboard representation of the table, you will get a pop up.

12. Navigate to **Quick Filters** and select **Sum of SalesAmount**; you'll see the filter appear in the dashboard, as shown in the following screenshot:

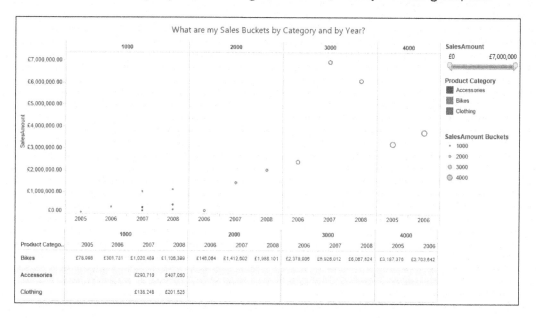

13. You can see the resulting dashboard in the next screenshot. Note that you can use the legend to filter along with the slider bar and the data points themselves. Users have many ways of interacting with the data, thereby increasing adoption.

How it works...

Filters are one of the most important features that automatically come with Tableau. As we did earlier, we set up everything visually, and the programming code is automatically generated behind the scenes. This means that it is easy to create Tableau dashboards, as well as use them.

There's more...

Using filters is a key part of dashboards, since it allows people to understand the data better so that they can make decisions based on the data. Filters help business users by allowing them to interact with the data. Further, "brushing" the data is a technique whereby we highlight the selected data points in order to see more details and gray out the irrelevant items.

Humans are thought to be able to hold only a limited amount of information in their heads at any one time; the "magic number" is thought to be seven, but it can often depend on the researcher. Highlighting selected data points helps us by focusing our attention on these data points and filtering the irrelevant material.

4
Using Dashboards to Get Results

In this chapter, we will cover the following recipes:

- ▶ Enriching data with mashups
- ▶ Page trails
- ▶ Guided analytics with Tableau
- ▶ Sharing your results in a meeting
- ▶ Notes and annotations
- ▶ Using external data to enrich your dashboard

Introduction

Dashboards are more than visual tools to display data; they are tools that can help to move your business forward. Dashboards are used as decision-making tools to obtain results quickly.

You can help your business users to make decisions fast by producing dashboards that are in line with the current research and thinking about dashboard structure. You can help users get results from their dashboard by:

- ▶ Improving the availability of data
- ▶ Facilitating the user to explore and understand the data quickly
- ▶ Sharing information with team members and beyond
- ▶ Providing adaptability in the dashboard
- ▶ Allowing flexibility for users to add notes to their dashboard

Enriching data with mashups

Business intelligence is all about people. We need to help people understand data as quickly as possible so that they make strategic decisions more quickly.

Unfortunately, decision makers can end up being distracted by a need to mash data together in Excel. Worse, they may even expend time in trying to understand the data in the first place, rather than using the time to analyze the data to make an informed decision. This has a pernicious impact on the organization since decision makers are diverted from their role and contribution to the organization.

One proposal is to take a step back and re-evaluate the business questions and how they are answered. Due to the requirement that the data is correct and current, users could be provisioned with data that is insulated from the operational systems and merged together. This could help to answer the business need for a decision to be made using the data on the dashboard.

In this recipe, we will load the fact table called `FactInternetSales` first, and then we will load the dimension tables. We will look at joining tables together and putting the tables into Tableau's memory. When we do this, we relieve some of the pressure that is produced when we create an unnecessary proliferation of snapshots of data. In turn, data silos need to be mashed up by business users in order to get the information they need. We will join tables together so that the business users can get results more quickly using Tableau, rather than trying to merge lots of smaller spreadsheets together.

Getting ready

For the exercises in this chapter, open a new Tableau workbook and name it `Chapter Four`.

How to do it...

1. On the initial Tableau page, select **Connect to Data** and navigate to the location where you stored the data files, as shown in the following screenshot:

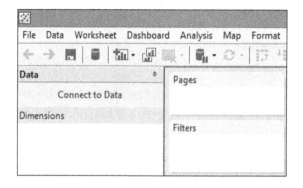

2. Click on the **Text File** option

3. Navigate to the `FactInternetSales` file and select it.

4. Next, we will add the date dimension first. Go to the **Files** heading on the left-hand side, and drag the file called `DimDate`, to the canvas on the right-hand side.

5. You should join the tables together. Under the heading **Data Source**, select the field list item called **Order Date Key**. On the right-hand side, under `DimDate.csv`, select **Date Key**. Your join should look like this:

6. You don't need to take all of the columns. In fact, it would be a good idea to take across only the columns that you need, or it will be confusing for the end user to see too many unnecessary columns. Here, we will remove the international language columns for clarity. For reference, we removed the following columns:

    ❑ Spanish Day Name of Week

    ❑ French Day Name of Week

    ❑ Spanish Month Name

    ❑ French Month Name

7. Now, let's add in a few more tables. Go to the **Files** section on the left-hand side, and drag `DimProduct.csv` to the white canvas. Tableau will do the join for you. It will join the `ProductKey` column in the `DimProduct` file to the `ProductKey` column in the `FactInternetSales` table.

8. Let's add in the product subcategory information. Drag the `DimProductSubCategory` file from the **Files** section on the left-hand side to the canvas. Again, Tableau will do the join for you. The join will use the `ProductSubCategoryKey` column in the `DimProductSubCategory` table to join with the `ProductSubCategoryKey` column in the `DimProduct` table.

9. Let's add in the product category information. Drag the `DimProductCategory` table to the canvas. As mentioned earlier, Tableau will do the join for you. Tableau will use the `DimProductSubCategory` key in the table to match with `ProductCategoryKey` in the `DimProductSubCategory` table.

10. Finally, let's add in some sales territory data. Drag the `DimSalesTerritory` file from the **Files** section, and drag it to the canvas area. Tableau will take the `SalesTerritoryKey` column in the `DimSalesTerritory` table, and use it to join with the `SalesTerritoryKey` column in the `FactInternetSales` table.

To assist you further, here is a table that shows the table name and its key:

Table name	Key
DimProduct	ProductKey
DimProductSubCategory	ProductSubCategoryKey
DimProductCategory	ProductCategoryKey
DimSalesTerritory	SalesTerritoryKey

Your canvas should now appear as follows:

11. For each additional table, we will add an inner join. What are these joins? An inner join, also known as an equi join, selects only the rows from both the tables that have matching values. Rows with values in the joined field that do not appear in both of the database tables will be excluded from the result set. So, for example, if there is a row in the `FactInternetSales` table, which does not have a value in the `DimDate` table, then it will not be returned, and vice versa.

> One or more fields can serve as the join fields. In this simple example, we have selected only one field for clarity.

12. Go to the **File** option at the top, and click on **Save**. This will import all the data into Tableau's data engine. Then, click on the **Go To Worksheet** button to go back to the main Tableau canvas.

13. Now, let's extract the data to make our data go faster. Go to the **Data** menu item, and navigate to **FactInternetSales+**. From the pop-up menu, select **Extract Data**. Here is a screenshot:

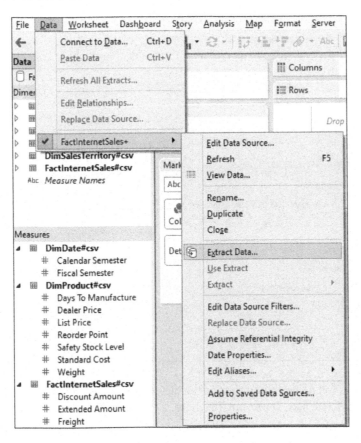

14. You will now be taken to an **Extract Data** dialogue box. We will import all rows, so you simply need to press the **Extract** button and the work is done. Here is an example:

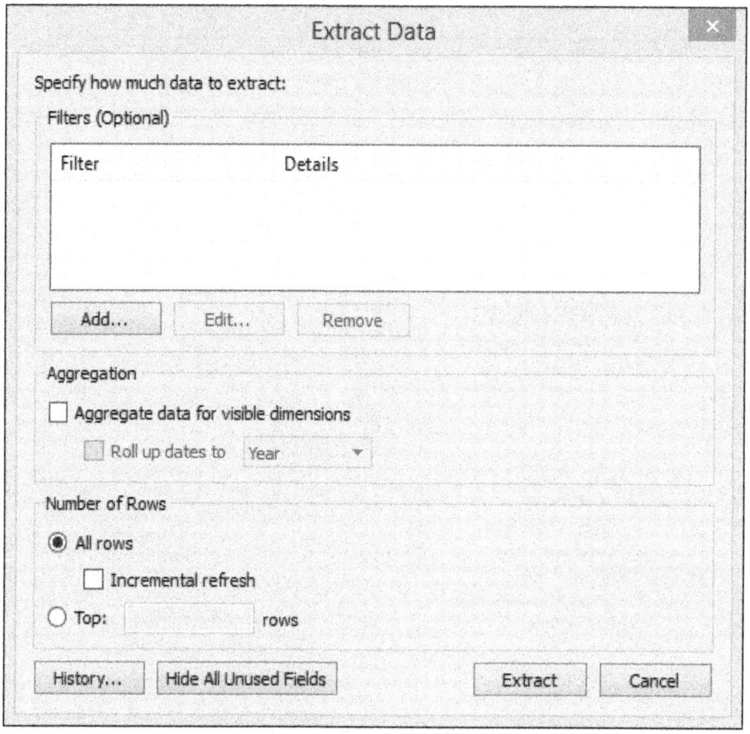

Extract Data

Specify how much data to extract:

Filters (Optional)

Filter	Details

Add... Edit... Remove

Aggregation

☐ Aggregate data for visible dimensions

☐ Roll up dates to Year ▼

Number of Rows

◉ All rows

☐ Incremental refresh

○ Top: _____ rows

History... Hide All Unused Fields Extract Cancel

15. Next, you will be prompted to save the file. Make a new folder on your computer, and call it TDE files. Save your TDE here.

16. Once you have imported your data, your Tableau worksheet will show all of the tables on the left-hand side.

17. As a quick check that all of your data is imported, select the **Number of Records** metric from the **Measures** pane. You will find it at the bottom of the **Measures** pane on the left-hand side. You can refer to the next screenshot as an example:

As you can see, the tables are located in the **Data** pane on the left-hand side.

How it works...

To summarize, in this section, we have shown different ways of joining tables in order to alleviate a situation where people are copying and pasting data all over the place. By unifying all the data that the users need into one distinct place, it will save them time and energy that they could use to make better decisions.

Tableau has its own data engine, which is an analytics database. It uses compression, which means that it can store a lot of data. It also involves techniques to make data retrieval very fast. It is a flexible data model, and you can work on the data very quickly in the same way as it is represented on the disk.

We saved the data extract, which is a separate file from the Tableau workbook. It has the file extension `.tde`, which stands for Tableau Data Extract. This extract file can be reused directly without having the source connection details. This is extremely useful for portability. You can also use it as a way to prototype the dashboard. Further, you can anonymize a dataset and load it into an extract file. Then, you can ask the developer to work from the anonymized extract file. Once the development is complete, you could change the source connection so that Tableau connects to real-world data.

There's more...

Here is a trick—if you want to verify the number of rows loaded into Tableau's data engine, then take the **Number of Records** metric and put it into the **Marks** shelf. This will give you a quick check to see if the number of rows loaded matches what you expect. If the number is much lower or higher, then one of your joins may be wrong. It's best to do this before you start or you will have to redo the work!

What happens if you have made a mistake and want to delete worksheets? You can delete worksheets by right-clicking on the worksheet tab, and selecting **Delete Sheet**.

When you attempt to delete a worksheet, you will notice that there is no option to delete the sheet. You can see an illustration of this feature in the following screenshot:

If the worksheet is used in a dashboard, Tableau will not allow you to delete a worksheet if it is reused elsewhere. In order to get around this feature, you need to delete the dashboard first, and then you'd need to delete the original worksheet. Tableau doesn't let you delete all the worksheets; however, it needs a worksheet in order to show data!

Page trails

Websites often have page trails that help users to find their way around the site. Similarly, in Tableau, we can add features that will help business users to reduce the number of actions that they need to take in order to navigate through the workbook. These actions can help to make worksheets more findable in a Tableau workbook. Findable refers to the ease with which a website can be found, and it is also relevant to finding pages within a Tableau workbook.

Linking workbooks together is an effective visual tool that helps the user to understand where they are in terms of the user's location within the workbook. It also helps to add context. In this recipe, we will look at user-oriented trails in a Tableau workbook.

Getting ready

In this recipe, we will use the existing workbook that you created earlier in this chapter. If you have taken the **Number of Records** field and put it onto the white canvas, remove it.

How to do it...

1. First, let's rename the worksheet to `Overview`.

2. Let's take the **SalesAmount** metric from the `FactInternetSales` table, and place it onto the white canvas.

3. Then, navigate to the **DimSalesTerritory** dimension, look for the `SalesTerritoryCountry` attribute, and drag it onto the white canvas.

4. Once you have the fields in place, let's select the filled map from the **Show Me** panel. To help you find it, you can see the next screenshot:

5. Let's work with the visualization of data. An example of data visualization is given in the next screenshot:

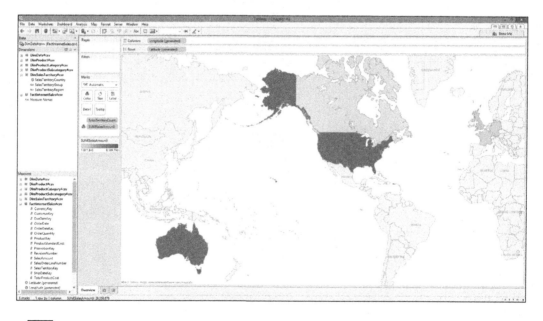

6. Now, let's work on the color and the size. For the color, let's drag the **SalesAmount** metric from the `FactInternetSales` table, and place it onto the **Color** button on the **Marks** shelf.

7. When you see the **SUM(SalesAmount)** metric on the **Marks** shelf, right-click on the arrow on the right-hand side of the dialog box. Select the **Edit Colors** option. You can see this in the next screenshot:

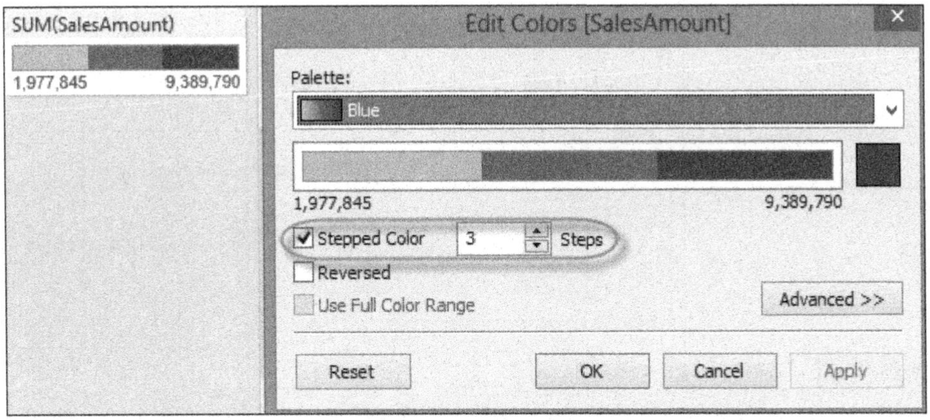

SUM(SalesAmount)	Edit Colors [SalesAmount]	✕
1,977,845 9,389,790	Palette: Blue ⌄	
	1,977,845 9,389,790	
	☑ Stepped Color 3 ⬍ Steps	
	☐ Reversed	
	☐ Use Full Color Range Advanced >>	
	Reset OK Cancel Apply	

8. From the drop-down list, select the **Blue** option for color.

9. Then, we will select the **Stepped Color** option.

10. Next, select **3** steps and click on **OK**.

11. Some of the colors might appear a little pale on the screen, so we will give a very light border to the shapes. To do this, click on the **Color** button on the **Marks** shelf.

12. Look for the **Effects** section for the **Border** option. Here, you will get a drop-down list that gives you the option to change the color. In this example, the border has been changed to a mid-purple color, since it is softer than black or dark grey, as shown in the following screenshot:

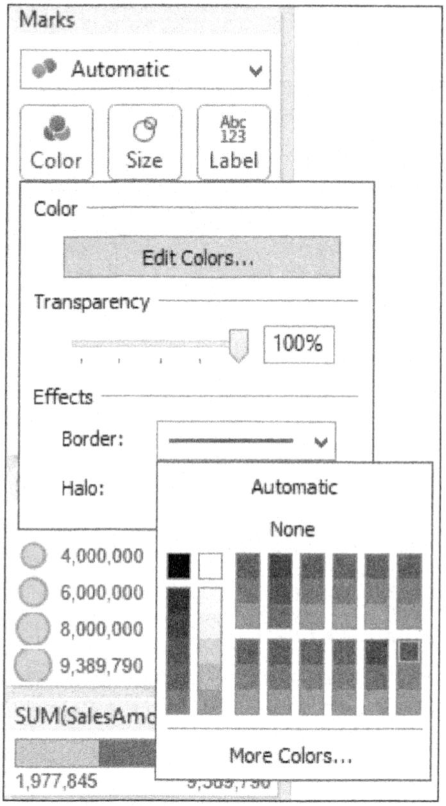

Once you have made these changes, the screen will appear as you can see in the following screenshot:

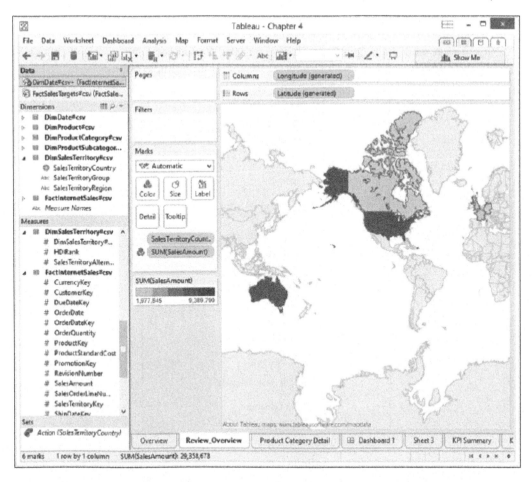

13. So, let's proceed towards creating our `Product Category Detail` worksheet. Now that we have an `Overview` worksheet, we will create a `Product Category Detail` worksheet that we would like to navigate to. To do this, simply right-click on the tab and select **Duplicate Sheet**.

14. Rename the duplicated worksheet to `Product Category Detail`.

15. Navigate to the `DimProductCategory` dimension, look for the `EnglishProductCategoryName` attribute, and drag it to the **Rows** shelf.

16. Next, let's add an action that will allow the user to simply right-click on country on the `Overview` worksheet, and they are presented with the `Product Category Detail` worksheet. To add an action, go to the **Worksheet** menu item and choose the **Actions...** option. The following screenshot is an example of this:

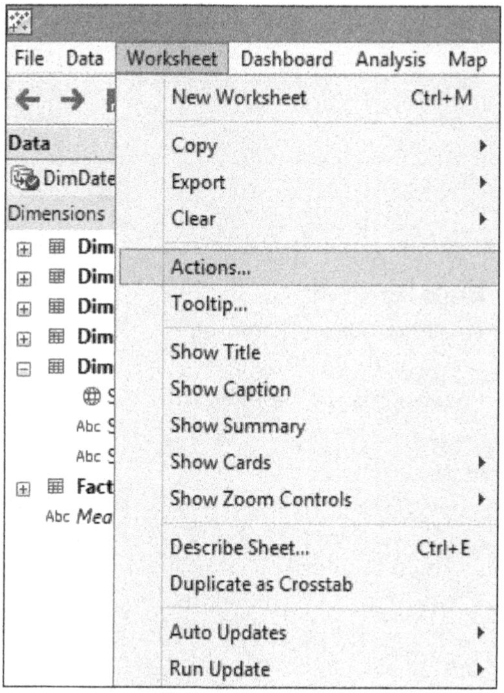

17. Now, when we click on the **Actions...** menu item, we get a dialog box. We should now click on the **Add Action >** button, and this will give us a number of options, as shown in the next screenshot:

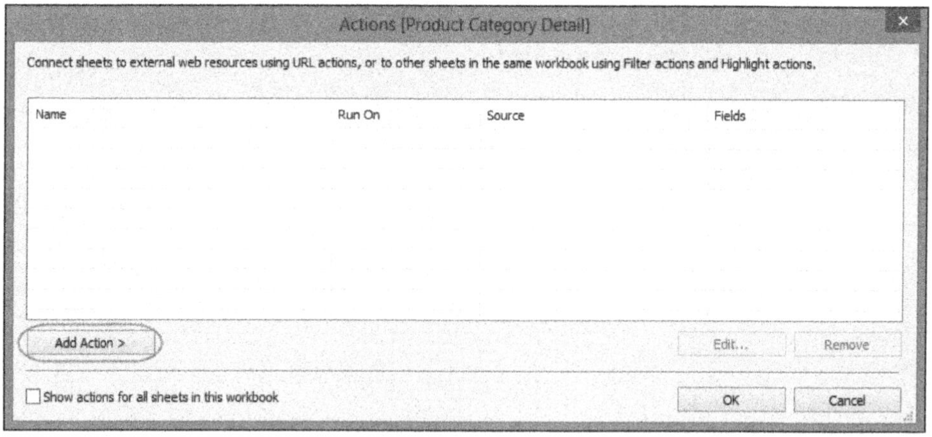

We have three options, as follows:

❑ **Filter**: This action means that you can make a trail between worksheets— from the summary to more specific data—going down to the details

❑ **Highlight**: This action emphasizes specific data points dependent on the rules you set up

❑ **URL**: This action allows you to link to external data, such as a website or a SQL Server Reporting Services report

18. In this example, we will choose a straightforward **Filter** example. When you select the **Filter** option, you will get the dialog box that appears in the next screenshot:

Add Action >	⅄	Filter...
	✎	Highlight...
☐ Show actions for all s	☑	URL...

19. Set the Name field to `ProductCategoryFilter`. We will set the `Overview` worksheet as the source sheet, and press on the `Select` button on the right-hand side. Then, set the `Product Category Detail` worksheet as the target sheet.

20. When you've selected the correct sheets, click on **OK**, and your action is all set up.

21. We can test whether the action works simply by going to the `Overview` worksheet and right-clicking on a country, and then click on the `Product Category Detail` option at the bottom of the pop-up menu. So, for example, if you click on Australia, then the `Product Category Detail` worksheet will appear with Australia in the middle of the page.

22. To summarize, we have set up a simple Tableau action that links worksheets together. This improves the user's experience in navigating through the data, in that, they can get the results from the dashboard quickly.

How it works...

In this recipe, we have used actions so that we can create worksheets that are more detailed than the `Overview` worksheet. Research has shown that people tend to prefer navigating from the summary data down towards the details, so our page trails will work in the same way.

There's more...

An important item to note is the item marked **Target Sheets**, in the **Edit Filter Action** dialogue box. There are options to **Leave the Filter, Show All Values**, or **Exclude all Values**. These features allow you to preserve the filter or release the filter when the user goes from one worksheet to another.

In our example, we preserved the filter. This means that we are facilitating user navigation by going from a summary view to a more detailed, filtered view.

Why did we only choose three colors to represent the **SalesAmount** value? We are not distinguishing the colors at a fine-grained level. Instead, we are using color to broadly distinguish the value of **SalesAmount** into three categories. The lower values are represented by a light color, and the higher values are represented by a darker color—a more intense blue. Research has shown that people tend to associate lighter colors with smaller values, and more intense, bright, or dark colors with higher values. You can follow this up by looking at *Show Me the Numbers: Designing Tables and Graphs to Enlighten, Second Edition, Stephen Few, Analytics Press*.

Using color in this way does not provide you with any details, but it can help you to see patterns in the data very quickly. This is extremely useful for dashboarding.

See also

▶ *Designing the User Interface: Strategies for Effective Human-Computer Interaction, Fifth Edition, Ben Shneiderman, Catherine Plaisant, Maxine Cohen, Steven Jacobs, Prentice Hall*

▶ *Show Me the Numbers: Designing Tables and Graphs to Enlighten, Second Edition, Stephen Few, Analytics Press*

Guided analytics with Tableau

Industry reports have shown that guided analytics is becoming an increasingly important requirement for mobile business intelligence requirements (Dresner (2013)). What is guided analytics? Guided analytics is defined as cases where knowledge workers can use data models to follow pathways of investigation towards their own results.

Users follow a pathway down the data, starting at a high-level summary of all of the available data, down to the specifics that they are interested in. Users don't have to start with a specific business question, but they can be directed down a pathway towards data that might be interesting and produce results.

Tableau can be used to create dashboards that can be adaptable in response to users' data explorations, while also providing them with a pathway that is intuitive and helpful towards the goal of producing results using the dashboard. The topics in this recipe will help you to create dashboards that use guided analysis.

In order to enrich the guided analysis, we will add some new target data, which we can use to compare with the actual data. The comparison between actual and target data is fundamental to dashboards. We will set up actions to highlight fields in one worksheet based on input from another worksheet. We will set up some menu actions, which will pop up some additional menu items in order to help users to flow naturally through the data.

Getting ready

In this topic, we will use the existing workbook `Chapter Four`. To proceed, we are going to import some more data.

How to do it...

1. Create a new worksheet and call it `KPI Summary` by going to **Worksheet** and then selecting **New Worksheet**.

2. We will import new data that will give us target metrics for the purposes of our visualization. To do this, go to **Data** and then select the option **Connect to Data**.

3. For our purposes, we will select the file called `FactSalesTarget` and open it. Click on the **Text File** option on the left-hand side, and navigate in order to select this file.

4. Then, select the **Go To Worksheet** button to go back to the main Tableau canvas.

5. When we have imported the additional data, the **Data** shelf will hold two connections—one for the original data and another for the target data. We need a way to tie the two connections together. To do this, go to the **Data** menu item and select the **Edit Relationships...** option from the list.

6. The **Relationships** dialog box helps to associate the data sources with each other. The data has the country, region, and group information in common, along with the year, and we need to link the data using these columns. We need to link the following columns, which have the same name in both columns: **Calendar Year**, **Sales Territory Country**, **Sales Territory Group**, **Sales Territory Key**, and **Sales Territory Region**.

    To do this, we will need to link the columns together by multiselecting them. Select the highlighted columns below, and then click on **OK**.

We are aiming to have the **Relationships** dialog box look like the example in the following screenshot; remove all of the fields, except the fields shown here:

Relationships

Relationships determine how data from secondary data sources are joined with primary data sources.

Primary data source:

FactInternetSales+

Secondary data source: ○ Automatic   ● Custom

FactSalesTargets

Sales Territory Country	Sales Territory Country
Sales Territory Group	Sales Territory Group
Sales Territory Key	Sales Territory Key
YEAR(Date Key)	YEAR(Date Key)

Add...   Edit...   Remove

OK   Cancel

7. Once we have set up the relationships, we can now add the data to the Tableau canvas. Click on the **FactInternetSales+** data source in the **Data** shelf of the sidebar.

8. Drag **SalesAmount** from the **Measures** pane and onto the **Column** shelf.

9. Click on the **FactSalesTargets** data source in the **Data** shelf of the sidebar.

10. In the **Dimensions** tab, select the broken chain symbol next to **Sales Territory Country**.

11. Now that we have blended our data together, we can create a calculated field in order to show very quickly whether there is a difference between the actual amount and the target amount.

12. To set up the calculated field, click on the data source **FactInternetSales+** and then go to the **Analysis** menu item and select the **Create Calculated Field...** option from the list.

13. We will call our **Difference between Actual and Target** calculation, and this should be inserted into the **Name** field. It is a very simple calculation to do. We will work out the difference between the actual and the target profit. The target profit is called `SalesAmountQuote` in the dataset.

14. To do this, go to the **Fields** drop-down list, and select **FactInternetSales+** from the options. Select `Sales Amount`.

15. Next, we subtract the target sales amount, called `SalesAmountQuote` in the dataset, from the actual sales amount. To do this, insert a subtraction symbol, and then select `FactSalesTargets` from the **Fields** drop-down list.

16. You can see an example in the following screenshot; when you have set up the calculation, click on **OK**:

17. Now, we have set up our actual metric, our target metric, and the difference between the two. We can now proceed to do some interesting guided analytics in putting the data together.

18. We will start by creating KPIs, which will serve as our summary data. From this vantage point, we can drill down into the detailed picture of the data.

19. Drag the **SalesTerritoryCountry** dimension attribute onto the **Rows** shelf.

20. Take our **Difference between Actual and Target** calculation and drag it to the canvas area.

21. Drag our **Difference between Actual and Target** calculation to the **Color** button.

22. Click on the **Color** button and choose the **Edit Colors...** option.

23. In the **Edit Colors** dialog box, choose **Red-Blue Diverging** from the **Palette** drop-down list. We will use the red and blue diverging color palette.

24. We will use stepped color as before. However, instead of using the default five steps, we will use only three. Enter 3 in the stepped color **Steps** box and then click on **OK**.

25. In the **Marks** shelf, change the mark type from **Automatic** to **Square**.

26. Drag the **Difference between Actual and Target** calculation onto the **Label** button. Let's add some labels so that the boxes appear more like KPI tiles.

27. Change the text color to white by clicking on the **Label** button, and navigating to the **Font** option. Here, you can select the color white.

28. Click on the **Label** button and change the font so that we can use the **Segoe UI** font with size **12**.

29. Next, we will make the KPI look more like a tile than a table. To do this, drag the **SalesTerritoryCountry** dimension attribute onto the **Label** button, as shown in the following screenshot:

30. Now, we will concatenate the **SalesTerritoryCountry** name and the **Difference between Actual and Target** calculation value together so that the label reads nicely. When you click on the blue edit label button, a dialog box appears, which you can see in the next screenshot.

31. Next, we will format the text so that we can use the **Segoe UI** font with size **12**.

32. When you click on the downward-facing arrow on the **Insert** button, you can select the **SalesTerritoryCountry** name and the **Difference between Actual and Target** calculation, in order to show the country and the associated difference.

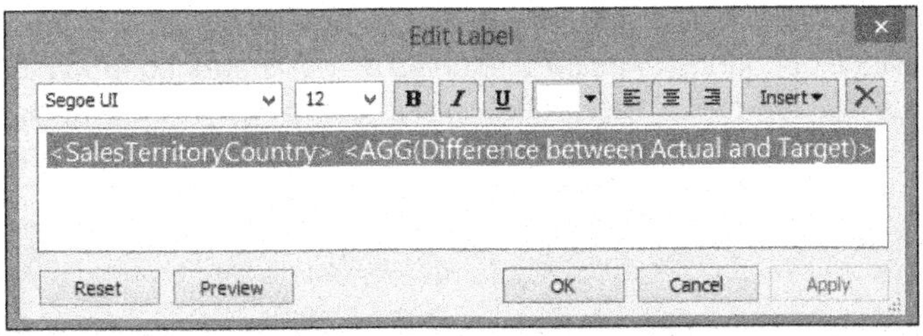

33. You will find that the number format for the **Difference between Actual and Target** calculation means that the whole number is shown. This isn't very clear. In order to stay with our principles of eliminating chartjunk, let's amend the format so that it simply shows the million figure. To do this, right-click on the **Difference between Actual and Target** calculation.

34. Go to **Default Properties** and click on **Number Format…**. This will bring up the **Default Number Format** box.

35. Choose **Number (Custom)**, as shown in the following screenshot:

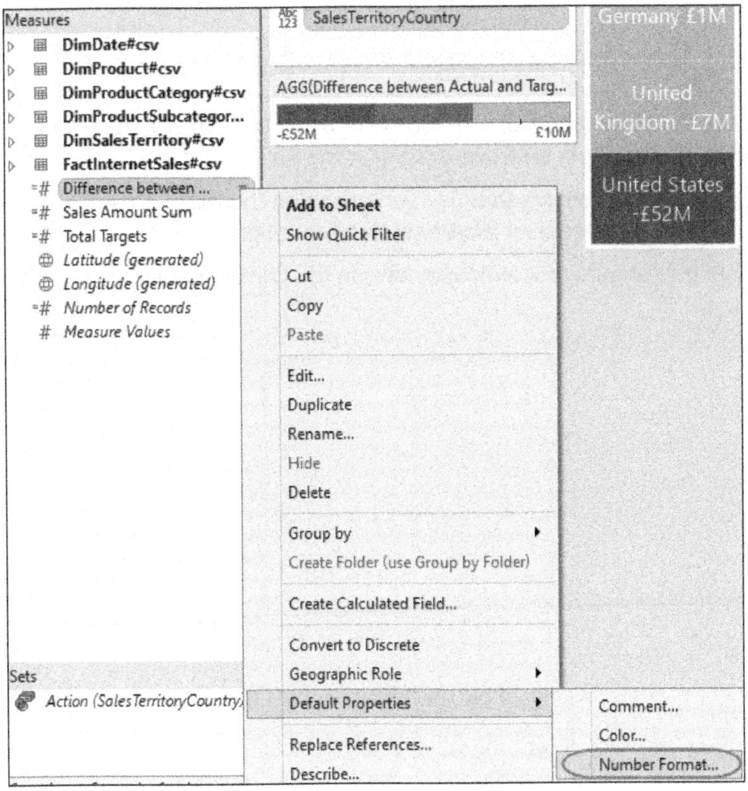

36. Firstly, let's get rid of the chartjunk. Let's get rid of the pennies; when we are talking about millions of pounds or dollars, pennies do not matter so much. Let's put the units to **Millions (M)** and prefix the amount with a pound sign or a dollar sign—whatever you prefer! Once you have done this, click on **OK**, as shown in the following screenshot:

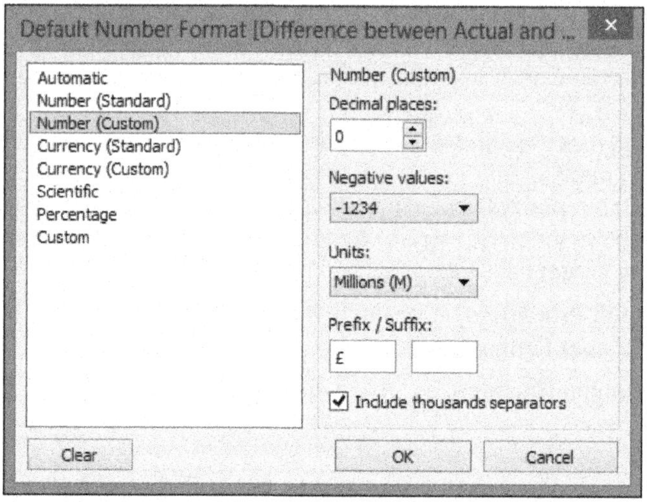

37. Remove the row headers from the canvas by right-clicking on the heading and selecting the **Hide Field Labels for Rows** option for the Sales Territory Country dimension.

38. Go to the **Sales Territory Country** dimension on the **Rows** shelf, and click on the downward arrow. Deselect the **Show Header** option.

Our KPI tiles should now look as shown in the following screenshot:

39. Let's add some actions so that we can navigate around. Before we move forward, let's duplicate the existing `KPI Summary` sheet and rename it to `KPI by Year`.

    We can now add some actions so that we can navigate around.

40. In the new `KPI by Year` worksheet, click on the **DimDate#CSV** dimension, look for the **Calendar Year** dimension attribute, and drag it across onto the **Columns** shelf.

41. Let's add the row labels back to the left-hand side so that we can compare more easily. To do this, click on the **SalesTerritoryCountry** dimension member in the **Rows** shelf and select the **Show Header** option.

42. Let's change the color settings so that we show five steps rather than three, as per the previous example. This will reveal more fine-grained variations in the data.

43. Click on the **Label** button and edit the text by removing **<FactSalesTargets#csv (FactSalesTargets.csv).SalesTerritoryCountry>**. You can adjust the size of the tiles by clicking on the **Size** button and adjusting the slider bar. Once you have completed these simple steps, your Tableau visualization will appear as shown in the following screenshot:

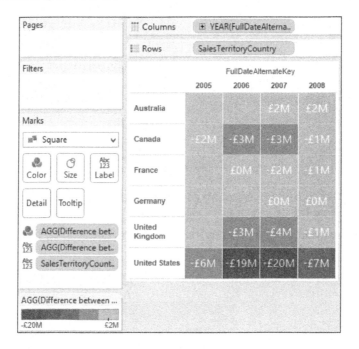

44. As per DW's comment earlier, remove the last comment. We can also format the borders of the cells so that they are neater. To do this, click on the **SalesTerritoryCountry** dimension and select the **Format...** option.

45. Using this dialog box, you can neaten the borders by making them all white in order to give a nice finish to the cells. You can see how to do this in the following screenshot:

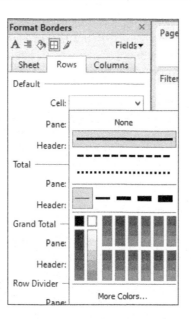

46. Let's add another worksheet that will provide more detail. Duplicate the KPI by Year worksheet and call it KPI by Q. This only requires a few simple changes in order to provide a more detailed chart.

47. To start, simply click on the green plus sign on the **Year(FullDateAlternateKey)** dimension so that we can see the **Quarter(FullDateAlternateKey)** dimension exposed on the **Columns** shelf. Now, we will see more columns on the visualization.

48. To summarize, we now have three sheets: KPI Summary, KPI by Year, and KPI by Q. We will now set up actions in order to link them together. Our Tableau actions will respond to user input. For example, if we click on **Canada** on the KPI Summary worksheet, then we can see that the Canada fields are highlighted on the KPI by Year worksheet. This is a very simple action that helps to draw attention to particular aspects of the dashboard, thereby helping the user interaction flow.

49. In all, we will create five actions that will facilitate all of these activities. Let's start with the actions to highlight fields. To do this, let's first go to the KPI Summary worksheet and begin adding some new actions by going to the **Worksheet** option and choosing the **Actions...** option.

50. Let's add in some highlight actions in the **Actions** dialog box by clicking on the **Add Action >** button and choosing the **Highlight...** option. We will create three highlights, one for each of the worksheets: KPI Summary, KPI by Year, and KPI by Q.

51. For the first filter, let's rename it to Highlight Country from Summary to Year. We will choose to run the action on the **Select** action. Otherwise, we will have a lot of noisy actions generated if the user simply hovers over a data point. This might mean that the user loses his/her thread in navigating the data, and we do not want that to happen.

52. For the **Source Sheets** option, let's stay with KPI Summary. For the **Target Sheets** option, let's choose KPI by Year. In the **Target Highlighting** section, let's choose to highlight some fields, which will be done by selecting the **Selected Fields** option. Once you've done this, your **Edit Highlight Action** dialog box should appear as shown in the following screenshot:

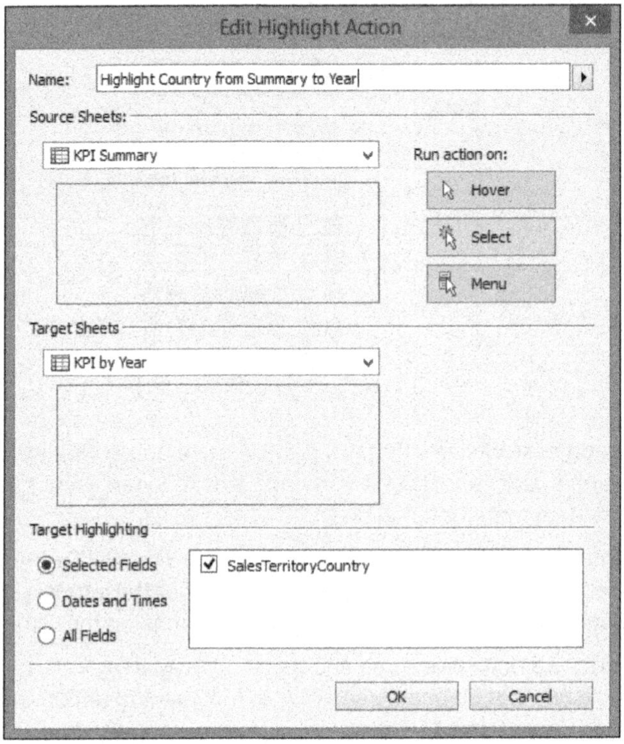

53. For the remainder of the actions, let's repeat them using the details given in the following table:

Name	Run on	Source sheet	Target sheet	Fields
Highlight Country from Summary to Q	Select	KPI Summary	KPI by Q	SalesTerritoryCountry
Highlight Country from Year to Q	Select	KPI Summary	KPI by Q	SalesTerritoryCountry. YEAR(FullDateAlternateKey)

Name	Run on	Source sheet	Target sheet	Fields
Filter Country from Summary to Year	Menu	Connection name, for example, `DateDate#csv` + `(FactInternetSales)`	KPI by Year	`SalesTerritoryCountry`
Filter Country from Year to Quarter	Menu	Connection name, for example, `DateDate#CSV` + `(FactInternetSales)`	KPI by Quarter	`SalesTerritoryCountry`

54. Once you have repeated the creation of the actions with these attributes, we can test out some action scenarios.

55. Let's test out the highlight actions first. On the worksheet, let's click on **United States** on the KPI Summary worksheet. When we do this, we can go to the KPI by Year worksheet, and you can see that United States is highlighted.

56. Now, let's create a set that will display only European countries. To do this, right-click on **SalesTerritoryCountry**, and select the **Create Set** option. In the **Create Set** dialogue box, select **France**, **Germany**, and **the United Kingdom**. Rename the set to Europe and click on **OK**. You will see that Europe set at the bottom of the data pane. Drag it to the **Filters** pane, then right-click on it to select the **Show In / Out of Set** option as shown in the following screenshot:

57. In setting up these actions, you have configured additional menu options as well. So, for example, if you right-click on the **United States** row in the KPI by Year workbook, you will be presented with a number of options for filtering, as shown in the following screenshot. These menu options were set up automatically for you by Tableau when you set up the menu actions.

58. So, if you select the **Filter Country from Year to Quarter** option, then you are taken to the KPI by Q worksheet, and you can see the relevant data for the United States. Note also that the years are highlighted; this is as a result of the addition of these fields in the **Selected Fields** option.

How it works...

To summarize, we have set up a lot of different options for navigating around worksheets and dashboards using Tableau actions. You can see that Tableau is extremely flexible and adaptable for customization, which helps users to get results from their dashboard explorations.

In setting up these actions, you have configured additional menu options as well. So, for example, if you right-click on the United States row in the KPI by Year worksheet, you will be presented with a number of options for filtering. These menu options were set up automatically for you by Tableau when you set up the menu actions.

When we changed the color, we removed the blue color completely from the visualization, and only red and grey remained. Using a neutral color conveys the message that those data points are OK, since they have been brushed out. This means that the strong red color, representing the high negative difference between actual and target totals for the United States here, is emphasized by default.

Depending on your version of Tableau, the **Label** button may be called the **Text** button. However, the rest of the items have stayed the same.

See also

▶ *2013 Wisdom of Crowds Business Intelligence Market Study: Buyer's Guide Edition, Howard Dresner, CreateSpace Independent Publishing Platform*

Sharing your results in a meeting

Dashboards are designed to communicate the meaning of the data to the decision maker. However, decisions are not usually made by one person, which means that dashboards need to be shared. This is very easy if you all have Tableau.

What about the case, however, where not everyone has Tableau? What do you do then in order to share your results? In Tableau, it is very easy to share your results in PowerPoint and via PDF files.

In this topic, we will look for different ways in which to embed a PowerPoint presentation into a Tableau workbook. Later on in this book, we will go through ways of embedding a Tableau workbook in a PowerPoint presentation, but in the meantime, we will start with the simplest option. Embedding a PowerPoint presentation in a Tableau workbook can help to share results since it might help to add context.

Sometimes, you may need to consider printing Tableau workbooks, and we will look at tips to make this easy.

Getting ready

In this recipe, we will continue to use the workbook we created for previous recipes in this chapter.

Before you proceed to do anything in Tableau, you should upload a PowerPoint presentation of your choice to SkyDrive. If you do not have a SkyDrive account, then you are welcome to use the following presentation, which you can access by putting the link into a browser `http://bit.ly/JenStirrupOfficialTableauBookCode`.

How to do it...

1. In this recipe, create a dashboard in the `Chapter Four` Tableau workbook.

2. First, we will add a web page component to the dashboard canvas by clicking on the **Web Page** element on the left-hand side of the dashboard canvas.

   You can see an example of this element in the following screenshot:

☐☐ Horizontal	🖼 Image
🗒 Vertical	🌐 Web Page
A Text	☐ Blank

   Add new sheets and objects as:
Tiled	Floating

3. When you drag the **Web Page** element onto the canvas, Tableau will present you with a textbox where you can put the website URL. You can see an example of this textbox in the next screenshot:

   Edit URL ✕

   `http://bit.ly/TableauChapter4PPT` ▶

   OK   Cancel

4. You can also add a textbox to the sheet and give it a title. When you have added a title, the Tableau dashboard will appear as follows:

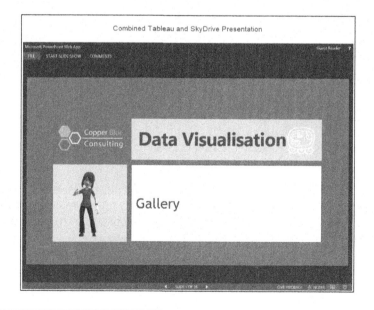

Combined Tableau and SkyDrive Presentation

Data Visualisation

Gallery

5. If you like, you can add some of the worksheets onto the dashboard in order to combine Tableau worksheets with the PowerPoint presentation.

6. What happens if you need to print out the Tableau workbook? To do this, go to the **File** menu item and select **Print to PDF...**. You can see an example of this in the following screenshot:

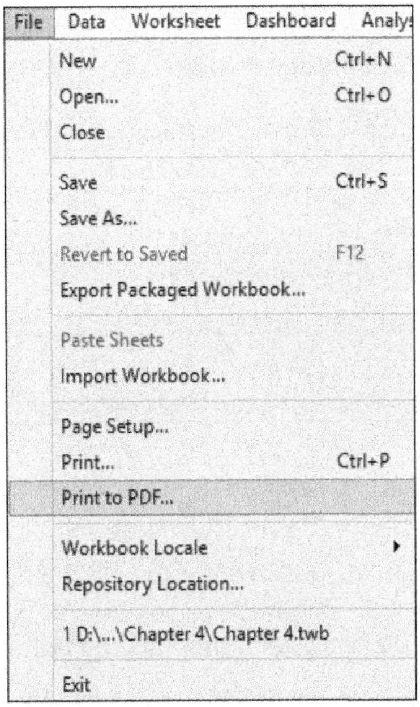

File	Data	Worksheet	Dashboard	Analys
New			Ctrl+N	
Open...			Ctrl+O	
Close				
Save			Ctrl+S	
Save As...				
Revert to Saved			F12	
Export Packaged Workbook...				
Paste Sheets				
Import Workbook...				
Page Setup...				
Print...			Ctrl+P	
Print to PDF...				
Workbook Locale			▶	
Repository Location...				
1 D:\...\Chapter 4\Chapter 4.twb				
Exit				

7. When you select the **Print to PDF...** option, you are presented with a small dialog box. There is an illustration of this dialog box in the next screenshot:

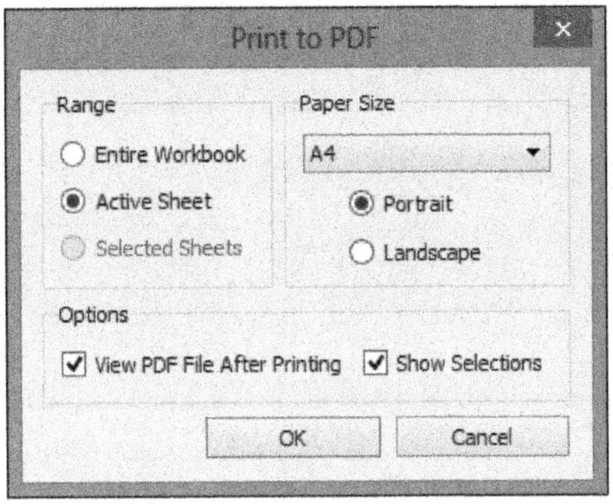

Print to PDF

Range
○ Entire Workbook
◉ Active Sheet
○ Selected Sheets

Paper Size
A4 ▼
◉ Portrait
○ Landscape

Options
☑ View PDF File After Printing   ☑ Show Selections

OK   Cancel

8. There are a few tips to note, however, when printing PDF files. For example, in the **Paper Size** drop-down list, there are a number of page sizes available. You can see a sample of the drop-down list in the next screenshot:

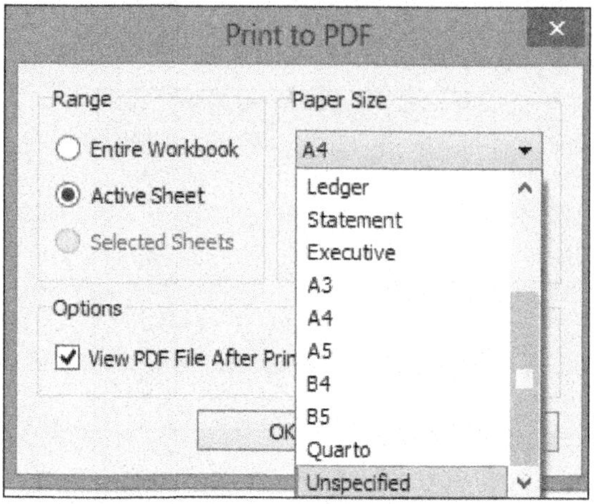

9. The highlighted option is **Unspecified**, and it is recommended that you do not select this option, or the paper size of your Tableau workbook will stretch and stretch!

10. You can also use the dimensions in order to split the printout into different pages. For example, you could have a new page per year, or per country as in our example here. Let's go through an example of this Tableau feature now.

11. Let's duplicate the KPI by Q worksheet and swap the dimensions around so that the **SalesTerritoryCountry** dimension is on the **Columns** shelf, and the **DimDate** dimension attributes are on the **Rows** shelf.

12. Now, let's drag the **Year(FullDateAlternateKey)** dimension attribute onto the **Pages** shelf, which is located above the **Filters** area. You can see an example of where it is located in the following screenshot:

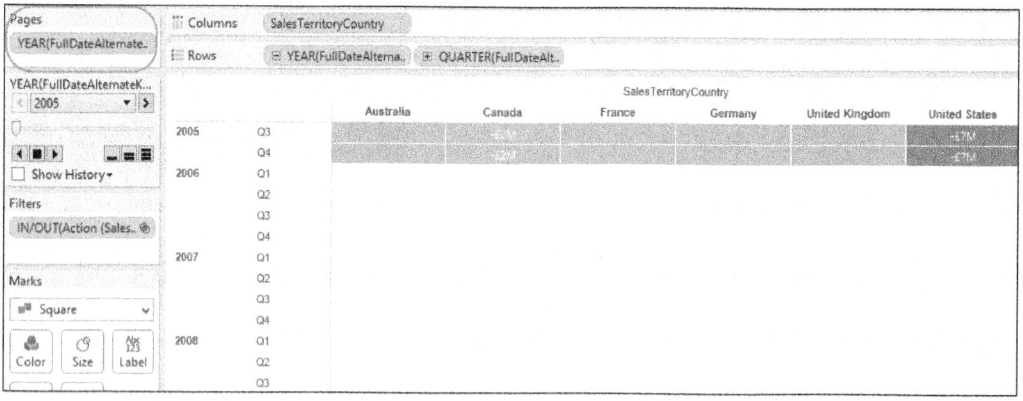

13. We need to do some work so that the PDF printout will have a new page per year. To do this, go to the **File** menu item and select **Page Setup...**.

You can see an example of this location in the following screenshot:

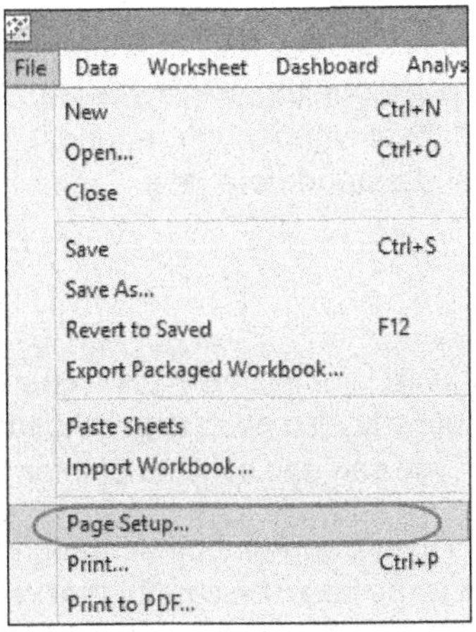

14. When you select this option, you are presented with a dialog box, where you can specify how you would like the pages to be printed out.

An example of the dialog box can be found in the following screenshot:

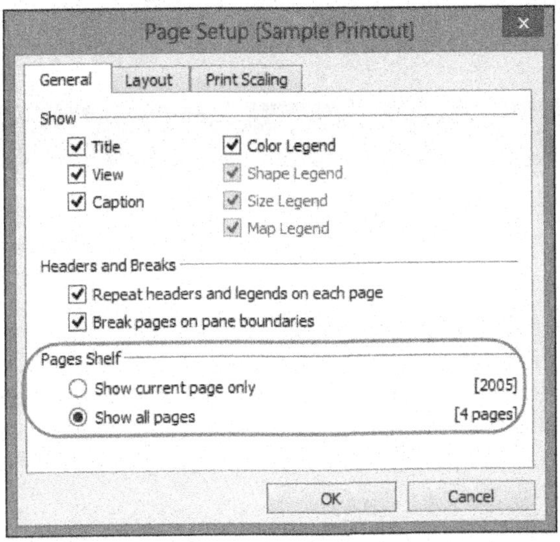

15. For our purposes, we will select the **Show all pages** option under the **Pages Shelf** configuration, since this will print out a new page for each dimension member. In our example, this will print out a new page for each year.

16. Once you have clicked on the **OK** button, you should now proceed to choose the **Print to PDF...** option, which you can find under the **File** menu option.

17. Tableau will ask you where you would like to store the file, and once you have saved it to the disk, you can review your file.

18. To summarize, Tableau has facilities that will help you to use dashboards as a tool for making decisions and sharing those insights with your colleagues. Even in today's world, some people work best with a printout, and it is good to be able to serve these people in the way they understand data best.

How it works...

The analytical power of the dashboard is amplified if it is shared with the right audience. Tableau is a great data visualization tool, but you also need to get the message out to the world. Adding it as part of PowerPoint means that you can add contextual information to the dashboard.

By embedding the dashboard and the PowerPoint presentation together, you might find that you end up with scroll bars. If this is the case, be careful that you are not scrunching everything together on one page. If so, it is time to rethink what you are showing on the screen. Less is more! You could think about increasing the interactivity so that it is not so confusing and scrunched up. You could also think about using filters or highlights in order to emphasize some data over others.

You can be careful with the dashboard size by emphasizing the most important data through the careful use of color, size, shape, or the inclusion of annotations, which we will discuss in the next recipe.

Notes and annotations

Annotations are little notes that help us to inform and engage the dashboard consumer, and they can make the difference between understanding the dashboard and even rejecting it due to a misunderstanding.

Annotations are useful for all sorts of reasons. For example, you might find them useful for jotting down ideas on the Tableau dashboard as we go along. Annotations can help to add context to your dashboard. For example, if a sales figure is an aberration in some way, then we can add an annotation to explain why this result has been found.

Getting ready

For the exercises in this chapter, we will continue to use the `Chapter Four` workbook. In this recipe, we will look at creating and formatting annotations. We will use the `KPI by Year` worksheet.

How to do it...

1. On the `KPI by Year` worksheet, right-click on the country **Canada** for the year **2007**.

2. On the pop-up menu, you will get the **Annotate** option, as shown in the following screenshot:

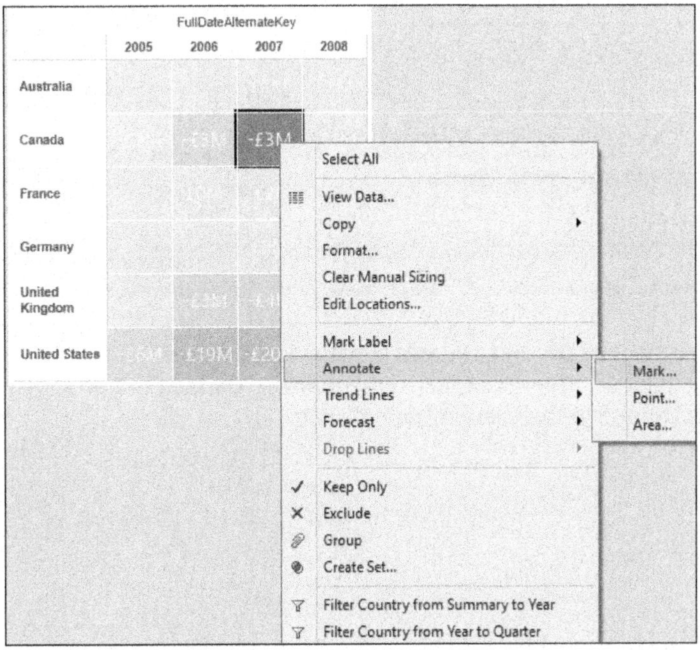

3. You have three options for how you would like to annotate: by the mark, the point, or the area. When you annotate using the **Mark...** option, the specific highlighted mark will be annotated. Alternatively, if you would like to annotate a specific point on the canvas that may not be at a specific data mark, select the **Point...** option. Finally, you could annotate an area of the canvas, and for this, you would choose the **Area...** option. For our example, we will annotate the specific mark for **Canada** in **2007**. When you choose the **Mark...** option, you are presented with a text editor with some prepopulated variables. You can see an example of this in the next screenshot:

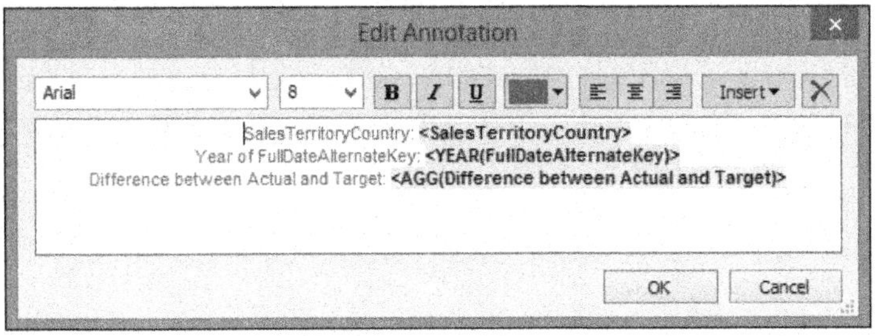

4. We can amend the default annotation, however, so that we can provide some more meaningful information. We can move around some of the features to make it more readable and add some additional text. For example, if we make the text black and add or remove some of the default text, we can take up the same amount of space on the page, but use it more meaningfully. An example of this is shown in the following screenshot:

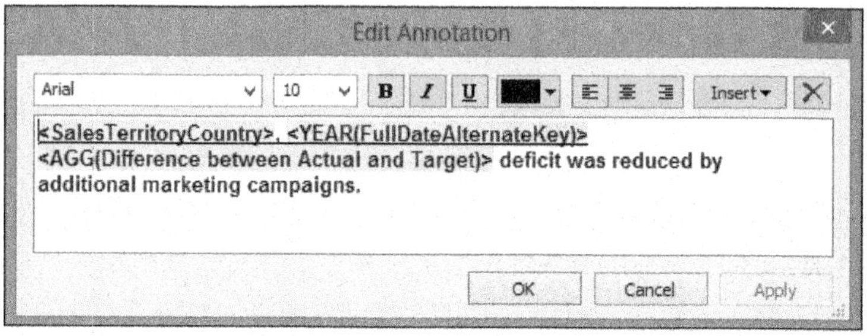

5. When we click on **OK** and return to the main screen, we can see that our annotation has been added. When we click on the mark for **Canada** in **2007**, we can see the mark, as shown in the following screenshot:

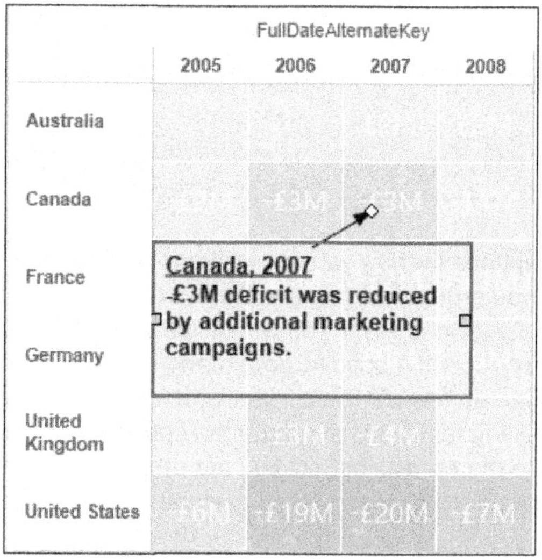

6. If the annotation is deemed noisy and is distracting, then we can try to reduce the font and move it to a location where there is less noise. An example of this is shown in the following screenshot:

	FullDateAlternateKey			
	2005	2006	2007	2008
Australia			£2M	£2M
Canada	-£2M	-£3M	-£3M	-£1M
France		£0M	-£2M	-£1M
Germany			£0M	£0M
United Kingdom		-£3M	-£4M	-£1M
United States	-£6M	-£19M	-£20M	-£7M

Canada, 2007
-£3M deficit was reduced by additional marketing campaigns.

7. To summarize, annotations can be a useful way of adding some context to the data visualization. One barrier for data visualization is that data consumers can get bogged down in the details if they do not understand a finer point. Adding an annotation can help the conversation to move forward, and hopefully help in the dashboard consumer getting results from your visualization.

Using external data to enrich your dashboard

We can provide a better perspective on data by adding external data sources. There are many applications where external data is extremely useful to the organization. For example, your marketing organization may be interested to know how your marketing campaigns impact your website, which in turn impacts your sales. Tableau is well suited to this type of analysis, and it provides a range of connectors so that you can mix external data sources together.

In an earlier chapter, we retrieved the country data from the Microsoft Windows Azure DataMarket. In this recipe, we will take a look at retrieving data from Google Analytics using the Tableau connector. Google Analytics is a tool that helps you to analyze traffic to your website, and many businesses make use of this free facility.

Getting ready

As in the case with the previous recipes in this chapter, we will continue to use the Chapter Four workbook.

How to do it...

1. Let's select the **Connect to Data** option on the Tableau welcome page on the Tableau desktop. Select the option for **Google Analytics** and the **Google** web page will ask you for a username and password for your user account, as shown in the following screenshot:

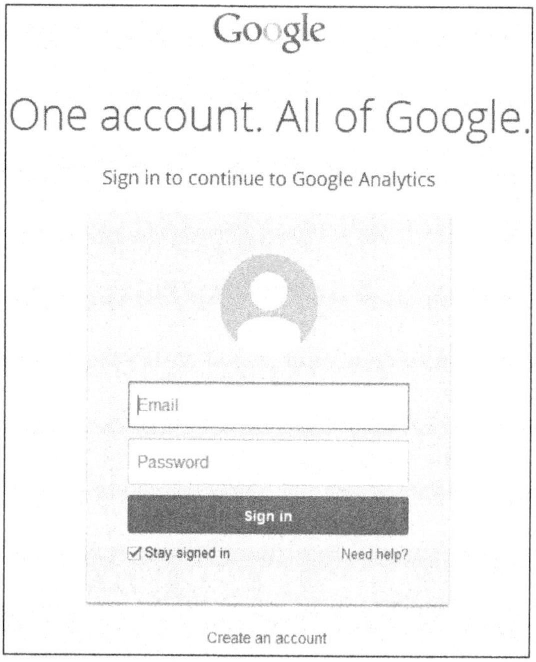

2. Once you have entered this information, you will be asked for the Google Analytics connection details. You can see an example of this feature in the next screenshot:

3. Once you see the **Google Analytics Connection** dialog box, you can fill in your details, such as **Account**, **Property**, and **Profile**.

4. When you click on **OK**, you can see the dimensions and measures in the Tableau worksheet.

5. Now that you can see your data, you can combine the data by simply grouping it together, which makes it easier to analyze.

6. For example, you can combine page groups in order to analyze web pages on a section-by-section basis, or even exclude certain groups from your analyses.

How it works...

To summarize, mashing up your external data with your internal data can mean that you get richer results and analyses from the data. This means your dashboards are essential tools for helping to drive decisions and insight throughout your organization, and your colleagues will thank you for it!

5
Putting the Dash
into Dashboards

In this chapter, we will cover the following topics:

- Choosing your visualization
- Using parameters in dashboards
- Using custom geocoding in Tableau
- Profiting from Big Data to rev your visualization
- Filtering your data for focus
- Creating choices in dashboards using conditional logic

Introduction

Dashboards are more than visual tools to display data; they are tools that can help to move business forward. Dashboards are used as decision-making tools to obtain results quickly.

You can help your business users make quick decisions by producing dashboards that are in line with the current research and thinking about dashboard structure. You can also get results from dashboards by performing the following actions:

- Improving the availability of data
- Facilitating the user's understanding of the data quickly
- Sharing information with team members and beyond
- Opening accessibility to users via adaptability
- Allowing users the flexibility to add notes to their dashboard

Choosing your visualization

Visualization is about democratizing data and making it accessible to the people who need it.

Today, there are many hot trends in both consumer and enterprise technology that increase accessibility by being highly visual. Think of the popularity of iPads, Surfaces, e-readers, and large screens. These devices are popular because everyone wants their data in the best resolution possible, with crisp graphics and colors.

Executives are engaging with the charm of visualization and putting it firmly onto enterprise business intelligence roadmaps. According to a survey by Howard Dresner, the extensive use of words such as color, size, shape, and motion were more appealing than other buzzwords such as Big Data and the cloud. A study by Dresner Advisory Services found that advanced visualization and dashboards ranked high in terms of importance.

Why is visualization so useful? It's more than pretty pictures. Data visualization helps us to understand meaning in data via a communication medium that we are "geared" towards every day—our vision. Through discrimination and the effectiveness of data visualizations, we obtain insights and make decisions. Technology allows us to create magic with our data, which engages us toward better decision making.

Given its power, how do we choose the right type of visualization? Throughout this book, we will talk about different visualization choices as we proceed. Because we are looking at dashboarding, we will look at dashboarding features, such as KPIs.

In this recipe, we will look at different considerations when choosing your visualization. We will look at some of the default settings of Tableau and how they are affected by color blindness. We will also look at **sparklines**, which aim to provide as much context in as small a space as possible. This will be very useful in creating dashboards.

Getting ready

For the exercises in this chapter, take a copy of the `Chapter 4` workbook and name it `Chapter 5`. This workbook already has the data for the exercises in this chapter, so we do not need to make any changes to the data. We will delete all of the sheets except the `KPI by Q` sheet.

The workbook will look as follows:

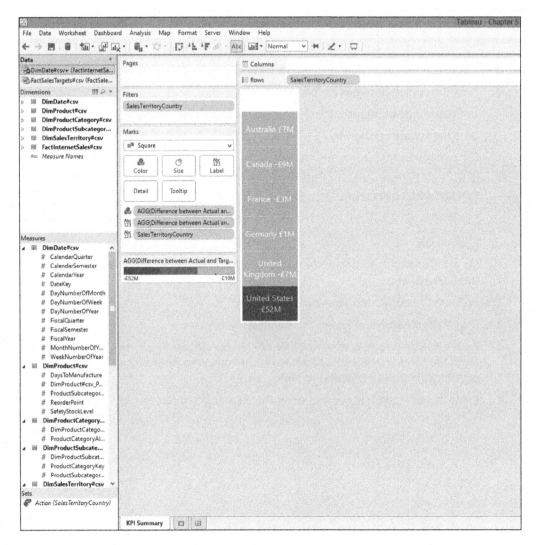

How to do it...

1. To start, let's rename the worksheet to `KPI Summary` by right-clicking on the tab at the bottom of the worksheet and selecting **Rename Sheet**.

2. Drag **SalesTerritoryCountry** to the **Rows** shelf.

3. Drag **Difference between Actual and Target** to the canvas area.

4. Drag **Difference between Actual and Target** to the **Label** button.

5. Drag **SalesTerritoryCountry** to the **Label** button.

6. Click on the **Label** button, and then click on the button with ellipses, next to **Text**.

7. In the **Edit Label** textbox, use the **Insert** drop-down box to choose the field names that should be displayed. This will read as follows:

   ```
   <SalesTerritoryCountry> <AGG(Difference between Actual and Target)>
   ```

8. Click on **OK**.

9. Let's duplicate the worksheet by right-clicking on the tab at the bottom and selecting **Duplicate Sheet**.

10. Rename the duplicated worksheet to `KPI by Q`.

11. Drag **FullDateAlternateKey** to the **Columns** worksheet.

12. We will start by creating a very simple KPI at first using the `KPI by Q` worksheet. To do this, create a new calculated field by going to the **Analysis** menu item and selecting the **Create Calculated Field...** option.

13. In the **Calculated Field** textbox, enter the following formula:

    ```
    IF [Difference between Actual and Target] > 0 THEN "Above"
    ELSEIF [Difference between Actual and Target] <= 0 THEN
    "Below"
    ELSE "Not Known"
    END
    ```

This appears as seen in the following screenshot:

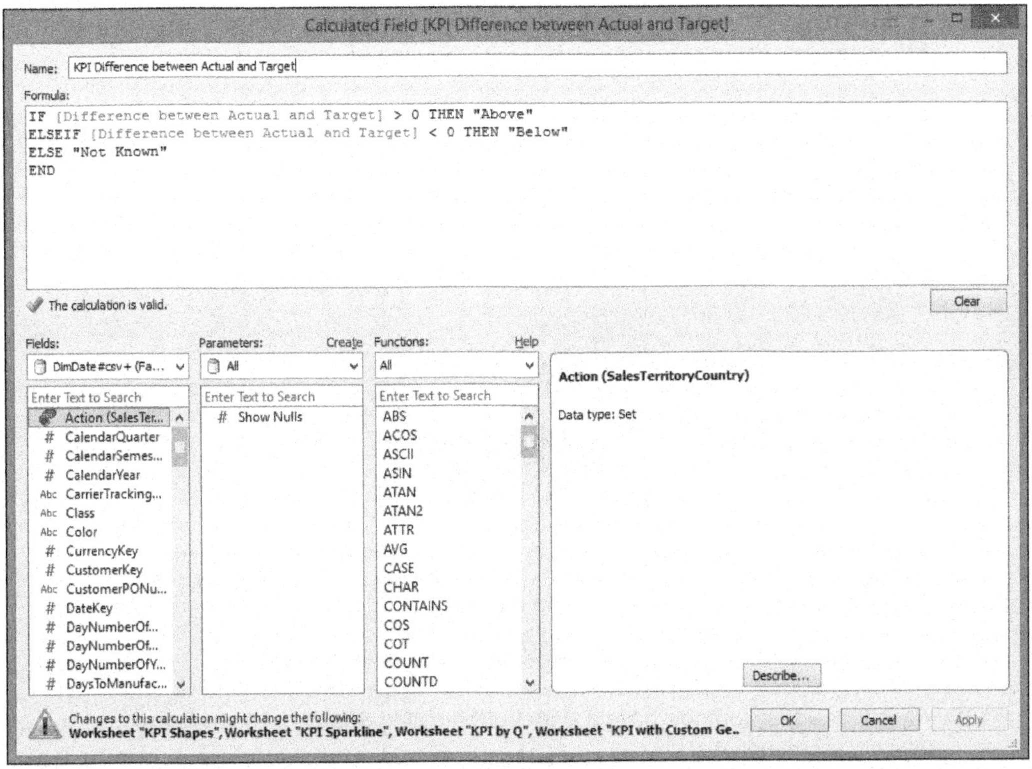

14. Once you've created your calculation and returned to the main Tableau canvas, you'll see that there are five buttons in the **Marks** shelf. You can add a sixth button: **Shape**. To do that, go to the drop-down list below **Marks** and select **Shape**, as shown in the following screenshot:

Marks

x+ Shape

    Automatic
ıιl Bar
∿ Line
◢ Area
▪ Square
● Circle
x+ Shape
Abc Text
🗺 Filled Map
● Pie
▀ Gantt Bar
▪ Polygon

15. You will see that you now have a sixth button called **Shape**, as seen in the following screenshot:

Marks

x+ Shape

| Color | Size | Abc 123 Label |
| Detail | Tooltip | Shape |

AGG(Difference bet..
AGG(Difference bet..
SalesTerritoryCount..

AGG(Difference between ...

-£23M   £3M

16. Click on the **Shape** button to edit the shape's style and appearance. Drag the **KPI Difference between Actual and Target** calculation onto the **Shape** button.

17. When you click on the **Shape** button, a dialog box offering a number of options appears. Choose the **Edit Shape** option, which brings up the following dialog box:

18. Here, we have selected the default **KPI** palette. A more traditional KPI selection selects the green tick for the **Above** option, which identifies the metrics that exceed the KPI success criteria. It is followed by the **Below** option, which is indicated by a red cross. Finally, the **Not Known** criterion identifies the areas where there is no value present; in other words, it is a NULL value.

19. Remove the color marks from the **Marks** shelf. At this point, you will probably have **AGG(Difference between Actual and Target)** as a color mark, but this will prevent the KPI shape from working properly.

20. Remove the **Label** marks from the **Marks** shelf.

21. Drag **Action(SalesTerritoryCountry)** from the **Sets** pane in the **Data** sidebar to the **Filters** shelf. On the downward arrow at the right-hand side of the **Action(SalesTerritoryCountry)** pill, select **Show In/Out of Set**.

22. In the dialog box, select **In** and then select **OK**.

23. Once you have selected this option, click on **OK**. Upon doing so, the visualization will appear as in the following screenshot:

24. Although we have created a KPI image, we would like to change it in order to cater to people who have color blindness. How can we show a KPI so that color blindness is taken into account?

25. Let's take a look and see what Tableau does when we try to create a sparkline. To do this, duplicate the existing visualization so that we have a "point in time" of our work to date.

26. Make sure that the **SalesTerritoryCountry** attribute is in the **Rows** shelf. Then, drag the **Difference Between Actual and Target** calculation to the **Rows** shelf.

27. Select a line graph visualization from the **Show Me** panel. Make sure that the **SalesTerritoryCountry** attribute is in the **Rows** shelf.

28. Ensure that **Year(FullDateAlternateKey)** is discrete by clicking on the pill in the **Columns** shelf and selecting **Discrete**.

29. Drag the **KPI Difference Between Actual and Target** calculation to the **Color** button.

30. Click on the **6 nulls** button on the bottom right-hand side of the screen.

31. You'll now get the following options. Select **Show Data at Default Position**.

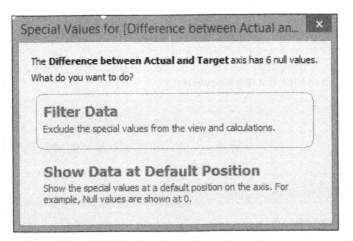

The Tableau visualization appears as follows:

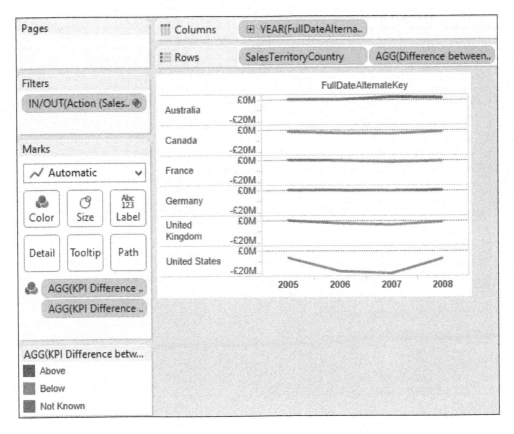

32. This still leaves us with the problem of showing data that isn't there—in other words, NULL data. While we are building up to a sparkline, it can look misleading because the data looks as if it starts from 0 and curves upwards; in fact, there isn't any data there for the highlighted marks, which you can see in the following screenshot. We can opt to **Hide** the **Not Known** data.

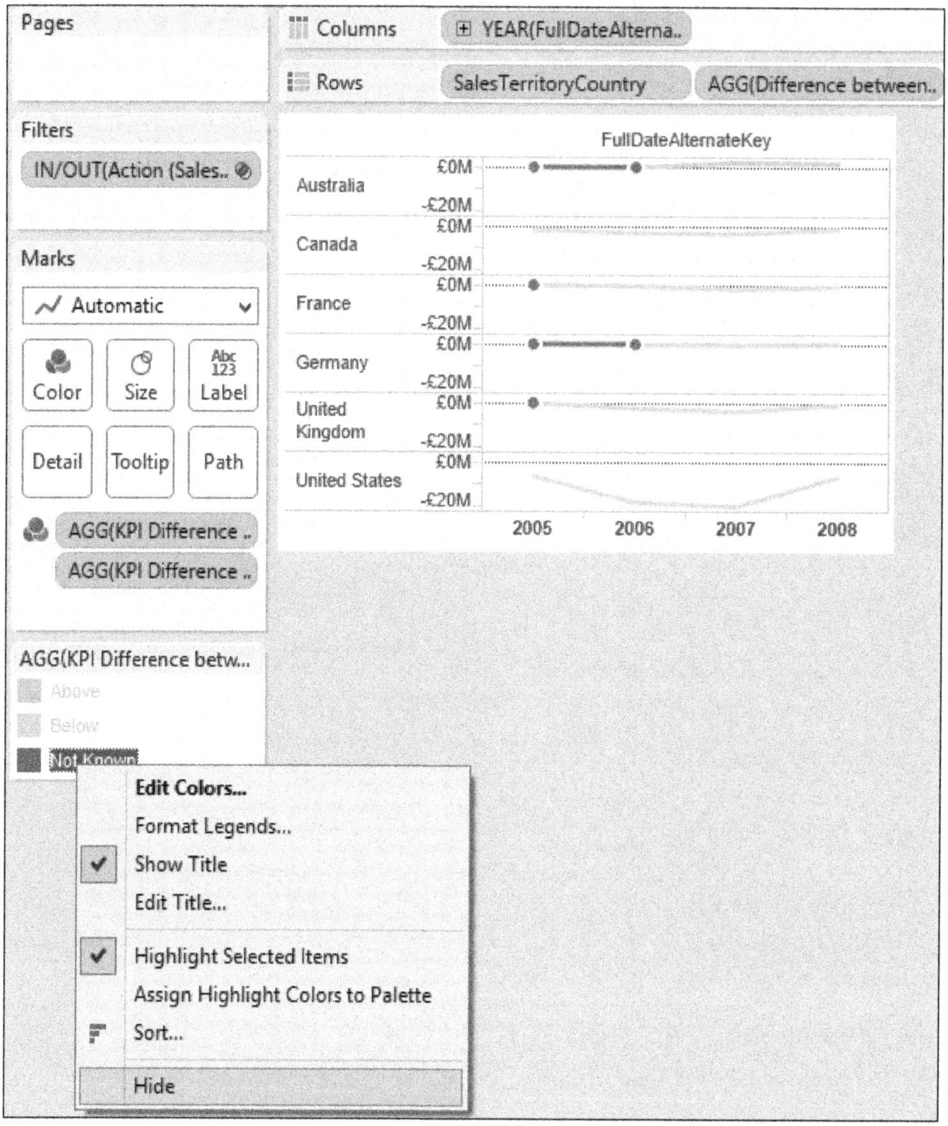

33. First things first, let's fix the colors so that they are more appealing. To do this, click on the **AGG (Difference between Actual and Target)** metric and select the **Edit Colors...** option, as shown in the following screenshot:

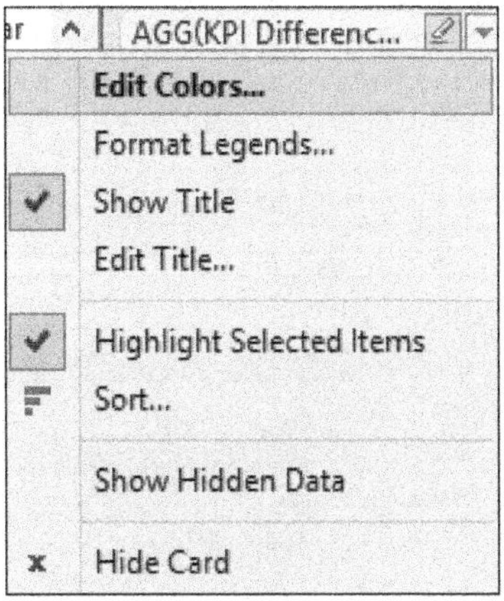

34. Since we have hidden the **Not Known** data, we only have the **Above** and **Below** data to worry about. For now, let's choose blue for the **Above** value and gray for the **Below** value. You can see a sample selection in the following screenshot:

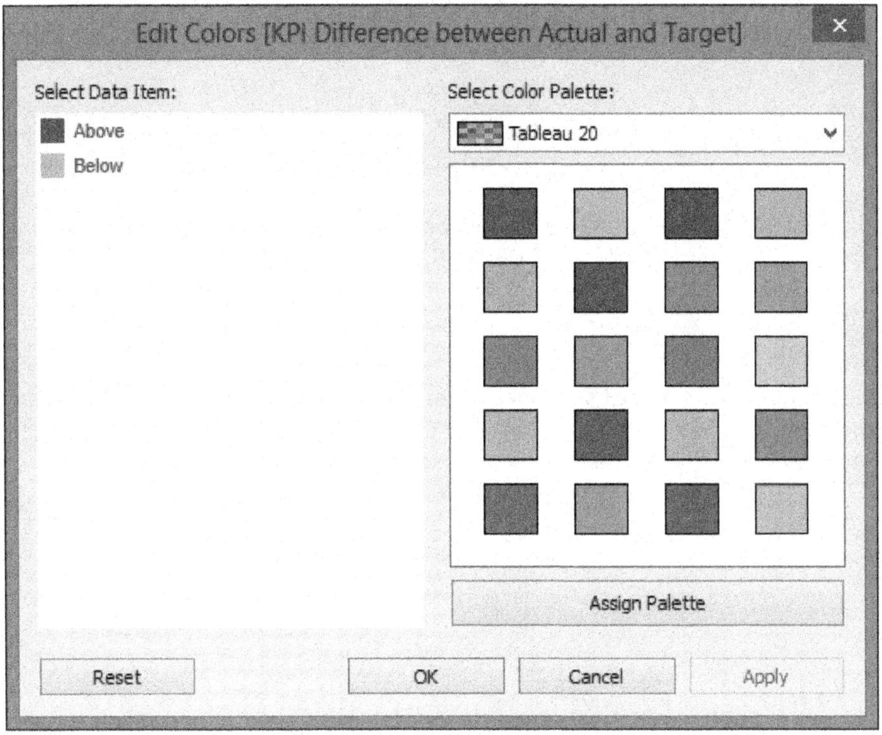

Now, let's see how the completed visualization looks once we have resized it, as shown in the following screenshot:

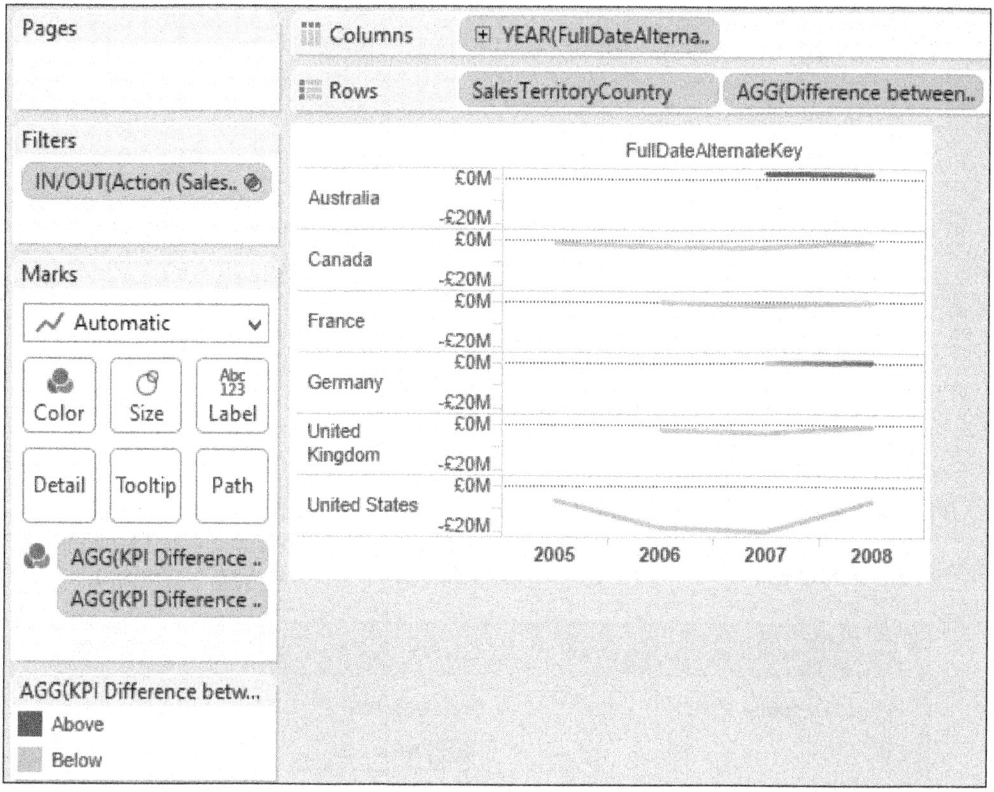

To summarize, in this recipe, we have started looking at some dashboard visualizations. We will look at other visualizations throughout the rest of the chapter.

How it works...

In this recipe, we have looked at some of the default settings in Tableau to create KPIs along with some options to configure them. It is clear that we can drastically change the appearance of the visualization by simply making a few changes to the default settings.

2. Once you have clicked on the **Create Parameter** option, you will get a dialog box named **Create Parameter**. This allows you to configure the parameter. We will set up a parameter that will allow users to choose whether they want to display Null values.

3. First, let's give our parameter a name so that its purpose is explained precisely. We will call it Show Data Points. This parameter is very simple. It is set to 1 if NULL values are to be shown and set to 0 if the NULL values are to be hidden. Since we are using integers as a setting, we should keep the **Data Type** setting as **Integer**. The **Current Value** option gives the parameter a value as a starting point. Once these fields have been completed, the **Create Parameter** dialog box should appear exactly as shown in the following screenshot:

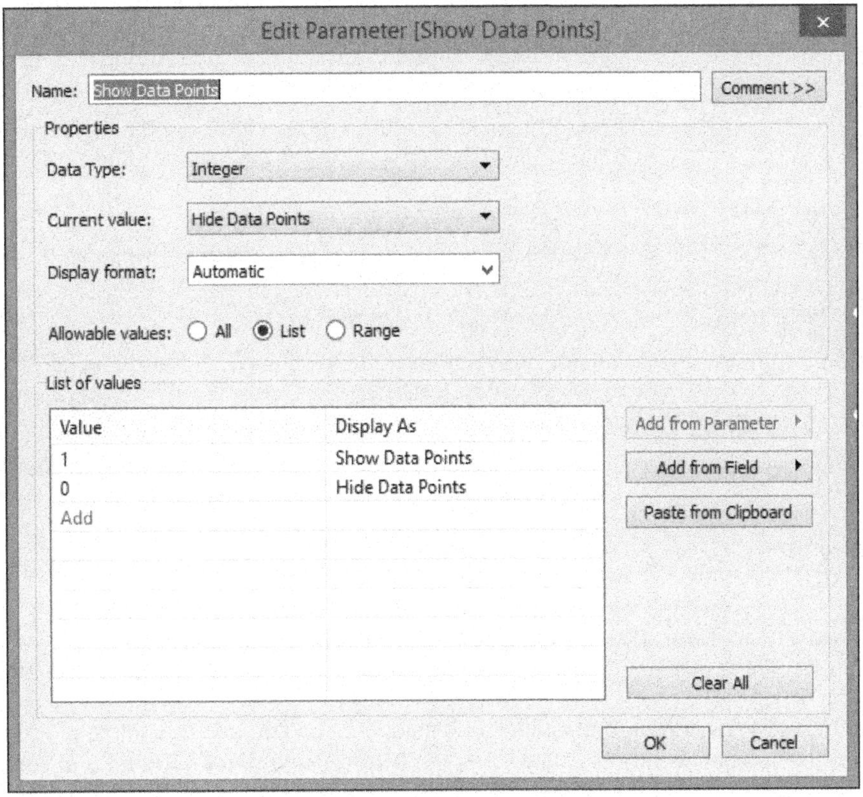

4. We need to set up a calculation to control the parameter. To do this, create a new calculated field by right-clicking in the **Measures** box again and choosing the **Create Calculated Field** option. We will use the calculation to make a rule that will drive the parameter. Our rule will specify that if the parameter setting is to show the NULL values, the parameter value is set to 1. This will display the second copy of the difference between the **Actual** and **Target** measures. If it is set to 0, only then will the line graph show on its own, which will show the NULL values as well as the actual data.

5. The calculated field is called **Difference (Show or Hide)**. The calculated rule incorporates a rule that says that if the **Show Data Points** parameter is equal to 1, then show the **Difference between Actual and Target** metric. If **Show Data Points** is not equal to 1, then the rule fails, and it does not show anything at all. You can see our calculated field in the following screenshot:

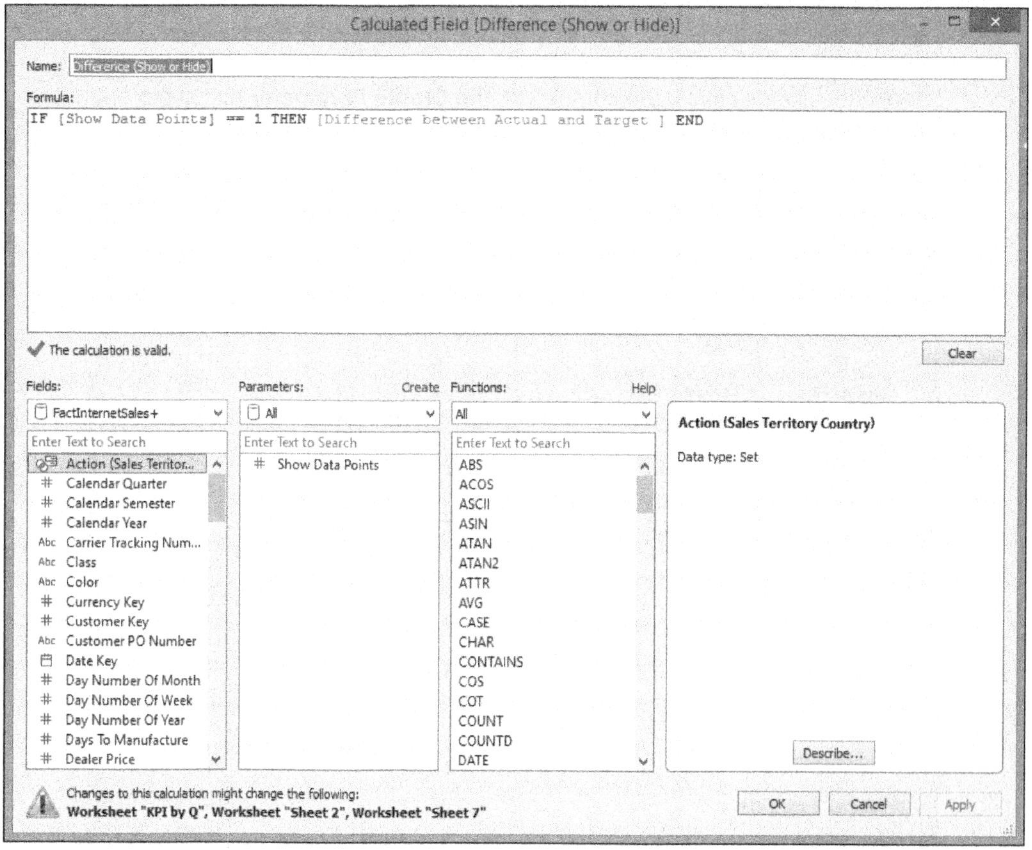

6. Once you have created the calculated field, click on **OK**, and this will take you back to the Tableau workbook. Then, drag the **Difference between Actual and Target** measure and **Difference (Show or Hide)** to the **Rows** shelf, making sure that **SalesTerritoryCountry** is also on the rows.

7. Click on **AGG(Difference (Show or Hide))** on the **Marks** shelf, and drag **Difference (Show or Hide)** to the **Color** button. The lines will now appear in different shades of red.

8. Then, choose the **Dual Line Axis** option from the **Show Me** panel. Your Tableau worksheet will look similar to the following screenshot:

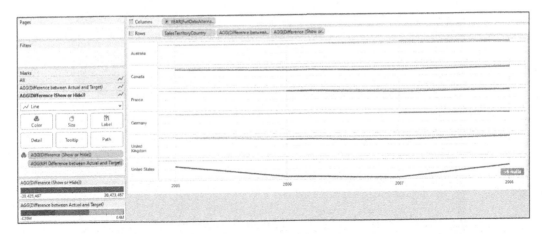

How can we clearly define where the actual data points are? The problem with the dual axis, as it stands, is that it will start at 0 if there is no data. This is because the axis is aligned to the year and the country, and if there is no data, it will simply map the data as having a value of 0. This can be misleading, however. For example, the data for Germany is represented by a line for 2005 and 2006, which ends up presenting a value of £1 million for the year 2008. However, this is a bit misleading; in fact, there was no data for the years 2005 or 2006; there was only data for 2007 and 2008. It would be better if this was clearer to the user.

Let's make the story of the data clearer to the business user by setting the colors and the line chart. This KPI panel illustrates data to answer a business question: which countries failed to meet their targets and when? This means that we are interested in emphasizing the losses made. We can do this by coloring these data points in red—a color normally used to denote a warning or a loss. Since we are not so interested in data where the countries met their targets, we will use the color gray so that this data goes into the background. Let's do this first for the **Difference between Actual and Target** data by dragging this measure onto the **Color** button. This will give us the following **Edit Colors** dialog box. Although we choose the option for **Red-Blue Diverging**, if we select the **Stepped Color** option and set it to **3** steps, we can get two different shades of red and one gray color.

You can see this setting in the following screenshot:

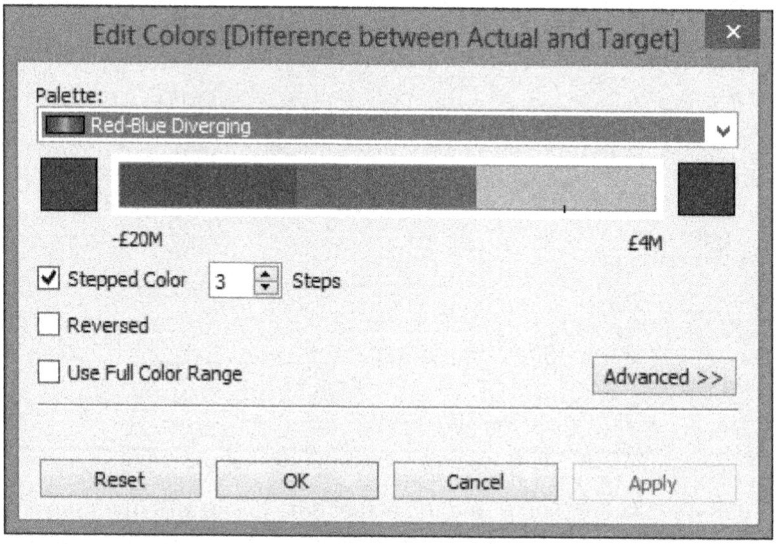

9. Once you have configured the color for the **Difference between Actual and Target** metric, set the color for the **Difference (Show or Hide)** metric. Drag the **Difference (Show or Hide)** metric onto the **Color** button and you will get the **Edit Colors** dialog box. This time, select the same **Red-Blue Diverging** option, but choose **2** steps in the **Stepped Color** box, as shown in the following screenshot:

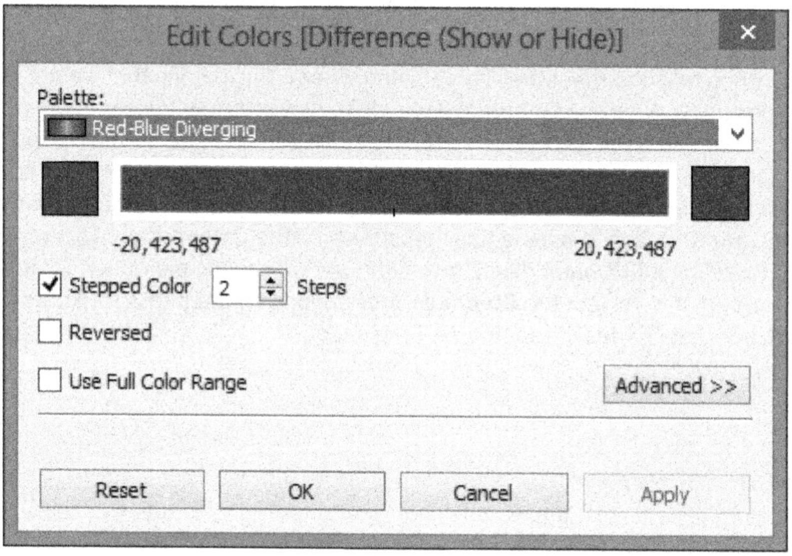

10. Now, let's make sure that the **Difference between Actual and Target** metric is set to a line. We can see this because the mark for the **Difference between Actual and Target** metric has a small line next to it, denoting that it is set to a line chart, as shown in the following screenshot:

Marks

All

AGG(Difference between Actual and Target) ⟋

⟋ Line ⌄

| Color | Size | Abc 123 Label |
| Detail | Tooltip | Path |

Measure Names

AGG(KPI Difference between Actual and Target)

AGG(Difference (Show or Hide))

Measure Names

⬛ Difference (Show or Hide)

⬛ Difference between Actual and Target

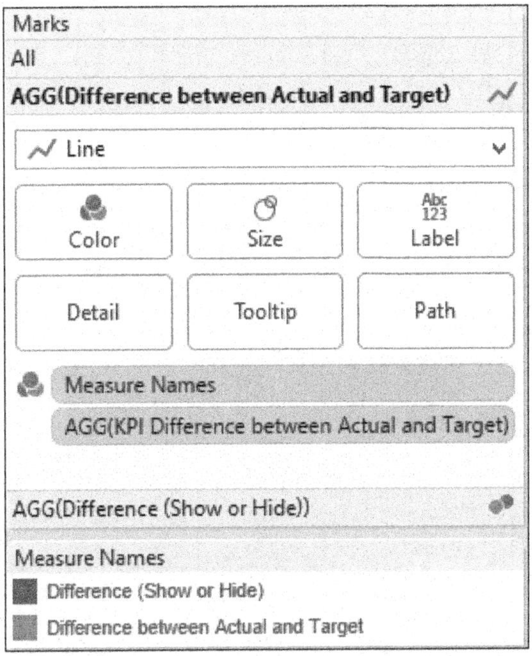

11. Now, click on the **AGG(Difference(Show or Hide))** metric under the buttons, and this will reveal the buttons to edit this metric. In the drop-down list, choose **Circle** for the **AGG(Difference(Show or Hide))** metric. This will distinguish it from the **Difference between Actual and Target** metric, which is denoted by a line graph, as shown in the following screenshot:

AGG(Difference (Show or Hide))

Circle ⌄

| Color | Size | Abc 123 Label |
| Detail | Tooltip | |

Measure Names

AGG(KPI Difference between Actual and Target)

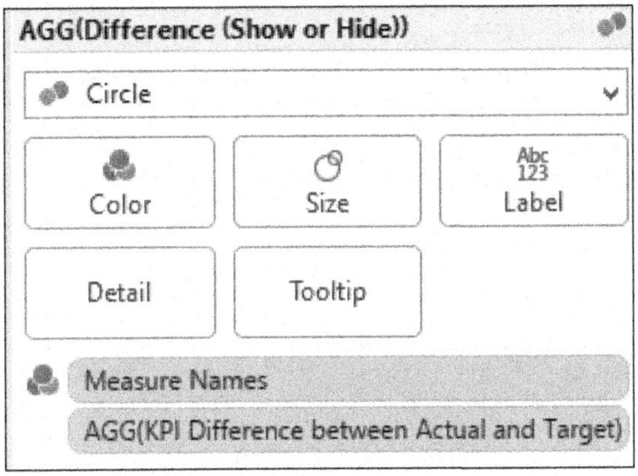

12. We can set a border around the circles so that they are defined. At the same time, we can make the color transparent so that we get a layered effect. To do this, click on the **Color** button, and you will get a pop-up menu. Set the transparency to 50 percent and choose a light purple color for the border. You can see the options in the following screenshot:

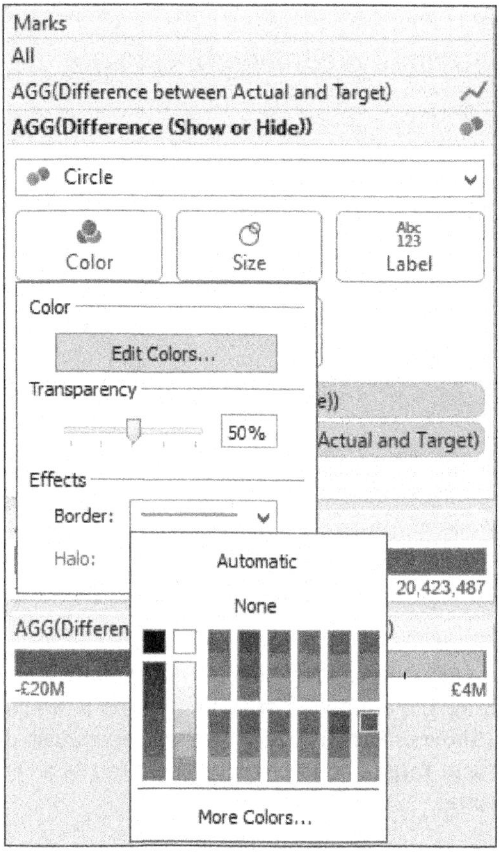

13. The last thing we need to do is to show the parameter control, which will give the user the option of explicitly showing the data points that are not NULL or leaving the chart as is. To show the parameter control, right-click on the **Parameters** section and select the **Show Parameter Control** option from the pop-up list.

Add to Sheet
Show Parameter Control
Cut
Copy
Paste
Edit...
Duplicate
Rename...
Hide
Delete
Create Folder...
Create Calculated Field...
Create Parameter...
Default Properties ▶
Replace References...
Describe...

14. The data visualization has now been completed, so let's test it out to see how it looks. The following screenshot shows the parameter control at the top-right corner:

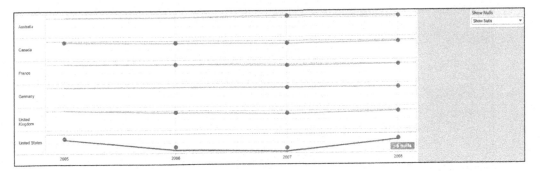

15. Let's configure the data visualization so that the NULL points are displayed at the default position, zero. To do this, click on the downward arrow on the **AGG(Difference Between Actual and Target)** pill and select the **Format...** option.

16. Go to the **Pane** option in the **Format Data** pane on the left-hand side of the screen. At the bottom of the pane, go to the **Marks** option and select **Show at Default Value**.

17. Click on the downward arrow on the **AGG(Difference(Show or Hide))** pill, and select the **Format...** option.

18. Go to the **Pane** option in the **Format Data** pane on the left-hand side of the screen. At the bottom of the pane, go to the **Marks** option and select **Show at Indicator**.

19. If we choose the **Hide Data Points** option, then we can see that the United States has engendered an unacceptable loss, but the other countries have not. However, this shows the NULL values, which assumes that all the countries have commenced at the same starting point, as shown in the following screenshot:

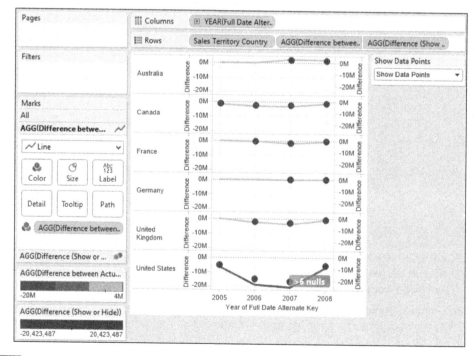

20. If we choose the **Show Data Points** option, we can see the data points that are not Null.

To summarize, using parameters to drive the data visualization, we can make our dashboards interactive and more sensitive to data quality.

How it works...

To sum up, in this recipe, we have looked at data quality, calculations, parameters, and data visualizations. These are all interesting topics in their own right, and the objective of this recipe was to show that we can put them together in interesting ways in order to produce a dashboard. Tableau allows us to be creative with our data to satisfy user requirements.

How did we use parameters in Tableau? To set up this visualization, we set up a dual line axis which has two measures on it: one is **Difference between Actual and Target**, and the other is a calculated field that has a rule in it, which shows or hides a copy of the **Difference between Actual and Target** measure. Yes, in other words, we show this measure twice on the dual axis or only once depending on the choice of the user. The difference is in the way in which we represent each copy of the measure. One copy of the measure is a line graph, which is always shown, and the second copy is a dot plot, which only shows the data that is present. The parameter shows, or hides, the second version of the measure in order to show which data points actually exist.

Using custom geocoding in Tableau

Organizations often have their own definitions of geographic data. Although country names stay relatively static, their classification can change as the organization emerges from one level of maturity and progresses to another. Sometimes, for example, an organization can start with a very simple division: North America and EMEA. However, as the organization grows, it may split into North America, Europe, Asia Pacific, and Rest of the World. This can mean that the geography has a business context and meaning; it also describes a physical location.

Since some geography is fairly standard, Tableau offers a default interpretation of certain geographic data to help you automatically create maps from your data, for example, the default interpretation includes countries, states, and area codes. However, Tableau's default interpretation can be tailored to align with the business interpretation of geographic data.

In this recipe, we will add some customized geographic data by importing a custom file and then using the customization to create a data visualization. The data is taken from the Human Development Index research, which is part of the United Nations Development Programme, an organization with the goal of "advocating for change and connecting countries to knowledge, experience, and resources to help people build a better life." The **Human Development Index** (**HDI**) is a new way of measuring development by using metrics such as life expectancy, educational success, and income and combining them into one measure. You can find more information about the HDI metric at `http://hdr.undp.org/en/statistics/hdi/`.

In this recipe, we will look at importing custom geocoding. One interesting feature of this exercise is how we go about using color to indicate rank.

Getting ready

Let's continue to use the `Chapter 5` workbook. You have an amended `DimSalesTerritory` to reimport, which contains the HDI rank of each country in the `AdventureWorks` database. To reimport this, replace the existing `DimSalesTerritory.csv` file with the `DimSalesTerritory.csv` file found in the `Chapter 5` workbook. If you open the new file, you will see that it contains an additional column: `HDIRank`. To refresh the data, simply go to the **Data** menu option and select **Refresh All Extracts**. You should see a new column called `HDIRank` in the `DImSalesTerritory` dimension.

The data created to customize geocoding in Tableau must follow a number of rules:

► The filename must be the same as the key of the data
► The file must be in CSV format

For the purpose of this example, download a small file called **HDIRank** from `http://bit.ly/JenStirrupOfficialTableauBookCode`. The data file contains three columns: a nominal latitude and longitude of the countries contained in the `AdventureWorks` database along with their HDI ranks according to the HDI 2013 report.

How to do it...

1. Once you have made a copy of the data file, open the `Chapter 5` workbook in Tableau and proceed to import the custom data file. Doing this is simple. Go to the **Map** file menu item, then to the **Geocoding** file menu item, and then select the **Import Custom Geocoding** option, as shown in the following screenshot:

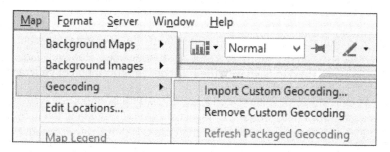

2. Once you have selected this option, a small dialog box will appear asking for the location of the file. The following is an example of the **Import Custom Geocoding** textbox:

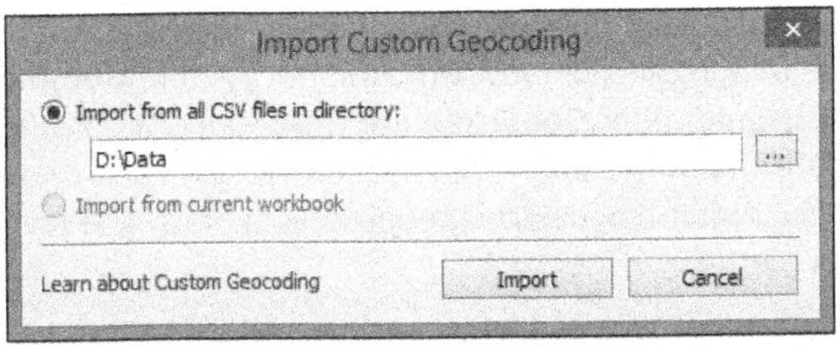

3. When you have navigated to the file, select the **Import** button to complete your import. Once you have imported the customized geography, you should be able to see it as part of the geographical role options in the Tableau drop-down list. You can see this in the next screenshot.

4. If you go to the **DimSalesTerritory** measures pane in the sidebar, you will see the new **HDIRank** column. Drag it to the **Dimensions** pane to make it a dimension.

5. Now, if you right-click on the **HDIRank** column and look under **Geographic Role**, you will see a new option called **HDIRank**, as shown in the following screenshot:

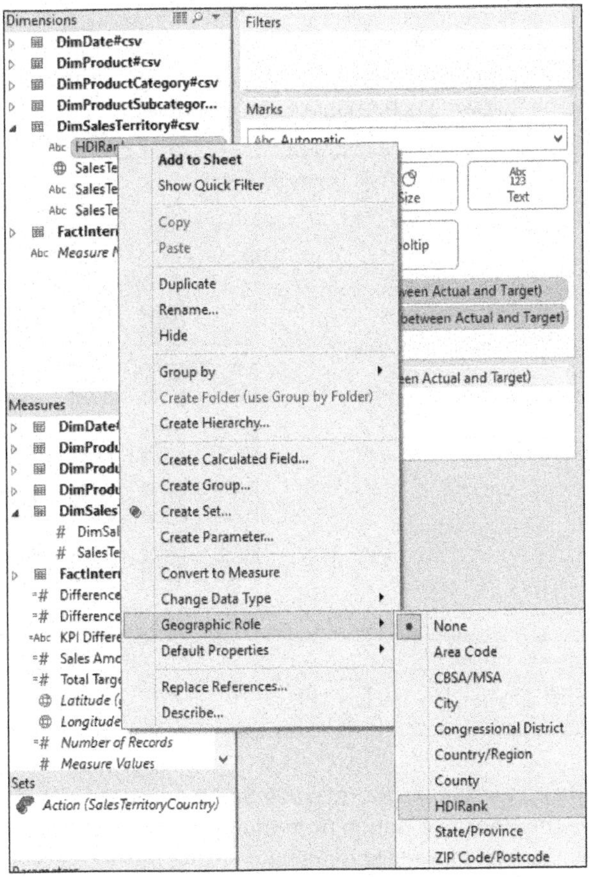

6. The next step is to assign the **HDIRank** geographical role to the **HDIRank** dimension attribute. To do this, right-click on **HDIRank**, navigate to **Geographical Role**, and then select **HDIRank** under **Geographical Role**. Once you have done this, you will be able to use **HDIRank** in the data visualization. You will see that the **HDIRank** symbol changes to show that it has custom geographical data. The following screenshot shows the new symbol:

7. For example, we can use **HDIRank** to drive the color that denotes each country. To do this, drag it to the **Color** button. Since we are using a rank to distinguish the countries, we can use a sequential palette to show that the data is on a continuum rather than in separate categories.

8. In this example, we will select the color orange.

9. Colors can be changed quite easily using the **Edit Color** dialog box. You will need to change each color so that the lower values have brighter and darker colors than the lower ranks. The following screenshot is an example:

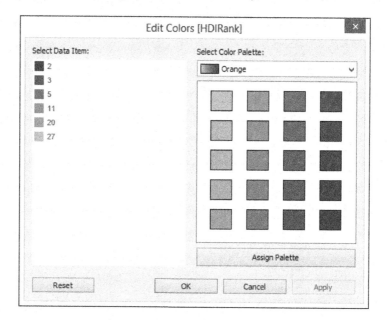

10. Once you have edited the colors, let's use **Sales Amount** to denote the size. Then, choose the **Heatmap** option from the **Show Me** panel. The visualization will now look like the following screenshot:

Pages				Columns

				Rows	HDIRank		SalesTerritoryCountry

Filters

2	Australia	■
3	United States	■
5	Germany	■
11	Canada	▓
20	France	▓
27	United Kingdom	▒

Marks

Automatic	∨

Color	Size	Abc 123 Label
Detail	Tooltip	

🔵 HDIRank

⬭ SUM(SalesAmount)

SUM(SalesAmount)
- ☐ 1,977,845
- ▢ 4,000,000
- ▣ 6,000,000
- ▤ 8,000,000
- ▥ 9,389,790

HDIRank
- ■ 2
- ■ 3
- ■ 5
- ▓ 11
- ▓ 20
- ▒ 27

To summarize, we have used our custom geography to help identify the rank of each country. Since the new role appears in the drop-down list as part of the Tableau interface, it is easy for report developers to use it as part of their dashboards.

How it works...

Once again, we see that color plays a vital role in conveying the message of the data. In line with research on how to visualize data, Tableau will assume that the lower values should be assigned a less intense color, and higher values should be assigned a darker, brighter, or more intense color. This would apply if our data was rational or interval in nature. However, we are looking at ranking data, so the situation is reversed. In other words, the lower the number, the higher the rank.

See also

▶ If you'd like to see the full HDI 2013 report, you can find it at `http://hdr.undp.org/en/media/HDR2013_EN_Summary.pdf`.

Profiting from Big Data to rev your visualization

We live in a world where everything is Big Data. Many organizations are burdened with too much data, and this is a common problem. The problem is made worse by the fact that many people aren't sure what to do with the data due to its size and complexity. In today's enterprises, data is often in disparate locations, and it is growing in size. This situation is reflected in this recipe, since it requires a lot of "moving parts" to be put together, such as downloaded data, the Hortonworks Sandbox, and Tableau.

For the purposes of simplicity and clarity, we will simply use a small amount of data rather than a Big Data source. This will help you to manipulate the data more easily since it is in an accessible format. Often, the key factor in the importance of data is how often it is used and how many business processes depend on the data, rather than its size. So, don't ignore the little data!

If you don't have access to Big Data technologies, don't feel excluded from the party. There is no need for you to skip over this chapter. We will base our example on the Hortonworks Sandbox, which is freely available over the Internet for you to use. It is also already preconfigured for you, so it is the easiest way possible to ramp up toward Big Data for free.

Getting ready

To use Windows Azure DataMarket, you will need a Microsoft account, such as a Live account, Hotmail, an MSN account, or others of the kind. This is free to set up if you don't already have one. To do this, visit `https://login.live.com/` and look for the **Sign Up Now** link to follow the wizard through the process.

To learn more about Big Data solutions, a great place to start is the **Hadoop Sandbox**, generously provided for free by Hortonworks and preconfigured for you to get started straightaway. To get started, download the Hortonworks Sandbox from the Hortonworks website at `www.hortonworks.com`. Sandbox is a virtual machine, and Hortonworks offers it using Hyper-V or VMware. You can download it to your preferred VM mechanism. If you are not sure about using Hyper-V or VMware, you can download the free VMware Player, which is easy to use and will work with the Hortonworks Sandbox. You can find it at `https://my.vmware.com/web/vmware/free#desktop_end_user_computing/vmware_player/6_0`.

Once you have configured the Sandbox, you need to download some sample code to put into the Sandbox. To enrich the data, we will use a country code set of data, which will give us a lot of information about individual countries. For this example, we will reuse the country file that we downloaded from Azure in *Chapter 1, A Short Dash to Dashboarding!*. Instead of connecting directly to the file, we will download it to a CSV file in Excel. To do this, connect to the Windows Azure DataMarket using a Windows Live ID by visiting `https://datamarket.azure.com/`.

The data can be found at `https://datamarket.azure.com/dataset/oh22is/` `countrycodes#schemaAbout`. Halfway down the page, look for the link to **Explore this Dataset**. On the right-hand side, you will see **Download Options**. Select the option to download as CSV.

You will see that there are several columns in the downloaded CSV, and we won't need them all for this example. To make the example simple, let's keep only the following columns:

- `Area`
- `Capital`
- `Continent`
- `Countrycallingcode`
- `Countryid`
- `Countryname`
- `Currency`
- `Fips`
- `IOC`
- `ISO3`
- `Isonumeric`
- `Nato2`
- `Nato3`
- `Population`

Now we are ready to use Big Data technology to enrich our data in Tableau.

How to do it...

1. Start by uploading the CSV file into the Hortonworks Sandbox. This is straightforward. Once you have the Hortonworks Sandbox open in your browser, create a directory called `GoldenRecord`. To proceed, go to the **File Explorer** option and select **Upload File** to upload it to the `GoldenRecord` directory.

2. Once you have uploaded the file, create the table. To do this, run a query in the **Query Editor** interface. The following screenshot shows this interface:

3. Copy the following script and paste it into the Query Editor, as shown in the preceding screenshot:

```
CREATE TABLE IF NOT EXISTS CountryInformation (
    countryID INT COMMENT 'Country ID',
    CountryName STRING COMMENT 'Country Name',
    ISO3 STRING COMMENT 'ISO3 Column',
    ISONumeric INT COMMENT 'ISO Numeric',
    FIPS STRING COMMENT 'FIPS',
    Continent STRING COMMENT 'Continent',
    Currency STRING COMMENT 'Currency',
    CountryCallingCode INT COMMENT 'Country Calling Code',
    IOC STRING COMMENT 'IOC',
    NATO2 STRING COMMENT 'NATO2 Classification',
    NATO3 STRING COMMENT 'NATO3 Classification',
    Capital STRING COMMENT 'Capital City',
    Area STRING COMMENT 'Country Area in SQ M',
    Population STRING COMMENT 'Population'
    )
ROW FORMAT DELIMITED
FIELDS TERMINATED BY ','
LOCATION '/user/hue/GoldenRecord'
```

4. Once you have done this, click on the **Execute** button, and the script will create a table called `CountryInformation`. When you click on the **Tables** option, you will see the `CountryInformation` table as shown in the following screenshot:

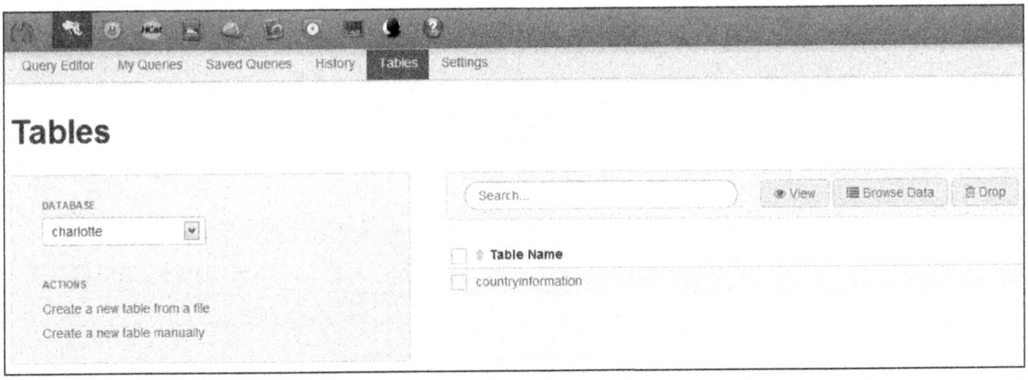

5. If you click on the **countryinformation** link, you will see the columns that you created. The following is an example of the columns as seen in the Hue browser:

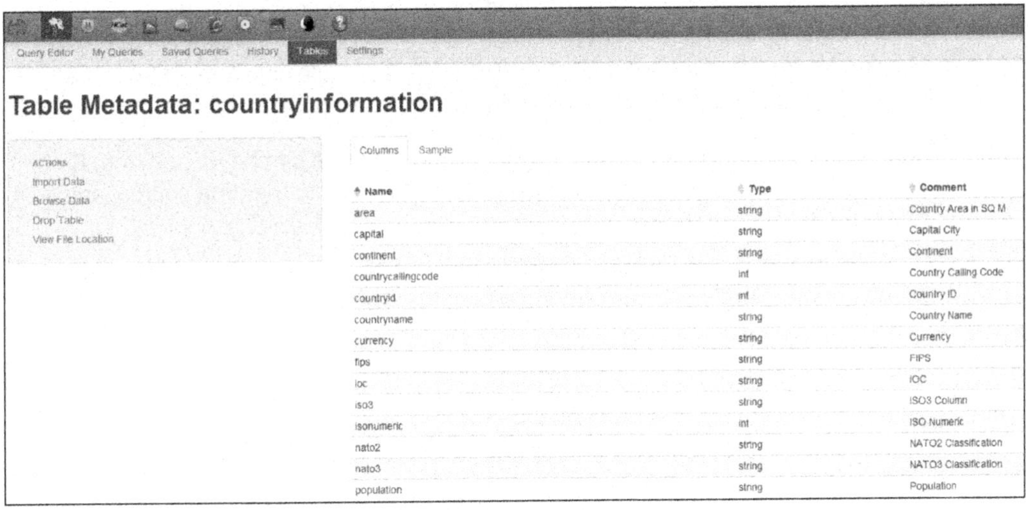

6. You can also see a sample of the data by clicking on the **Sample** link, as seen in the following screenshot:

We are now finished working with the Hortonworks Sandbox. Next, we need to use Tableau to connect to the Hortonworks store. There are two ways to do this. If you have the Tableau Professional edition, then you have enabled connectivity to Hortonworks. You can see this if you go to **Connect to Data** on the Tableau workbook. If you have the Tableau Desktop edition, you will need to use Excel to connect to the Hortonworks Sandbox and download the data from there. Once the data is downloaded to Excel, you can store it and connect to it easily. If this was a real-life scenario, this wouldn't be satisfactory because the data might go out of date very quickly.

7. However, for the purpose of our simple example, the data can be loaded from Excel into the Tableau Desktop edition. However, we'll connect to the data source, and let's call it GoldCountryCodes.

8. Once the data is in the Tableau workbook, we can join it to the other tables using the country name. Here's an example of the joining in the following screenshot:

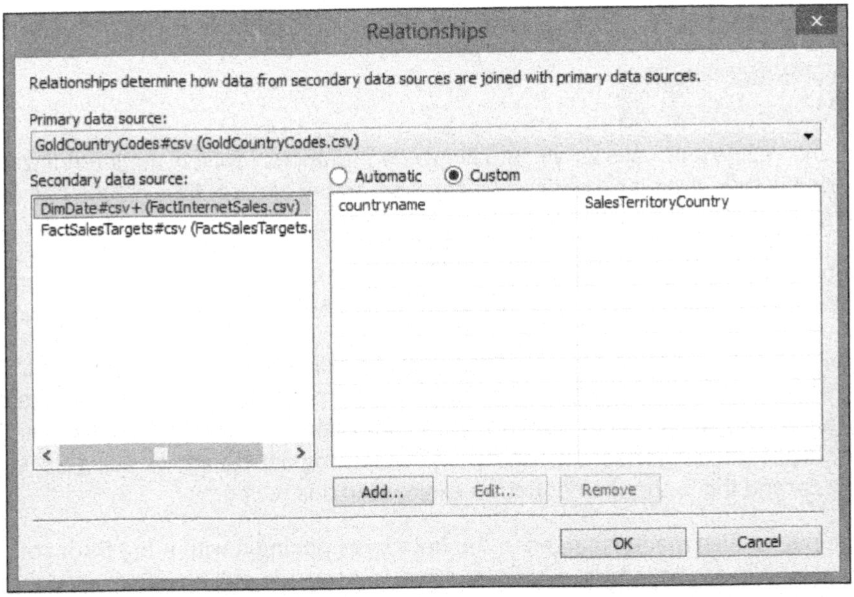

9. Once the data is joined together, we can visualize it in Tableau. We will have a mashup of the CSV files and Big Data technology—all in the same Tableau workbook.

10. For example, you could use the **SalesAmount** measure and put it next to the **Population** data from the external file. As a starting point, you could make a table and then see where the data takes you! The following screenshot shows your starting point:

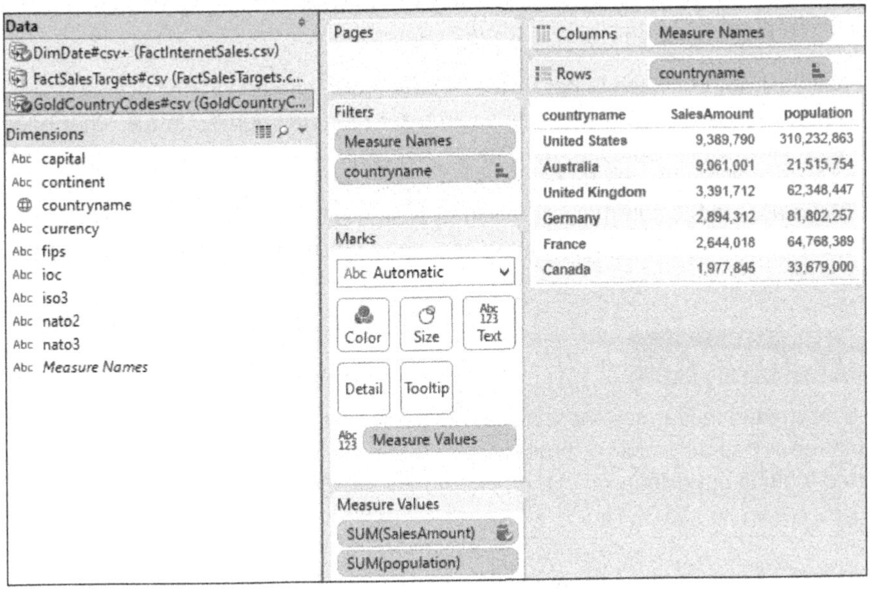

Why not try some of the visualizations in Tableau based on this data to see how it looks?

How it works...

Note that this recipe only uses small data files as an example, and it is not intended to be a real-world Big Data exercise where we transfer petabytes of data. Excel is used as an accessible example of a data source for training purposes.

The beauty of mixing Big Data sources with Little Data is that the user is insulated from the size of the data. Instead, they can visualize their data from different stores and different formats.

Fortunately, Tableau offers us a royal road to understanding the data by helping us to visualize it quickly and easily. It also allows us the ability to explore the data so that it starts to make sense regardless of whether it is Big Data or the important Little Data that makes up the data currency of the enterprise. We can enrich our existing data stores by using Big Data technologies, and this is the theme that we explored in this recipe.

In this recipe, we also made changes to the data by enriching it with a Big Data source. Big Data solutions are becoming more prevalent, but there is still a need for simplicity in accessing data regardless of its size. In this example, Tableau used a simple ODBC connector to access the data held in the Hortonworks Sandbox. A common experience among data analysts is not being able to get access to the data they want. Therefore, the simplicity of accessing the data is vital, and ODBC is a common way of accessing data that is familiar to IT professionals.

Once we have access to the data via ODBC, there is no stopping us! Tableau then sees the data as another data source, in the same way as it sees data from Excel or OData, for example. In other words, this mechanism is a great "leveler" of data access since the data is accessible regardless of its size.

Tableau obviously cannot suck in petabytes of data (yet!), and this is one scenario where Big Data will need to stay outside of Tableau as an external data source. On the other hand, as we saw earlier, business intelligence requirements often involve summarizing data for averages, counts, and so on. It can be useful to break the data down into manageable summaries, and Tableau could access the summary data rather than the full Big Data itself. These issues are architectural questions, but a summary is a good place to start before moving forward to bigger questions.

There's more...

If you are interested in learning more about Big Data, you will find that the Hortonworks Sandbox already has a number of preconfigured tutorials. This is a great resource to get you started looking at Hadoop.

Filtering your data for focus

Dashboards offer compact ways of communicating data because they are constrained by space. One way in which we can make more of the real estate on the dashboard is by using filters.

Tableau has three ways to filter dashboards. Global filters apply to every part of the workbook that uses the same data source. This might be a problem, though. What happens if you want the filter to apply in some cases but not others?

Local filters are specific to only one region of the dashboard. However, this may make them too restrictive. Tableau 8.1 now has a new filter feature, which allows you to stipulate a selection of worksheets for the filter rather than being specific to a data source. You can apply the filter to all the worksheets that use the data source, and to do this, you can choose the **All Using This Data Source** option. It is also possible to let the filter apply to only the current worksheet; you should select the **Only This Worksheet** option for this.

In this recipe, we will look at the new filter advancements of Tableau 8.1. We will work toward changing a chart into a filled map to show the sales amount filtered by year. We will add some new dashboard elements and get them to talk to one another by the use of filters. We will apply our filter to selected worksheets, where in the previous editions of Tableau, it was more "all or nothing" in terms of filtering the data visualization.

For the purpose of this recipe, we will want to select only some of the worksheets, so we'll select the **Selected Worksheets** option.

Getting ready

In this recipe, we will continue to use the workbook we created for the previous recipes of this chapter. There is no need to add more data sources.

How to do it...

1. Create a new dashboard called **KPI Analysis**.

2. Take the **KPI Summary** and **KPI Sparkline** worksheets and put them in the dashboard by dragging and dropping them into place.

3. Next, add a title at the top of the dashboard, asking the question: How well did the countries perform?

4. Place a **Blank** object below the two worksheet objects so that the countries are aligned and read left to right. Your dashboard should now look like the following screenshot:

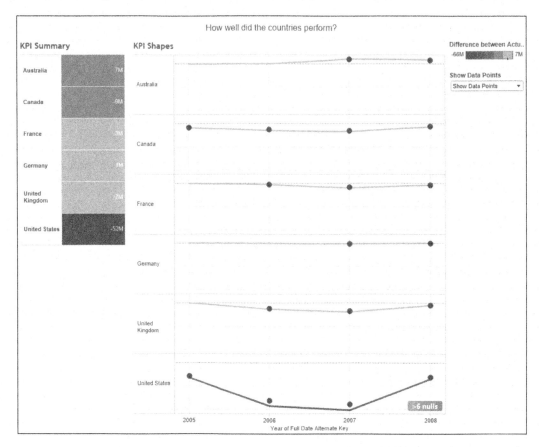

5. When you go to the original **KPI Sparkline** sheet, add the **SalesTerritoryCountry** filter so that you can filter by country. Do this by dragging the **SalesTerritoryCountry** attribute to the **Filters** shelf. The following screenshot shows this:

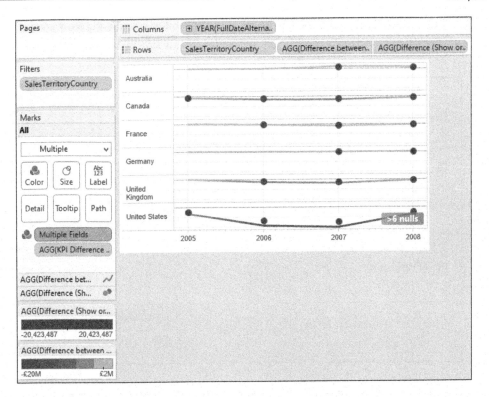

6. This option is fulfilled by selecting the **Selected Worksheets** option as follows:

7. For the purpose of this recipe, select the **KPI Sparkline** worksheets by simply checking the boxes next to **KPI Summary** and **KPI Sparkline**. The following screenshot shows the dialog box:

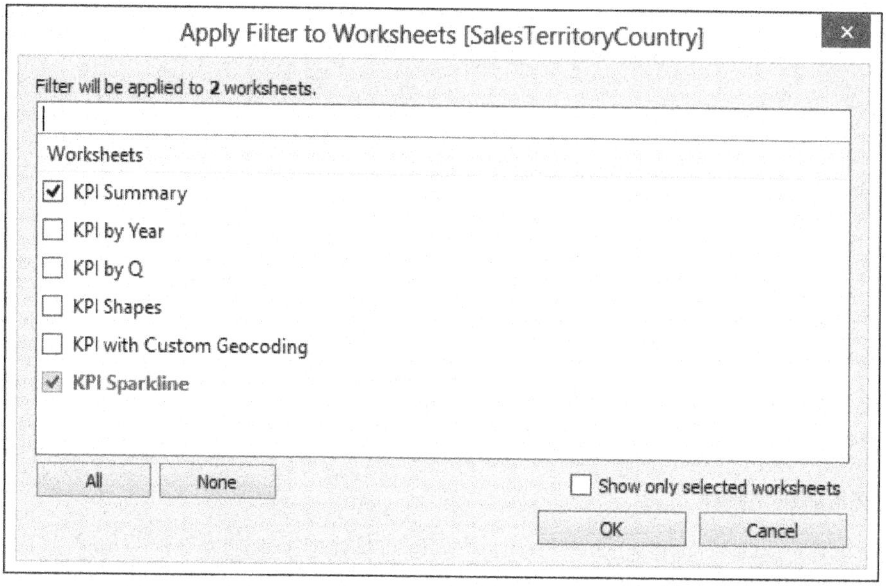

8. Once you have clicked on the checkboxes next to the worksheets, click on **OK** to create the filters. Next, to display the filters, click on the filter and choose the **Show Quick Filter** option.

9. Now, create a worksheet called **Golden Record**.

10. Drag **Longitude** to the **Columns** shelf.

11. Drag **Latitude** to the **Rows** shelf.

12. Drag **SalesTerritoryCountry** onto the canvas.

13. Drag **SalesAmount** onto the **Size** button on the **Marks** shelf.

14. Drag **SalesAmount** onto the **Color** button on the **Marks** shelf.

15. To change the **Golden Record** visualization to a filled map, simply select the **Filled Map** option from the **Show Me** pane.

16. Remove **Population** if it is present, and use **SalesAmount** to illustrate the sales amount value. In the following example, red has been used because it represents the sales amount for the other components of the dashboard:

Edit Colors [SalesAmount]

Palette:

Red

1,977,845   9,389,790

☑ Stepped Color   3 ⬍ Steps

☐ Reversed

☐ Use Full Color Range   Advanced >>

Reset   OK   Cancel   Apply

17. Let's filter the filled map to only show the latest year's data by simply taking
FullDateAlternateKey and dragging it to the **Filters** shelf. This will initiate a **Filter
Field** dialog box. Select the **Years** filter and restrict the data so that only the data
from the latest year is shown, which in this case, is the year 2008. You can see an
example of this in the following screenshot:

Filter Field [FullDateAlternateKey]

How do you want to filter on [FullDateAlternateKey]?

🗺 Relative date
🗺 **Range of dates**

\# Years
\# Quarters
\# Months
\# Days
\# Hours
\# Minutes
\# Seconds
\# Week numbers
\# Weekdays
\# Month / Year
\# Month / Day / Year
🗺 Individual dates and times

\# Count
\# Count (Distinct)
🗺 Attribute

Next >   Cancel

18. The next step, as shown in the next screenshot, is to select the year **2008** from the **Filter** dialog box; this will filter the map. However, we are not applying this filter to the rest of the dashboard. This means that the map will stay static even though we have filters shared across the other components of the dashboard, **KPI Summary** and **KPI Sparkline**.

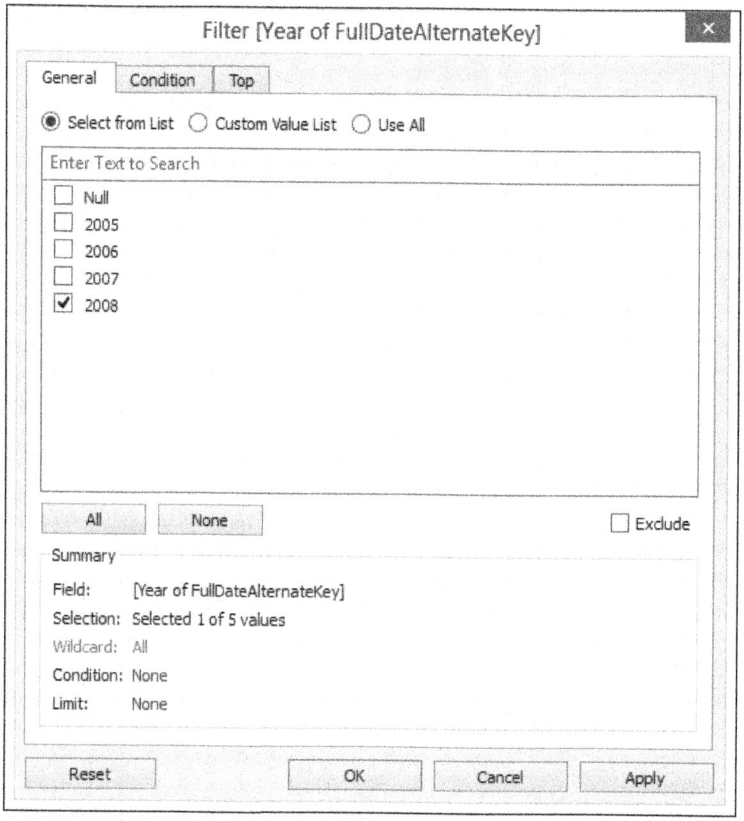

Filter [Year of FullDateAlternateKey]

General | Condition | Top

( ) Select from List ( ) Custom Value List ( ) Use All

Enter Text to Search

- [ ] Null
- [ ] 2005
- [ ] 2006
- [ ] 2007
- [x] 2008

All   None   [ ] Exclude

Summary

Field: [Year of FullDateAlternateKey]
Selection: Selected 1 of 5 values
Wildcard: All
Condition: None
Limit: None

Reset   OK   Cancel   Apply

19. Once you have selected the year **2008**, click on **OK** to return to the map.

20. Finally, let's put the **Golden Record** worksheet with the filled map into the **KPI Analysis** dashboard. It is static data, and we will place it down at the bottom so that it acts as an anchor for the rest of the more detailed data.

21. Click on the **KPI Sparkline** worksheet in the dashboard. At the top right-hand corner, click on the drop-down arrow and select **Quick Filters** and then **Sales Territory Country**. Your filter should now appear.

The Tableau dashboard will now appear as follows:

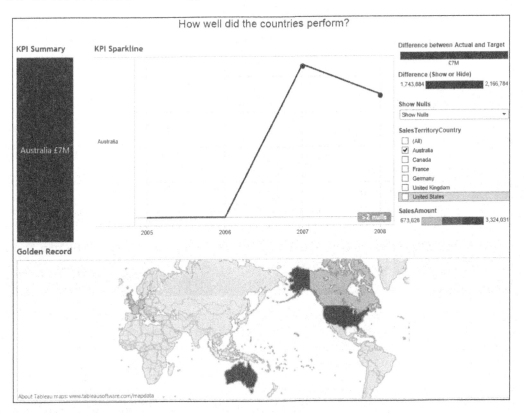

How it works...

Filtering data is a key part of the *Visual Information-Seeking Mantra* article by Professor Ben Shneiderman, and users expect to be able to filter and interact with their data. Although the principles will not hold if people only want very detailed row-level data, the mantra works when you are thinking about designing your dashboard. Dashboards are about actionable overviews rather than the detail about one row. Hence, the summary is an essential part of providing the overview.

Filtering is a good way to promote engagement with your dashboards. In marketing, stickiness refers to anything that encourages readers to stay on your website. In dashboard creation and reporting, stickiness can refer to features that increase the likelihood that users will stay on your dashboard and use it.

We can use filters to make our dashboards more flexible in response to user input, which may help to keep the dashboard engaging and interesting for data consumers. A key aspect of dashboarding is that we need to make the most of the space while engaging the user in the key facts of the data. Filters can help us to do that easily in Tableau.

Once again, color is key to conveying the message of the data. In this example, red is used in both the **KPI Summary** and **KPI Sparkline** worksheets, and the color is split into three steps in order to simplify the classification of the sales amount. People don't always distinguish fine-grained nuances of color, and hence, using the **Stepped Color** feature of the **Edit Color** panel makes the data simpler to understand.

There's more...

For the purpose of this recipe, we have only selected some of the worksheets, so the **Selected Worksheets** option serves our purpose.

See also

▸   http://www.ifp.illinois.edu/nabhcs/abstracts/shneiderman.html

Creating choices in dashboards using conditional logic

Logical calculations can make your analyses richer. They can also make things easier for a dashboard consumer. For example, logical calculations can help you funnel the analysis to specific dimension members, combine members to follow a business rule, or even remove values that are irrelevant to your investigation.

Normally, when we use filters, we select the attributes within a dimension. In this recipe, we will implement logical calculations so that users can choose different dimensions to describe the data. We will place a small control on the dashboard so that users can simply click to choose the dimension they would like to see, which describes the sales amount data. Users can simply click on which dimension they would like to see, for example, by color, country, or product line.

In this recipe, we will need to make a calculated field using a logical calculation and a number of parameters, amend the colors, and so on. Our sequence is to set up some parameters, a calculated field, and then some filters. So, let's get started!

Getting ready

For the exercises in this recipe, we will continue using the Chapter 5 workbook. There is no need to add any more data. Let's make a copy of the **KPI Sparkline** worksheet and call it KPI Dimensions. We will also make a copy of the dashboard and call it KPI Dimension Analysis.

How to do it...

1. First, let's set up a parameter so that the user can choose a metric. To set up a parameter, right-click on the **Measure** box and select the **Create Parameter** option. Call the parameter `Choose Characteristic` and set up a list for each metric. Make sure that you set up **List** as an allowable value and type each metric name into the list of values.

The following is an example of the resulting parameter:

Edit Parameter [Choose Characteristic] ✕

Name: | Choose Characteristic | Comment >>

Properties

Data Type: String ▾

Current value: Color ⌄

Display format: ⌄

Allowable values: ◯ All ⦿ List ◯ Range

List of values

Value	Display As	
All	All	Add from Parameter ▸
Color	Color	Add from Field ▸
Country	Country	Paste from Clipboard
Product Line	Product Line	
Add		
		Clear All

OK   Cancel

2. Next, we need to add a calculation that will help us choose different dimensions. We will use a `CASE` statement, which is simply like lots of `IF...THEN...ELSE` statements strung together. The calculation will execute the first statement that it finds to be true.

3. We will set up a `CASE` statement that chooses between dimensions dependent on the user selection. We will offer the following choice of different measures so the dashboard consumer can select the measure they would like to see on the dashboard:

   ❑ Sales amount
   ❑ Sales amount quote

4. To do this, right-click on the **Dimension** part of the Tableau workbook and select the **Create Calculated Field** option. The logical calculation is written as follows:

```
CASE [Choose Characteristic]
WHEN "All" THEN "All"
WHEN "Color" THEN [Color]
WHEN "Country" THEN [SalesTerritoryCountry]
WHEN "Product Line" THEN [ProductLine]
END
```

5. The CASE calculation allows us to simply show all of the data not described by any dimension, or show by color, country, or product line.

6. The logical calculation can be seen in the calculation editor, as shown in the following screenshot. Simply copy and paste the mentioned calculation into the textbox and call the calculation Calc_ChooseCharacteristic.

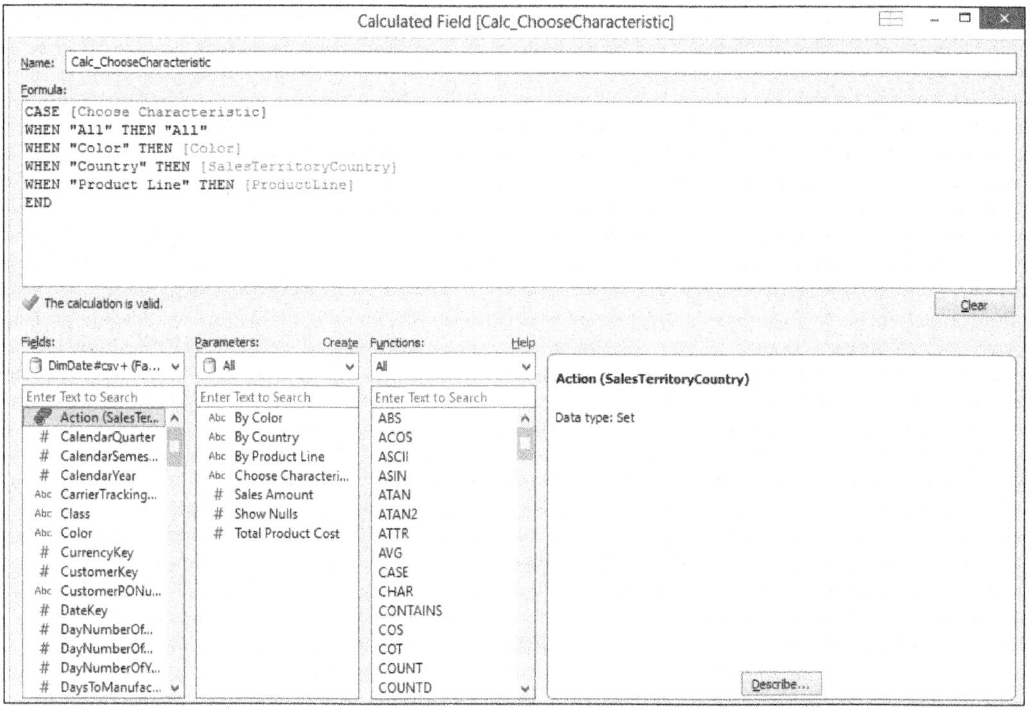

7. Once you have clicked on **OK**, you will see the calculation in the **Dimensions** pane in the sidebar in the Tableau workbook.

8. Now, we need to set up some pills so that our workbook visualization is filtered according to the user-selected dimension. Take the **Calc_ChooseCharacteristic** filter and drag it to the **Marks** shelf so that the detail is retained.

9. Next, drag **Calc_ChooseCharacteristic** onto the **Color** button. This is vital because it tells Tableau that it needs to change the display depending on the selected dimension. The calculated fields implement the logic to denote which dimension should be displayed.

10. This selected **Dimension** value is held in the **Choose Characteristic** parameter. The color is dependent on the result of the CASE statement evaluation in the **Calc_ChooseCharacteristic** calculation, and this is how Tableau differentiates in the display. You will need to make sure that users can select their preferred dimension, and to do this, they will need to see the parameter control. And you will need to see it in order to test it out! Simply go to the parameter called **Choose Characteristic**, right-click on it, and select the **Show Parameter Control** option.

11. Since we are using **Color** as a potential dimension, we can make the palette-defined colors match the actual colors of the merchandise. To do this, click on the **Color** button and select the **Edit Colors** option. We can then set the color attribute **Red** to be red, set the color attribute **Blue** to the color blue, and so on, as seen in the following screenshot:

12. To finalize the visualization, ensure that **Year(FullDateAlternateKey)** is on the **Columns** shelf and that **Sum(SalesAmount)** is on the **Rows** shelf.

13. Set **Marks** to be **Circle** rather than **Automatic**.

14. We can also add **SUM(SalesAmount)** so that the diameter of each circle becomes representative of the **SUM(SalesAmount)** value.

15. Let's go to our dashboard called **KPI Dimension Analysis**, which we copied earlier. Let's remove the **KPI Sparkline** worksheet and insert the new **KPI Dimensions** worksheet instead. We will need to show our parameter control; to do this, click on the **KPI Dimensions** area of the dimension, select **Parameters**, and select the **Choose Characteristic** option. We should also add the **Calc_ChooseCharacteristic** filter, which is under **Quick Filters** in the same menu. This step is demonstrated in the following screenshot:

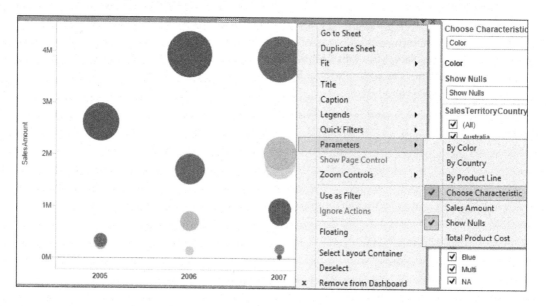

16. You can also remove the title and any headings to make the most of the space. Overall, in the dashboard, you will need to change the business question that has been posed. Here, we have changed it to `How well did sales perform, by different characteristics?`

17. On the dashboard, look for the drop-down list under **Choose Characteristic**. Try making different selections between color, product line, all, and country. You'll notice that the screen and the legend change in response to your actions.

You can see the final dashboard and the culmination of this chapter's work in the following screenshot:

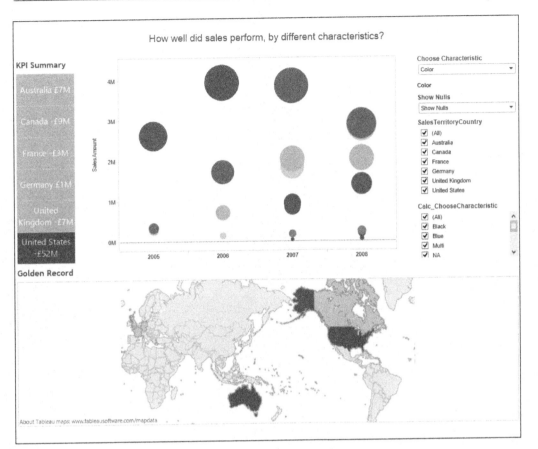

The dashboard is now complete, and you can have fun changing the parameters and switching dimensions. This will create interesting patterns in the data for your users.

How it works...

In this recipe, we implemented logical calculations that allow users to change the dimension that appears on the dashboard. We are now starting to make our dashboards look more interesting and more interactive.

Showing different dimensions helps the dashboard designer to make the most of the space while maximizing the choices available to the dashboard user. Setting up all of the moving parts is not as quick as other visualizations, but it is worth the effort to help users.

For this recipe, we will use the **KPI Dimension** worksheet and see the result in our dashboard.

There's more...

In this chapter, we have looked at many different ways to help users to engage with dashboards, such as choosing visualizations and making use of items to help with analysis, such as parameters, Big Data technologies, and conditional logic. These tools will allow us to create dashboards that are powerful and rich, and who knows, maybe even fun!

6
Making Dashboards Relevant

In this chapter, we will cover the following recipes:

- ▶ Adding an infographic to your Tableau dashboard
- ▶ String manipulation using dashboards
- ▶ Correcting data exports from Tableau to Excel
- ▶ Blending data
- ▶ Optimizing tips for efficient, fast visualization

Introduction

Performance dashboards are used by management to gauge performance and to identify how the business is progressing towards business goals. These can be hard to define, since they apply to a wide spectrum of objectives, such as evaluating a business strategy globally or looking specifically at one department or team.

Tableau is simple software to use. By now, you are probably running through lots of scenarios in which Tableau is useful to your business. Perhaps some of your colleagues are starting to eye your work so far, and are looking at ways in which Tableau could be applicable to their teams.

Although Tableau is easy to use, dashboards often fail in achieving their objectives because they are not aligned with the business goals. Perhaps the objectives themselves are poorly defined; in such cases, dashboards will simply reflect the poorly thought out objectives. It is possible that the dashboard will only show a mediocre strategy, and accordingly, the business will only be able to execute a mediocre strategy. However, this situation must be better than executing no strategy at all, and basing business decisions on a month-by-month reporting calendar. A dashboard is a picture that communicates the business vision clearly.

How can we be sure that a dashboard meets the expectations of the business audience? There are a number of important factors, which are as follows:

- Appropriate characterization of the target audience
- Who are the consumers of the dashboard, and what are their objectives and responsibilities
- How well do they respond to change

Often, the dynamics of an organization would be such that you cannot introduce a change too quickly. A dashboard can help you identify the key drivers that departments use when evaluating performance; then, you can start aligning them with the drivers of other departments so that end-user departments can start working together. Communication is often a key failure point in many organizations, and this alignment is a step in getting everyone headed in the right direction. The process of creating a dashboard can help in defining the clarity needed across the organization, since this process begins with communication.

It is essential to have a fitting definition of the metrics. What is going to be measured? If you are creating dashboards across the organization, then flexibility is going to be a key factor in order to facilitate the alignment. The metrics should be meaningful to the consumers, with a logical structure and repeatable results. The dashboard should help generate and translate the data into actions that are aimed towards the organizational goals.

Further, the metrics should be manageable. Who is going to manage the dashboard? Is there a data steward within the organization? Dashboards are no good if nobody looks at them. Within many organizations, a lot of work has gone into reports and dashboards that have then been ignored and gone into obscurity. Sometimes this happens because people do not like what the dashboards say! That said, placing unrealistic metrics on a dashboard is a certain route to dashboard failure, since it will result in a lack of support, ultimately rendering the dashboard irrelevant.

It can be hard to meet these success criteria for dashboards, as defining metrics that target strategic objectives such as return on investment or governance can often be a challenge. The most useful dashboards are those implemented with a project sponsor who is senior in the organization, and able to push the organization through a change. Is there a change champion within the organization? Are they onboard?

Dashboarding and the scorecard approach will become more prevalent with the emphasis on Big Data. Implementing Big Data approaches is only part of the Big Data story, and we will always need ways to learn from our data. This chapter will help us make our dashboards more meaningful to our organization using Tableau.

Adding an infographic to your Tableau dashboard

Sometimes people want an infographic rather than a data visualization. An infographic is a picture or a poster that illustrates a part of the story contained in the data so that the viewer understands it very quickly. Data visualization, on the other hand, allows viewers to make up their own minds about the data, which can often be a longer process.

In this recipe, we will look at adding an infographic or a picture to the Tableau dashboard and putting it together with data visualizations that tell a story of the comparison of certain results between the United Kingdom and Australia.

This recipe consists of a number of steps. Generally, we will use a background image and then configure the properties of the image using Excel. We will then go back to Tableau, and use the image and the Excel file to configure the appearance of the Tableau worksheet.

Getting ready

For the exercises in this recipe, make a copy of the Chapter 5 workbook and name it Chapter 6. We don't need to add in any more data for now.

Configure the dimensions of your image in an Excel workbook and save it separately to connect to it later. Record the length and width of the image as X and Y values.

How to do it...

First, choose your background image and use it as a base for your infographic. For the purpose of this recipe, we have provided you with a sample image that you can download from http://bit.ly/TableauImage. You can use your own background image as well. Then, perform the following steps:

1. Create a new Excel workbook and call it TableauImage.xlsx.

2. In the Excel workbook, create a headings row by typing the following three items into the following cells:

   ❑ Cell A1: Country

   ❑ Cell B1: X

   ❑ Cell C1: Y

3. Simply enter the word Country into cell A2.

4. Next, record the width of the image in pixels in cell B2, which is the X value. For our example, the width is 527. Your Excel workbook should look like the following screenshot:

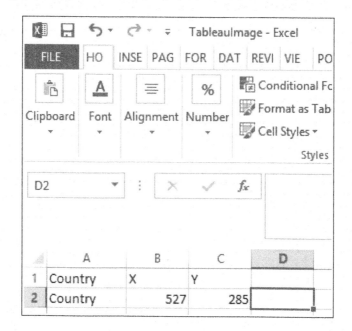

5. Now, record the height of the image in pixels in cell C2, which is the Y value. For our example, the height is 285.

6. Save your Excel workbook as TableauImage.xlsx and close it.

7. Go back to Tableau and create a new worksheet called KPI Poster.

8. Next, connect to the Excel workbook that you just created. To do this, go to **Data**, then click on **Connect to Data** and select the option **Microsoft Excel** on the left-hand side.

9. Navigate to the TableauImage.xlsx file and choose the option **Connect live**, and then select **Go To Worksheet**.

10. Next, connect to the image by setting it as a map. To do this, navigate to **Map | Background Images** and then select the Excel spreadsheet that contains the image dimensions, as shown in the following screenshot:

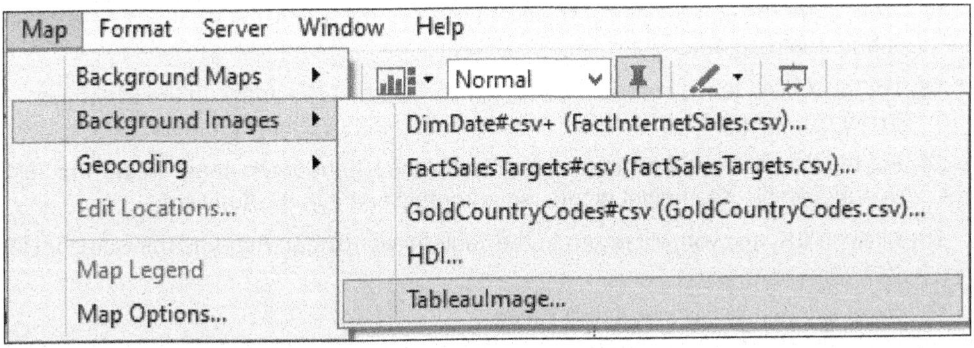

Map	Format	Server	Window	Help

> Background Maps ▶
>
> Background Images ▶   DimDate#csv+ (FactInternetSales.csv)...
>
> Geocoding ▶   FactSalesTargets#csv (FactSalesTargets.csv)...
>
> Edit Locations...   GoldCountryCodes#csv (GoldCountryCodes.csv)...
>
>   HDI...
>
> Map Legend   TableauImage...
>
> Map Options...

Normal ▾

11. Choose **Add Image** and then browse for the location of the image file in your `Chapter 6` folder. Now, select the file, and you will see it appear in the **Add Background Image** box, as shown in the following screenshot:

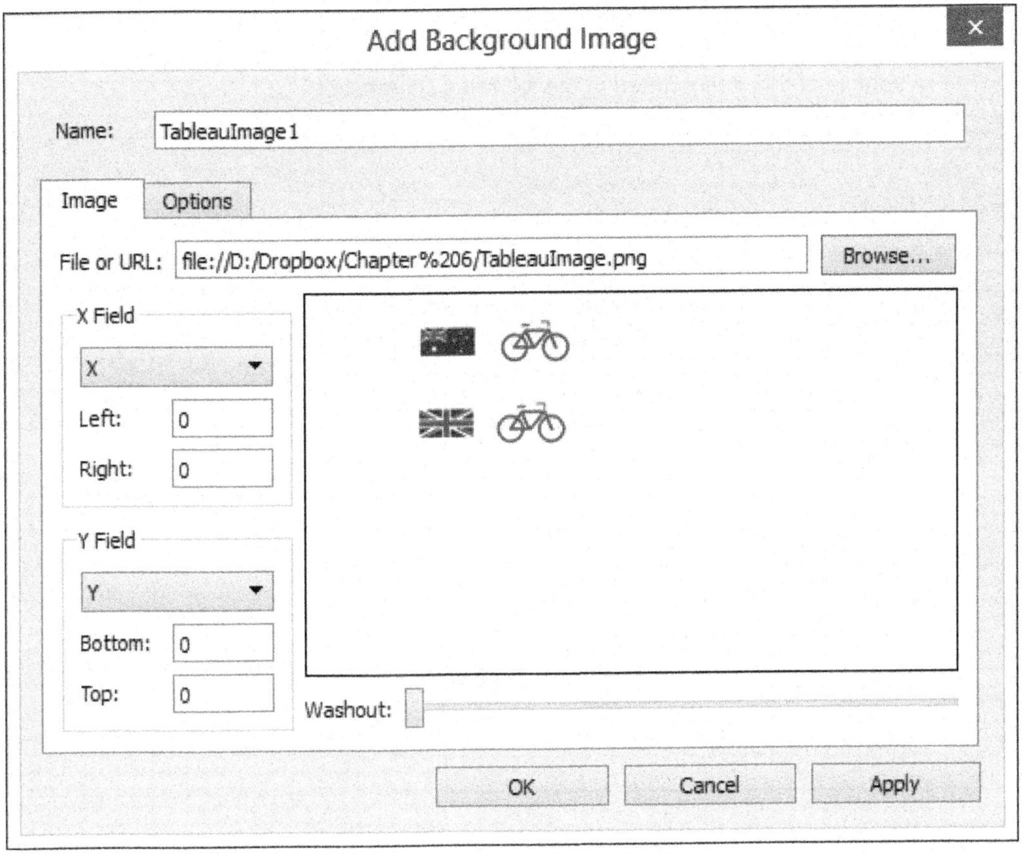

Add Background Image

Name: TableauImage 1

Image | Options

File or URL: file://D:/Dropbox/Chapter%206/TableauImage.png   Browse...

X Field

X ▾

Left: 0

Right: 0

Y Field

Y ▾

Bottom: 0

Top: 0

Washout:

OK   Cancel   Apply

12. Next, enter the dimensions of the file in the **X** and **Y** axis fields. For the X field, choose **X** from the drop-down list.

13. For the **X** field, leave **Left** as 0 and enter the width of the image in the **Right** field. In our example, the width is 527, so enter this value in the **Right** field.

14. For the **Y** field, leave **Bottom** as 0 and enter the height of the image in the **Top** field. In our example, the height is 285, so enter this figure in the **Top** field.

15. Click on **OK**, and you will return to the Tableau worksheet. Rename the worksheet to KPI Poster.

16. Now, we need to plot our **X** and **Y** fields.

    Drag **X** onto the **Columns** shelf, right-click on it, and select **Dimension**. Drag **Y** onto the **Rows** shelf. Your image will now appear.

17. Right-click on the **Y** green pill on the **Rows** shelf and select **Dimension** from the pop-up menu.

18. You may notice that you have the axis headers appearing on the *x* and *y* axes. To remove each axis, right-click on the axis and uncheck the **Show Header** option. A sample of this is illustrated in the following screenshot:

19. Now, we can select the point at which we would like the data to appear. To do this, pick a spot to the right of the Australian flag, right-click on it, and select **Annotate** and then **Point**. When you click on **OK**, you will see the *x* and *y* coordinates for any point.

20. Similarly, select a point for data related to the United Kingdom flag. To do this, pick a spot to the right of the United Kingdom flag, right-click on it, and select **Annotate** and then **Point**. When you click on **OK**, you will see the *x* and *y* coordinates for any point.

21. When you have the points that you want, open the Excel workbook called `TableauImage.xlsx`.

22. Enter `Australia` in cell A2.

23. Enter `United Kingdom` in cell A3.

24. Your spreadsheet should look like the following screenshot:

	A	B	C
1		X	Y
2	Australia	307.1	223.4
3	United Kingdom	309.1	57.6
4			

25. Save and close the Excel file.

26. Go back to your Excel worksheet.

27. To refresh the data source, go to the **Data** field at the top left-hand side and look for the `TableauImage` data source. Right-click on it and select **Refresh**.

28. Next, set up a relationship between the Excel worksheet and the Tableau **FactInternetSales+** table. To do this, go to **Data** and select **Edit Relationships**.

29. Now, place the **Country** field on the **Level Detail** shelf of the **Marks** shelf.

30. Drag **KPI Difference between Actual and Target** onto the **Color** button on the **Marks** shelf.

31. Now, **KPI Difference between Actual and Target** is driving the color of the KPI. So, for the KPI data above, the color should be blue, and for the KPI data below, the color should be gray.

32. You can choose to select the **Square** option to change the mark types. To do this, go to the **Marks** shelf, and then to the drop-down list right under the **Marks** label. Look for **Square** and select it, as shown in the following screenshot:

33. Let's now turn this into a dashboard. Don't worry if the images look strange; the dashboard will be fixed when we put it together.

34. Create a new dashboard, and call it `Infographic Dashboard`.

35. On the dashboard, drag our new image to the top left-hand side.

36. Drag the **Golden Record** sheet to the top right-hand side.

37. Drag **KPI Shapes** to the bottom of the dashboard.

38. For the **Golden Record** chart, simply right-click on France, Canada, Germany, and the United States and choose the **Exclude** option. Only the data for Australia and the United Kingdom should be displayed on the dashboard.

39. To filter the **Golden Record** sheet, right-click on the arrow located at the top of the chart and select **Go To Sheet**. From there, drag the **countryname** attribute onto the **Filter** shelf and choose the **Filter** option. In the list of countries, select **Australia** and **United Kingdom** and then click on **OK**.

40. Remove the title from each component of the dashboard. To do this, click on each of the components and look for the arrow at the top right-hand side. In the pop-up menu, click on **Title** to uncheck it.

41. Finally, let's add a title so that the intent of the dashboard is clear. Drag the **Text** button from the left-hand side of the dashboard over to the top of the dashboard. For the text itself, enter `How does Australia compare to the United Kingdom overall?` into the textbox, changing the font to royal blue.

Now, you've completed the steps. The dashboard will appear as follows:

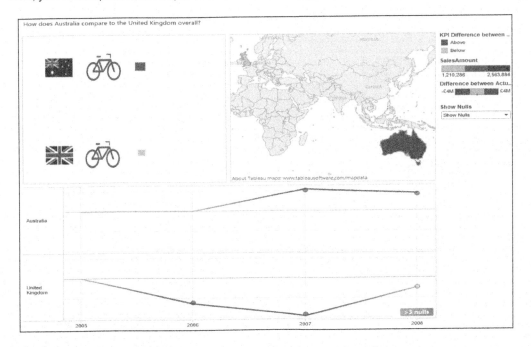

How it works...

In this section, we used a custom image and overlaid it with data points in order to produce an infographic that displays up-to-date data. This infographic can be used as part of a dashboard to complement and highlight the main message of the data.

To do this, we need a base image and an Excel workbook as a small data store. We use the Excel workbook to hold the image size of the picture, and we add to it throughout. When Tableau starts up, it loads the data, such as the file properties, from this Excel workbook so that the image is loaded properly. It provides some information that helps us locate the data points at particular points on the image.

There's more...

▸ If you want to know more about infographics versus data visualization, visit http://www.jenstirrup.com/2010/12/data-visualisation-and-infographics.html

String manipulation in dashboards

Data can be difficult to interpret without any context, and additional commentary can help save the business user from manually having to research additional information. Annotations are useful for providing additional context to a data visualization.

In this recipe, we will look at using calculated fields to amplify the message of the data and to automatically add new information to the annotations.

Getting ready

For the exercises in this recipe, we will build on the existing Chapter 6 dashboard. We don't need to add in any more data for now.

How to do it...

1. Let's start by adding an annotation to the dashboard. Right-click on the square that we created near the Australian flag in the last recipe. In the pop-up menu, select **Annotation** and then **Mark**. You can see an example of this activity in the following screenshot:

F1:	**Australia**
Sales Amount Sum:	**2,563,884**
KPI Difference between Actual and Target:	**Above**
X:	**307.100**
Y:	**223.4**

✓ Keep Only   ✗ Exclude   🔗   ⦿ ▾   ▦

	Select All	
▦	View Data...	
	Copy	▶
	Format...	
	Mark Label	▶
	Annotate	▶
	Trend Lines	▶
	Forecast	▶
	Drop Lines	▶
⊕	Hide Zoom Controls	
✓	Keep Only	
✗	Exclude	
🔗	Group	
⦿	Create Set...	

Annotate submenu:
- Mark...
- Point...
- Area...

2. Now, you will get a pop-up window that contains a default specification of the annotation. However, this must be amended so that it is relevant to the data points. The pop-up window looks like the following screenshot, by default:

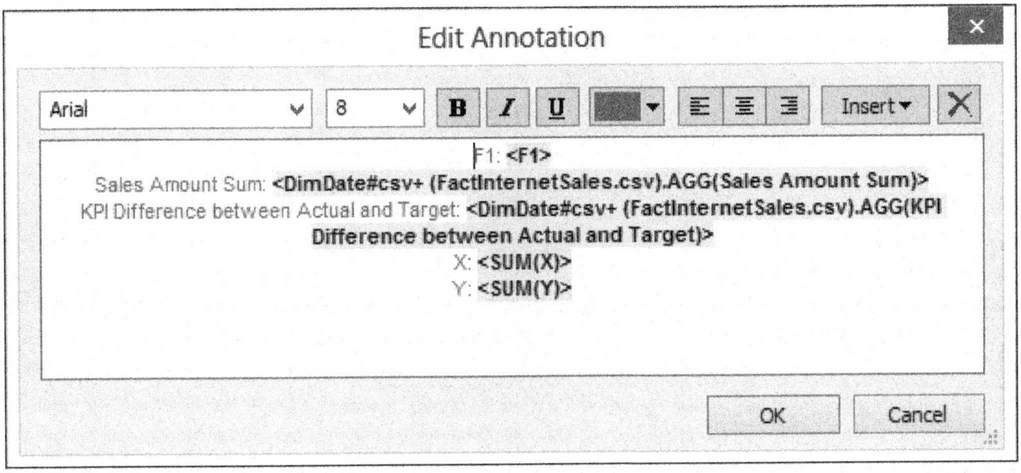

Edit Annotation

| Arial | 8 | **B** | *I* | <u>U</u> | | | | | Insert ▾ |

F1: **<F1>**
Sales Amount Sum: **<DimDate#csv+ (FactInternetSales.csv).AGG(Sales Amount Sum)>**
KPI Difference between Actual and Target: **<DimDate#csv+ (FactInternetSales.csv).AGG(KPI Difference between Actual and Target)>**
X: **<SUM(X)>**
Y: **<SUM(Y)>**

OK   Cancel

3. Next, let's make the annotation more relevant to the visualization. Remove the text in the annotation and enter `<F1> was <DimDate#csv+ (FactInternetSales.csv).AGG(KPI Difference between Actual and Target)> Target`. The pop-up window will now look like the following screenshot:

Edit Annotation

| Arial | 8 | **B** | *I* | <u>U</u> | | | | | Insert ▾ |

<F1> was **<DimDate#csv+ (FactInternetSales.csv).AGG(KPI Difference between Actual and Target)>** Target

OK   Cancel   Apply

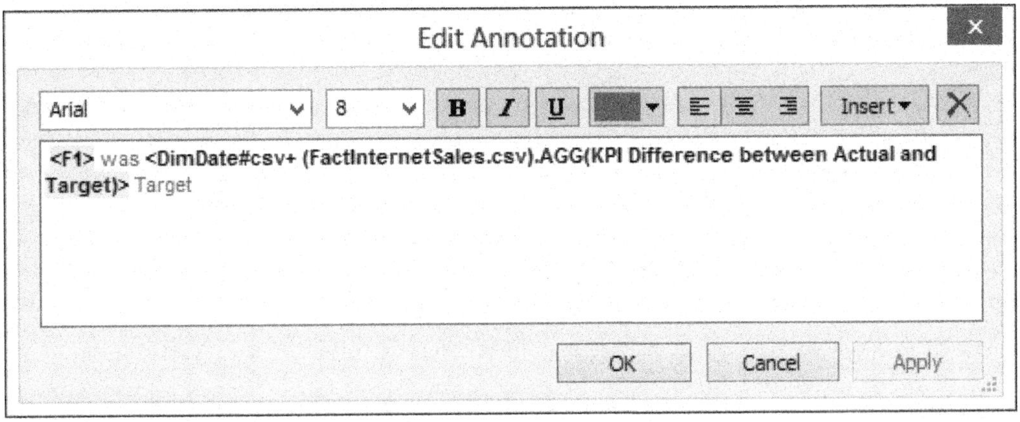

It is easy to add the content of the calculated fields using the **Insert** button on the right-hand side. When you click on the **Insert** button, it gives you a list of all the fields. You can see an example of this in the following screenshot:

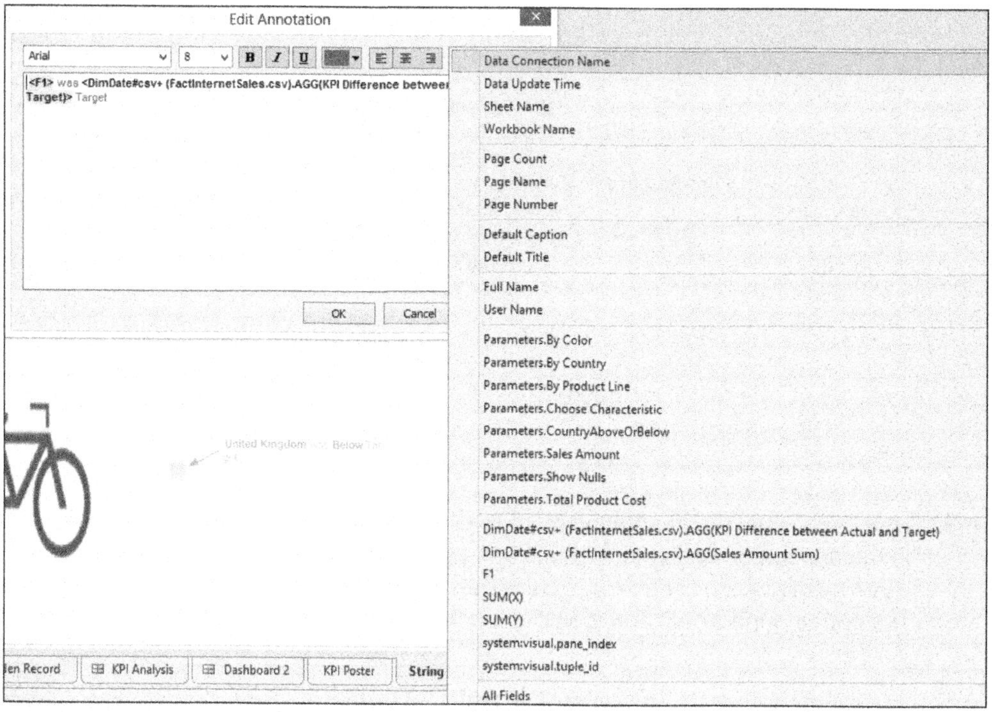

4. Go back to the **Edit Annotation** window by clicking on it and then click on **OK** in order to create the annotation.

5. The annotation uses a mix of calculated fields and field names to construct an appropriate annotation. The resulting annotation looks like the following screenshot:

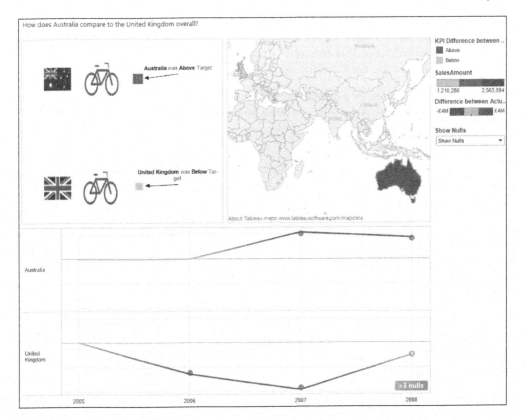

How it works...

Strings can be set up using calculated fields, parameters, field names, or a combination of these. It is a useful feature to make your visualization punchy.

Correcting data exports from Tableau to Excel

IT agility can be increased by improving the quality of the data, for instance, by creating enterprise data standards. However, how can you increase data quality if you can't see the problems in the data? Data quality isn't just about wrong numbers or missing data. It can also refer to surplus data stores that your IT team ends up looking after unnecessarily.

This is where Tableau steps in. By making data accessible and visible, the issues are made visible for all to see. It's at this point that the business needs to decide whether to tackle the problems head on or go along as they did before.

Sometimes, people don't like numbers. Numbers can deliver hard news, for example, something like job losses might be on the cards. People need to be completely sure of the data so they have confidence that they are taking the right decisions. They need to prove to themselves and their managers that the numbers are correct.

The information-seeking mantra defines drilling to detail as a key concept of people interacting with their information. This is particularly important if the numbers show a message that business consumers do not like.

When looking at the details, it is important to work out what details we want to see. Sometimes, people will want to see the detailed data behind the whole workbook. On other occasions, they will simply want to see the data that lies behind the particular dashboard that is currently on view. In this recipe, we will look at both these scenarios.

In Tableau, it isn't possible to export all of the data at the dashboard level. Instead, you need to export data at the worksheet level only. Therefore, if you go to a dashboard and try to export data, you will see that the option is grayed out. This makes sense because the dashboard-level data may appear confusing if it is placed in a crosstab format, and it may be hard to relate the columns to their appearance on the dashboard.

You can select the **Export the data to CSV** option. However, this will only export the data for the specific data points that you see. If you want to export all of the underlying data, then you need to select the **Underlying** tab, rather than the **Summary** tab. It is easy to miss this step, and we will call it out in this recipe.

Getting ready

For the exercises in this recipe, continue to work on the `Chapter 6` workbook.

How to do it...

1. To export all of the data, go to the `KPI Shapes` worksheet.

2. Go to the **Worksheet** menu item, and then choose the option **Duplicate as Crosstab**. This will then generate a new worksheet that has a neat crosstab that displays all of the data.

3. Rename your new worksheet as `KPI Shapes Crosstab`.

4. Now, let's export just a part of the data rather than the whole set. If you simply want to export the data of one particular data point, right-click on that data point.

5. Click on the **Above** label for Australia and you will see a pop-up appear.

6. Click on the **View Data...** button at the bottom-right corner of the pop-up window that appears, as shown in the following screenshot:

d Analysis Map Format Server Window Help

Pages		III Columns	⊞ YEA	Above			Names

Filter Country from Summary to Year ▸
Filter Country from Year to Quarter ▸

4 items selected · SUM of Measure Values: 7,821,337   of FullDateAlternateKey

✓ Keep Only   ✗ Exclude

Filters					2006	2007	2008
SalesTerritoryCountry							
Measure Names	Australia	Above	Difference (Show or Hide)			2,166,784	1,743,884
			Difference between Actual and Target	View Data...		£2M	£2M
		Not Known	Difference (Show or Hide)				
			Difference between Actual and Target				
Marks	United	Below	Difference (Show or Hide)		-2,568,413	-3,843,751	-1,001,714
	Kingdom		Difference between Actual and Target		-£3M	-£4M	-£1M
Abc Automatic ⌄		Not Known	Difference (Show or Hide)				
			Difference between Actual and Target				

Marks

Abc Automatic ⌄

Color   Size   Abc 123 Text

Detail   Tooltip

Abc 123 Measure Values

Measure Values

AGG(Difference (Show o..

AGG(Difference betwee..

7. Now, you will see the following **View Data** dialog box, which opens on the **Summary** tab, as shown in the following screenshot:

View Data: KPI Shapes Crosstab

✓ Show Aliases   Copy   Export All

Measure Names	SalesTerritoryCountry	Year of FullDateAlternateKey	Measure Values	KPI Difference between Actual and Target
Difference between Actual and Target	Australia	2008	1,743,884.29	Above
Difference (Show or Hide)	Australia	2008	1,743,884.29	Above
Difference between Actual and Target	Australia	2007	2,166,784.37	Above
Difference (Show or Hide)	Australia	2007	2,166,784.37	Above

Summary Underlying   4 rows

8. Click on the **Underlying** tab to reveal all the data. You can see this at the bottom-left corner of the **View Data** dialog box.

How it works...

In this recipe, we took a dashboard and conducted various exports on the data. We exported all of the data and then looked at taking filtered exports based on the data displayed on the screen. We also looked at obtaining the underlying data, which supports the summary that we see on the screen.

When you create a new crosstab worksheet, you could use this crosstab as the basis for further visualization, or to export data to other packages, such as Excel.

It is also helpful for checking the data. People get comfort from knowing about the data from the cradle to the grave, particularly if the data is contentious.

Blending data

If a workbook uses data from more than one data source, you can blend data. Blending data is different from joining tables. It enables you to combine data from different sources. Tableau makes it very simple to perform this activity.

If you have more than one source of data, you can blend it together in Tableau. Alternatively, you might want to blend the data in a data warehouse or a data store in a single place, outside of the Tableau software.

Sometimes, when we put data together, we get an error message saying **Fields cannot be used from the data source...**. This means Tableau could not associate the new imported file with the existing file because it could not match any of the column names. This recipe will explain how to get around this issue.

Getting ready

For the exercises in this recipe, let's continue working on the Chapter 6 workbook.

How to do it...

1. Duplicate the Golden Record worksheet and rename the copy to Blending Example.
2. Next, import the HDI.xlsx file by going to the **Data** menu item and then choosing the **Connect to Data...** option.
3. In the pane that appears, click on **Text File**, browse to find the HDI.csv, and click on **Open**.
4. Click on the filename and rename the data source connection to HDI.
5. Rename the columns. Rename F1 to **Level of Human Development**.
6. Rename the F2 column to **countryname**.
7. Rename the F3 column to Year.
8. Rename the F4 column to **HDI Rank**. Then, click on **Go To Worksheet**.
9. When all the data has been imported, you will see the new HDI connection on the **Data** shelf. Here is an example of this:

10. Drag the **HDI Rank** field over to the **Color** button on the **Marks** shelf.

11. You will get the following error message, and when you do, click on **OK**:

12. To sort the error message, click on the **HDI** data source in the **Data** shelf that you set up earlier in this recipe.

13. Right-click on the **Country** field and click on **Rename**.

14. Rename **Country** to countryname and click on **OK**. Note that the case must match exactly as is or Tableau will not be able to match the fields.

15. On the right-hand side of countryname, you should now see a data blend mark appear, as shown in the following screenshot:

Data	⇕
🗒️ DimDate#csv+ (FactInternetSa...	
🗎 FactSalesTargets#csv (FactSale...	
🗒️ GoldCountryCodes#csv (Gold...	
🗄️ HDI	
🗌 TableauImage	
Dimensions	▦ 🔍 ▾
⊕ countryname	⊖⊖
# HDI rank	
Abc Level of Human Development	
Abc *Measure Names*	

16. The **HDI Rank** field will appear as a measure, which means that Tableau will try to aggregate it. Drag the field up to the **Dimensions** pane so that it is used as a way of describing the data, rather than as an ordinal piece of data that can be added.

17. Now, repeat the step of dragging the **HDI Rank** field over to the **Color** button on the **Marks** shelf.

How it works...

In this recipe, we looked at blending two disparate data sources together, and we saw how easy it is to relate data sources together based on the column name.

Blending data is a key part of creating guided analytics for the user. This feature is useful in solving end-to-end problems, since the user can get up to speed quickly, without a detailed understanding of the underlying data sources. Further, it allows users to quickly connect to the data without having to associate the data together. With this, you can assume that the data is clean, of course. It also helps that non-matching column names can be associated with one another simply by renaming one of the columns so that the columns match and are recognized as the relationship between the tables.

One word of warning, however: it is easy to become blithe about setting up relationships in the data based on the column name if you are unfamiliar with the sources. It can be possible to have identical column names in different data sources, but the data can mean totally different things and refer to different business processes. It is easy to set up the relationships, but it's also imperative to check the relationships, too. What's technically correct may not be correct from the business perspective.

Optimizing tips for efficient, fast visualization

Tableau is a great tech toy, and people enjoy playing with data. By having access to a lot of data that you've never seen before, it is easy to get excited and engrossed in loading the data and pushing it around. If you are seeing lots of new data for the first time, how can you make sure that Tableau is interacting as quickly as possible with the data? People want to interact with data, and Tableau helps people to explore their data quickly. Nothing, however, puts business users off a new system more than poor response times. People want their data, and they want it now.

Evaluating a system often involves questions such as response time, data-load time, and utilization. However, it can often be difficult to work out the quickest way to access data. The best way is to test, but this recipe will offer some different ways in which you can get a head start in optimizing data.

This recipe isn't intended to suggest that Tableau is slow to access data; in fact, it is extremely fast. In today's world of ever-increasing data sources, it can be hard to work out the best way to access data quickly. It is important to make the right decision at the very start, and this topic is aimed at setting you on the right path.

If you have multiple data connections that are large and take a long time to query, using a join can increase query time dramatically. In this case, it is possible to consider joining the data earlier on in the process, before Tableau sees it.

Tableau can help you work out the relationships within the data. For example, by visualizing the data, it can help you see whether you need to bring data into a single platform or whether the data can live in its existing sources.

This recipe helps you to see a process for making your data as fast as possible. We prepare the data at the source. We import the aggregated data into the Tableau data source for speed.

In this example, we preaggregate the data by turning it into average data. This means that the calculation is already done when it goes into Tableau, and Tableau does not have to spend time making the calculation; it just lifts the data as it sees it.

Importing the whole data into Tableau's own engine is often a useful strategy since Tableau does not have to connect to large data sources, query them, and then bring the data back across the network.

Ultimately, the best way is to provide the best performance for your environment and your data. The method suggested here is one way to give you a head start.

Getting ready

Let's continue with the Tableau workbook `Chapter 6` as is.

As in the previous chapter, we will use the Hortonworks Sandbox to connect to some data and use it as a data source. Alternatively, if you don't have access to this source, you will find details of a location where you can download the sample files so that your work is not impeded.

You can download the data source file and the resulting CSV files from `http://sdrv.ms/1aHDtib`.

How to do it...

1. Upload the source file to the Hortonworks Sandbox using the file explorer to a directory called `/hue/WorldBank`, as shown in the following screenshot:

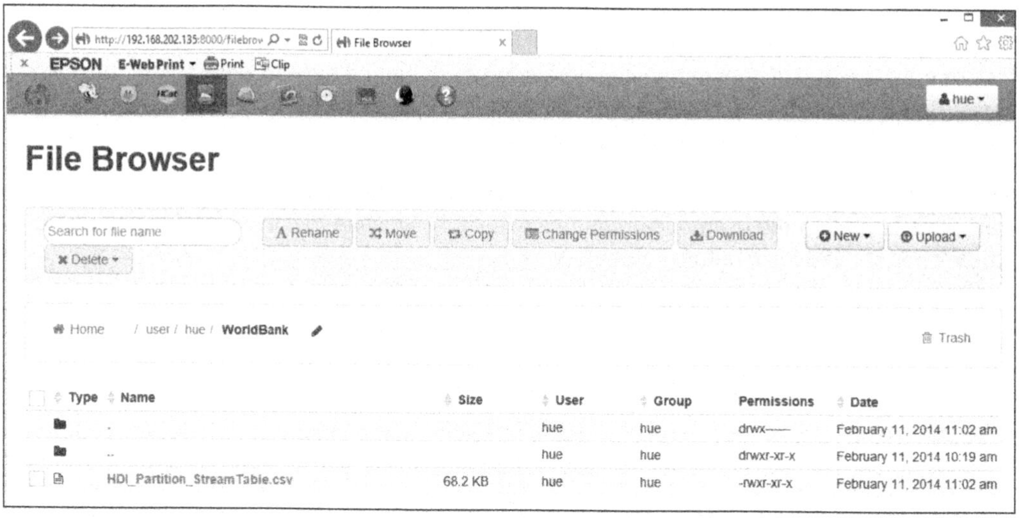

2. Create a table in Hive using the following command:

```
CREATE EXTERNAL TABLE IF NOT EXISTS HDI (
HDILevel       STRING,
CountryName     STRING,
Year           STRING,
HDIValue     FLOAT)
ROW FORMAT DELIMITED FIELDS TERMINATED BY ','
LOCATION '/user/hue/WorldBank';
```

The following screenshot shows how the query will look on the Hue web interface:

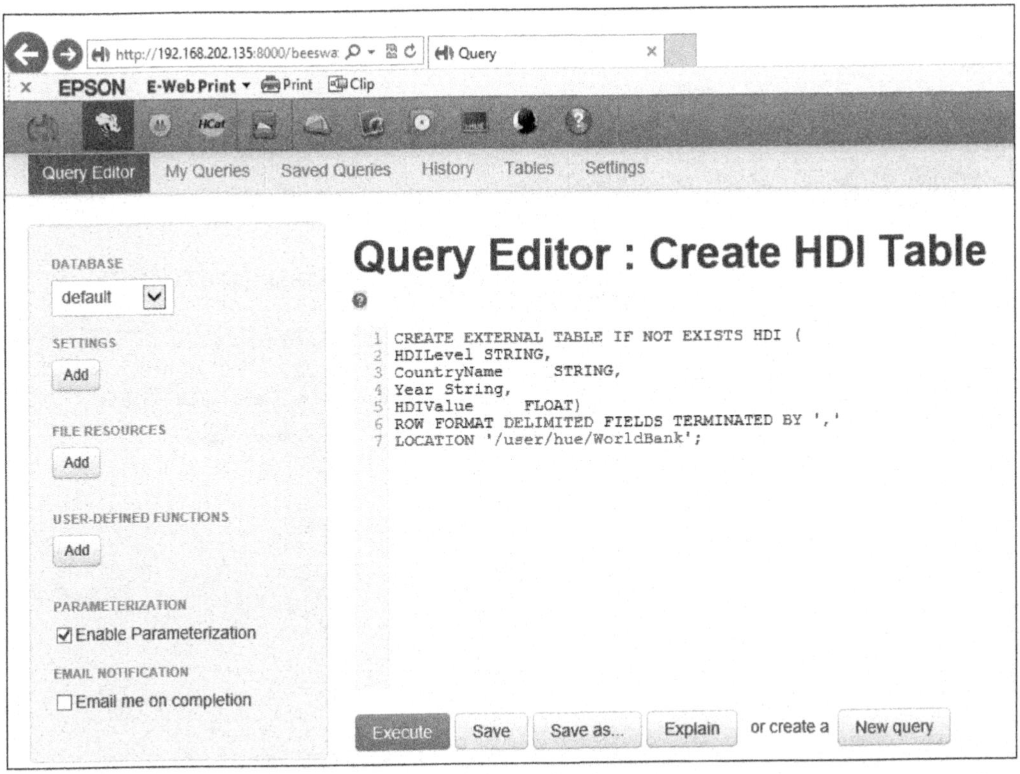

3. Run the following query in the Hortonworks Hive query table. It is designed to obtain the average HDI value, which is based on the HDI level and the country:

```
SELECT
a.hdilevel, a.countryname, avg(a.hdivalue)
from hdi a
GROUP BY a.hdilevel, a.countryname
```

The Hue screen will appear as follows:

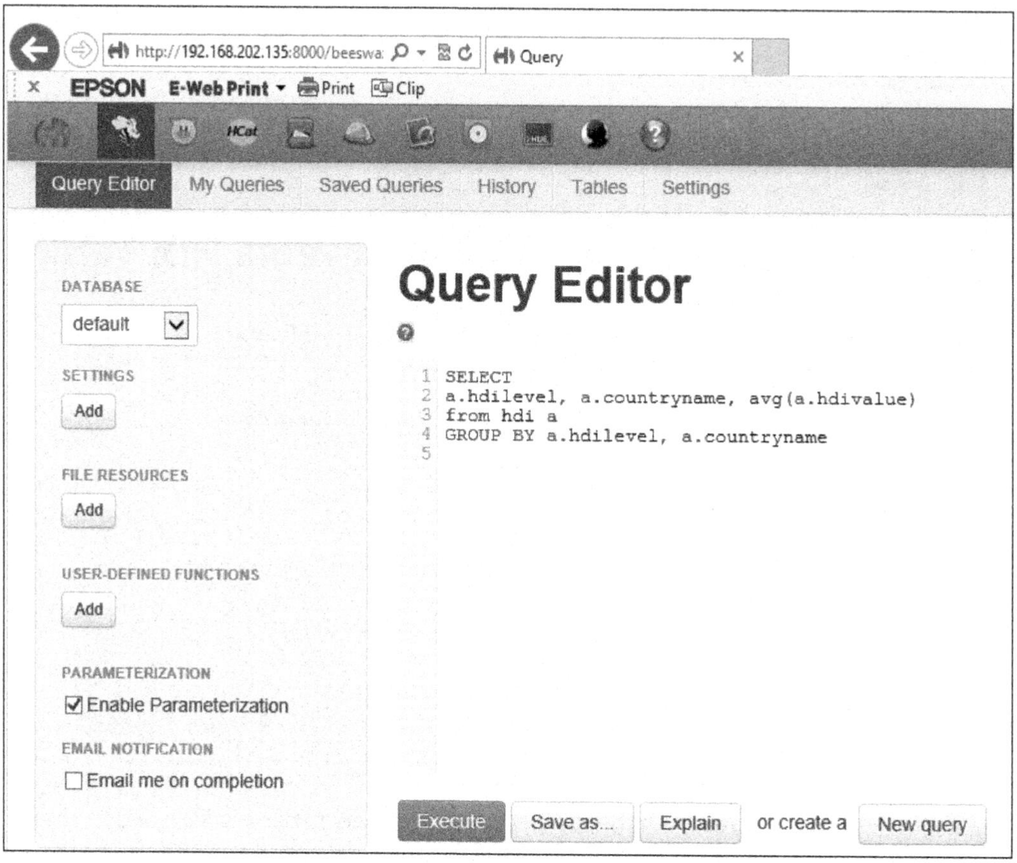

4. Once you have created the table, go to the **Results** view of the query to make sure that the data has been loaded, as shown in the following screenshot:

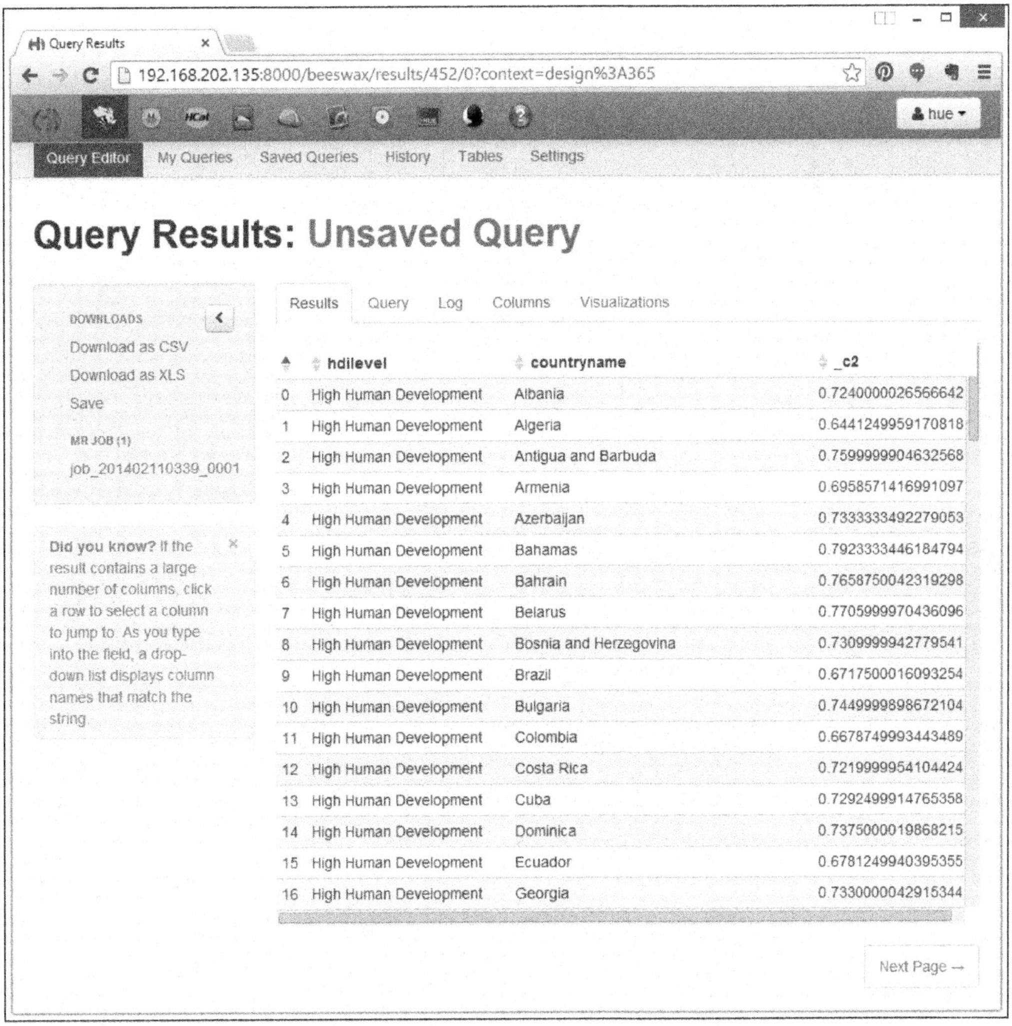

5. Next, you can save the file by navigating to **Download as CSV** on the left-hand side, as shown in the following screenshot:

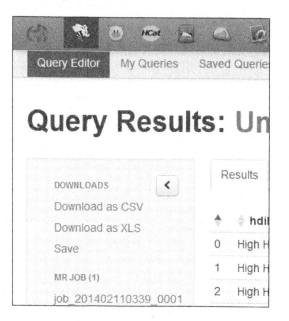

6. In case it isn't clear, there are a number of options, and you need the top one, which you can see in the following screenshot:

7. Alternatively, download the file from `http://sdrv.ms/1aHDtib`.

8. The CSV file will be downloaded with the name `query_results.csv`. Rename it to `HDI Average`.

9. Connect to the text file in Tableau. Open Tableau, create a new worksheet using the **Connect to Data** option, and navigate to the location where you have stored `query_results.csv`.

10. Next, rename the connection to `HDI Average`.

11. Click on **Return to Worksheet** and return to the Tableau worksheet.

12. Start a new Tableau worksheet by pressing *CTRL + M*.

13. Let's import all of the data into Tableau's internal data store. So, in the **Data** pane, right-click on the new connection, and select the **Extract data** option.

14. Tableau will then ask you where to store the data abstract as a TDE file; select a file location on your laptop that suits you best.

15. When the data is imported, you will see the fields on the left-hand side. The value field may be transported with a default column name. For example, it may read **c2**, which is simply Tableau's placeholder name for the column during the transport. It is shorthand for column 2. In this case, right-click on it and select the **Rename** option. Rename it to `HDI Average Value`, as shown here:

16. `HDI Average Value` will appear as a string, so we will need to make it a measure. To do this, drag it from the **Dimensions** shelf down to the **Measures** shelf.

17. The field will still be in the string format, so we will need to change it to a decimal format. To do this, right-click on the field and select **Change Data Type**, and change the type to a number, as shown in the following screenshot:

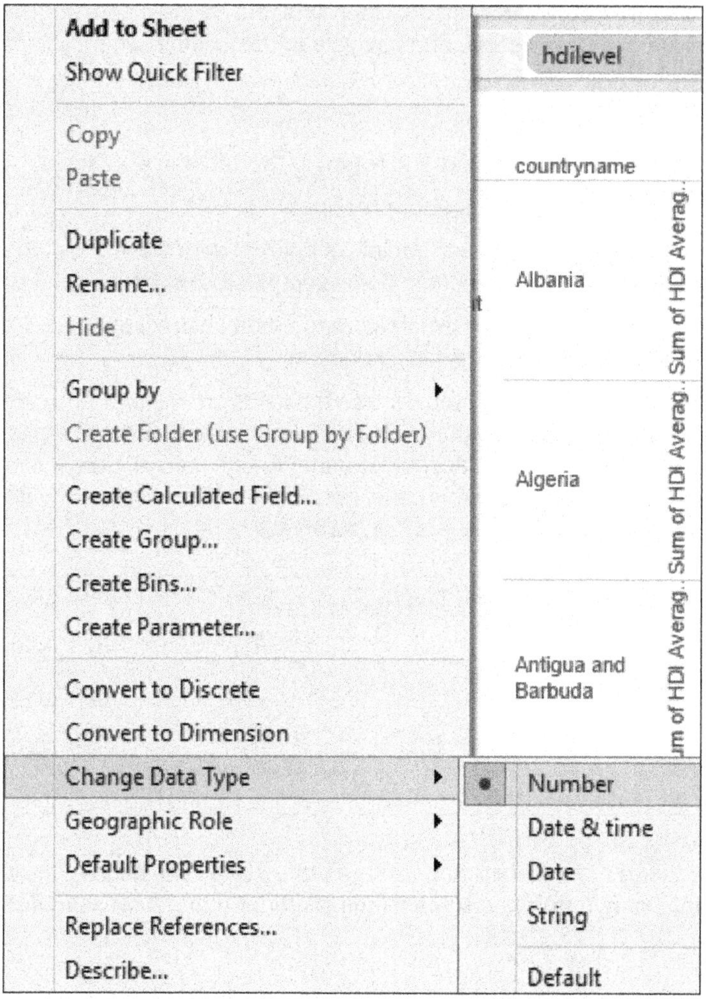

Add to Sheet		hdilevel
Show Quick Filter		
Copy		countryname
Paste		
Duplicate		
Rename...		Albania
Hide		
Group by ▶		
Create Folder (use Group by Folder)		
Create Calculated Field...		Algeria
Create Group...		
Create Bins...		
Create Parameter...		
Convert to Discrete		Antigua and Barbuda
Convert to Dimension		
Change Data Type ▶	●	Number
Geographic Role ▶		Date & time
Default Properties ▶		Date
Replace References...		String
Describe...		Default

18. Now, when you drag **HDI Average Value** over to the **Rows** column, you will notice that it is a **Count (Distinct)** measure rather than an average measure. Tableau does this because the measure was originally a dimension that could be counted rather than summed. To change the metric to **AVG**, right-click on the metric in the **Rows** shelf and then select **AVG**. Here is an example of this setting:

CNTD(HDI Average Value)

	Filter...
	Show Quick Filter
	Format...
✓	Show Header
✓	Include in Tooltip
	Dimension
	Attribute
●	Measure (Count (Distinct)) ▶
	Discrete
●	Continuous
Δ	Add Table Calculation...
	Quick Table Calculation ▶
	Remove

	Sum
	Average
	Median
	Count
●	Count (Distinct)
	Minimum
	Maximum
	Percentile ▶
	Std. Dev
	Std. Dev (Pop.)
	Variance
	Variance (Pop.)

19. Drag **countryname** onto the **Rows** shelf so it is on the left-hand side of **HDI Rank**.

20. Select a symbol map from the **Show Me** panel. You should have **Longitude** in the **Columns** shelf and **Latitude** in the **Rows** shelf.

21. Drag the **hdilevel** column onto the **Color** button. This will use **Color** to categorize the countries in terms of their development.

Your dashboard should now look like the following screenshot:

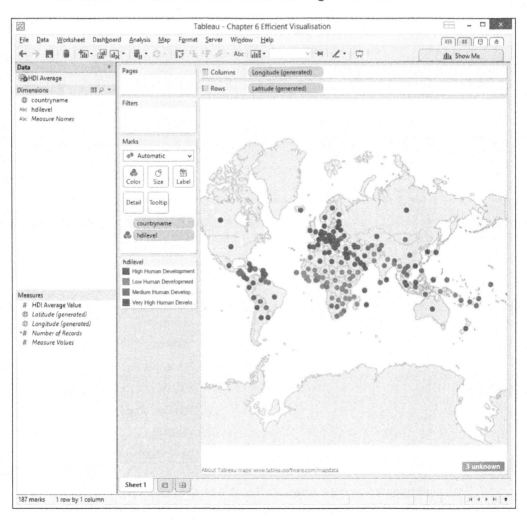

22. The data is now visualized very simply using a mix of data that was aggregated at the source, and then importing the data into Tableau's memory engine.

How it works...

Tableau can connect to live data or data that is held in memory, or both. The Tableau data engine uses different levels of memory at different times, so people can explore their data more quickly. It also means that the business users are not touching the underlying data source, which means that pressure can also be relieved from the system.

A nice thing about the Tableau data engine is that we can combine data that has been held in different formats, such as SQL Server, Excel, or Teradata, and combine it together into one source. Regardless of the source of the software solution, users can connect to the data, consolidate it, and then analyze and visualize the data.

It isn't always easy to work out when to use in memory and when to use the source. Live connections are better if you have fast-moving data and a fast database since the data is changing all the time and you need a fast connection.

In memory is better where the underlying data source is slow or has a lot of user and operational pressure on it. Also, by taking the data into Tableau, you can access it offline, for example, if you are working on a train or somewhere where you don't have good Internet access to connect to your company's data sources.

To summarize, it is good that Tableau gives us several options; we have looked at one method of connecting to data here, which combines the features of the source system as well as the fast features of Tableau.

7

Visual Best Practices

In this chapter, we will cover the following recipes:

- Coloring your numbers
- Dueling with dual axes
- Where is the three-dimensional data?
- Eating humble pie – Pie charts or not?
- Sizing to make a data story

Introduction

Why is data visualization so important, and how can we do it well? Data visualization is often the initial pain point in a project. People don't have enough reports and data visualizations, and they simply want more of them. In order to build a business strategy, leaders and decision makers need to understand what they want to achieve, and what the existing terrain of the organization is.

Businesses require that operational reporting solutions deliver results that can be predicted and are operationally efficient and robust while delivering corporate accountability and transparency. This makes operational reporting more important. If the stakeholder needs are not fulfilled, then they will simply resort to more homegrown solutions rather than insightful long-term decision-making tools.

Business intelligence can enhance and extend an enterprise by supporting its decision-making ability. It can have a direct impact on the overall performance of the organization by promoting a cycle of continuous innovation and enable better decision making. This is more important in today's fast-paced and demanding environment, particularly given the amount of data that we produce every day. By understanding the data better using visual best practices, we are giving ourselves the opportunity to make better decisions. This is particularly important in today's Big Data world.

This chapter will help you to see some of the theories and best practices that underpin visual design and display in a dashboard. Why is this important? You will want to share your dashboards with team members or perhaps with senior management in your organization. Even though each visualization is different, there are common themes that will help you create your dashboards so that you are more likely to get your message across to the right people in the right way.

John Stuart Mill, the English philosopher, once held the utilitarian principle that the right course of action is the one that maximizes utility. This usually translates as the one that maximizes benefit or the one that makes most people happy. In data visualization, ultimately, the goal is to build a visualization that suits your audience rather than building something that is best for you, the dashboard creator.

This is only a brief overview, and it's recommended that you follow up with the references provided in each section.

Coloring your numbers

In this recipe, we will look at the use of color to convey a message. Since we are looking at dashboarding, we need to know how to use color effectively to make the most of a small space. Here, we will use a box-and-whisker plot to convey a lot of information about the data in a small space, along with additional information on the figures themselves using color.

Getting ready

For the exercises in this recipe, let's start with a fresh Tableau workbook. There are no other requirements for this recipe.

How to do it...

1. In Tableau, navigate to **File | New** and rename the sheet to **Box Whiskers**.
2. Select the **Connect to Data** link at the top-left corner of the screen.
3. Click on **Text File** on the left-hand side. Navigate to the `DimProductCategory.csv` file, which is located in the folder where you downloaded the code samples, and click on the **Open** button to import it into the Tableau workbook.
4. Drag the `DimSubProductCategory.csv` file from the **Files** section on the left-hand side to the white canvas.
5. Drag the `DimProduct.csv` file from the **Files** section on the left-hand side to the white canvas.

6. Drag the `FactInternetSales.csv` file from the Files section on the left-hand side to the white canvas.

7. In the join clause, select **FullDateAlternateKey** for the `DimDate` table and **Order Date Key** for the `FactInternetSales` table.

8. Hide the columns in DimDate, keeping only the **Max year**, **FullDateAlternateKey**, **FiscalYear**, **FiscalSemester**, and **FiscalQuarter** fields.

9. Now, go back to the Tableau worksheet by navigating to **Go to Worksheet**. You should now see the Tableau worksheet with your data source on the left-hand side. Right-click on the data source and **Rename** it to `Chapter Seven`.

10. Drag **SUM(SalesAmount)** onto the **Columns** shelf.

11. Drag **EnglishProductCategory** onto the **Rows** shelf.

12. Select the **box-and-whisker** plot from the **Show Me** panel.

13. You'll see that the selected dimensions and measures change. Click on the **Swap** button, which you'll find under the **Map** menu item. The screen will look as shown in the following screenshot:

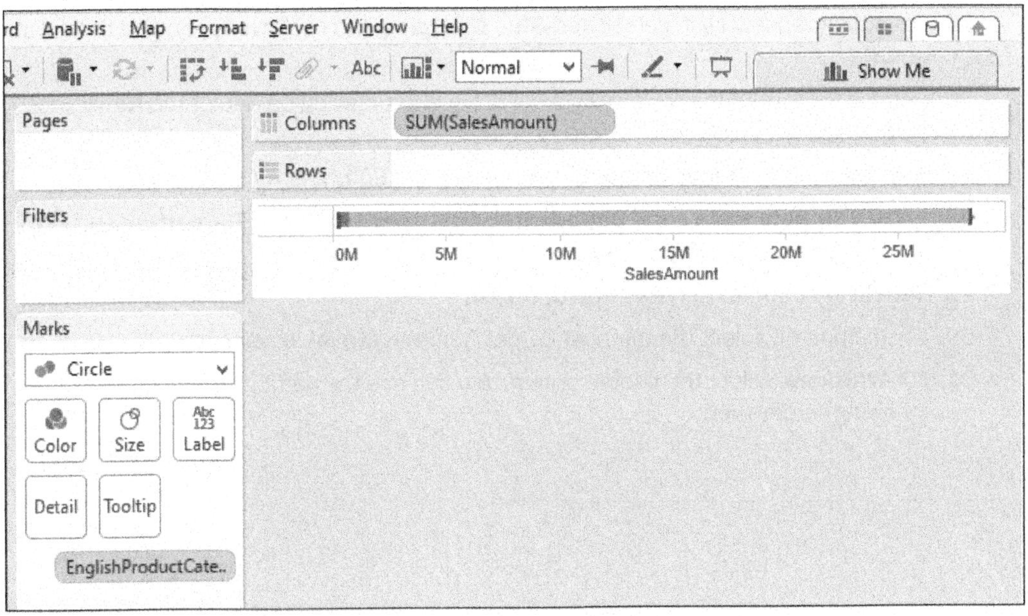

14. Drag **EnglishProductCategory** back onto the **Rows** shelf.

15. Drag **Year(FullDateAlternateKey)** onto the **Marks** shelf.

16. Filter **Year(FullDateAlternateKey)** so that only the year **2008** is selected. Drag **Year(FullDateAlternateKey)** onto the **Filters** shelf. In the pop-up dialog box that appears, select **Years**.

17. In the **Filter[Year of FullDateAlternateKey]** editor box, select **2005, 2006, 2007,** and **2008** and click on **OK**.

18. Drag **SUM(SalesAmount)** onto the **Rows** shelf. It should appear in the Columns shelf and the Rows shelf now.

19. Right-click on the **SalesAmount** axis and deselect **Show Header**.

20. Select **Circle** from the dropdown list on the **Marks** shelf.

21. Drag **SUM(SalesAmount)** onto the **Size** button.

22. Click on the **Size** button and move the slider so that it is half way between the start and the end of the slider. This will increase the size of the circles for **SalesAmount**.

23. Drag **SUM(SalesAmount)** onto the **Color** button.

24. Click on the **Color** button and select **Edit Colors...**.

25. From the dropdown list, select **Red-Blue Diverging** and click on **Apply**, and then click on **OK**.

26. Reduce the size of the rows by clicking down and pressing on one of the **Rows** lines and dragging it upwards.

27. Right-click on the **Sales Amount** x axis and select **Edit...**.

28. In the **Edit Reference Line, Band or Box** dialog box, under the **Formatting** section, choose **Glass** for the **Style** setting.

29. Set **Fill** to be white from the drop-down list.

30. For the border, select the thinnest border from the available selection.

31. For **Whiskers**, select the middle option. You can see the settings in the following screenshot:

Edit Reference Line, Band, or Box

Line	Band	Distribution	Box Plot

Plot Options

Whiskers extend to: `Data within 1.5 times the IQR` ▾

☐ Hide underlying marks (except outliers)

Formatting

Style: `Glass` ▾

Fill: `85%` ▾

Border: `——————` ▾

Whiskers: `——————` ▾

~~Cancel~~   Apply

The final result appears as in the following screenshot:

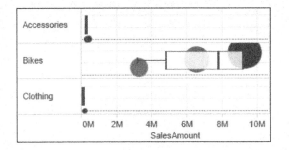

How it works...

Ever played with a Rubik's cube? Color is a vital way of understanding and categorizing what we see. We can't order colors in terms of low to high value, for example, red plus yellow gives blue, since people experience colors differently. However, we can use color to tell a story about the data. We can use color to categorize, order, and display quantity.

In this recipe, we chose color to highlight some elements over others, and we used it to convey a message. Red was used to denote smaller values, and blue was used to denote higher values. Red is often seen as a *warning* color in the West. We reduced the color intensity in the **box-and-whisker** plot so that the circles could be seen through them. This allows us to add visualizations on top of one another but not occlude one another. The users can click on the **box-and-whisker** plot to get more detail about the data.

Data visualization is about displaying high-dimensional data on a low-dimensional canvas. Color can help us to distinguish between the dimensions that you want to display. Bright colors pop at us, and light colors recede into the background. We can use color to focus attention on the most relevant parts of the data visualization. This is very important when we are dealing with Big Data sources. We tend to spot things that stand out.

In Tableau, we can see that there are a number of ways to choose colors. Further, we know that a percentage of the population is color blind, so their color perception is reduced. We can choose colors that feel natural, thereby bringing the dashboard closer to the viewer, and they can understand it better. Fortunately, Tableau often helps you to choose the right type of color for the data.

Color choice depends on the numbers that you are trying to represent. If you are looking at ordering data, you can choose a sequential palette. This is where you choose one color to reflect the metric, but the intensity, brightness, or darkness of the color increases as the value increases. You may want to use a sequential palette to represent age, for example, where lighter values represent younger age groups and darker colors represent older age groups.

Alternatively, if you are looking at distinguishing metrics, you could use a diverging palette. For example, the palette could diverge from red right through the spectrum to white and then on to blue. This palette could be used to represent profit and loss. For example, white could represent zero or thereabouts, red could indicate a loss, and blue could indicate profit.

If you are looking at categorizing data, you could use different colors to represent different dimensional attributes. For example, you could use a different color to represent a different country or a different product group.

Picking color isn't easy. We can't say precisely that this color of blue is twice as blue as another shade of blue. However, Tableau does give you a helping hand.

See also

If you want to know more about color choice and theory, there are plenty of resources. Here are some good places to start:

- *Show Me the Numbers, Stephen Few, Analytics Press* (2012)
- *Now You See It, Stephen Few, Analytics Press* (2009)

Dueling with dual axes

Charts with dual axes can be a mixed blessing. Adding another axis can help the purpose of comparison. Comparison is one of the essential tools to analyze data. You can often hear it expressed in user questions, such as how does that figure compare to last year's, or where are we in relation to our target?

On the other hand, dual axes are best used where the viewer genuinely understands the data. Dual axes can be very misleading. For example, if we have units on one axis and currency on another, the chart can be hard to understand. Further, if the axes are contracted whereby they don't start at zero, or only show a band of the data, then the naïve user may find it misleading. Normally, due to these issues, dual-axis charts are best avoided where people don't understand the data very well. This is particularly the case for a dashboard, where people are expecting to pick up information very quickly.

In Tableau, however, the use of dual axes can be useful to display the same data in different ways in order to enhance the message of the data. In this recipe, we will look at using dual-axes charts as another neat trick to visualize data.

Getting ready

For the exercises in this recipe, we will build on the existing `Chapter 7` dashboard. We don't need to add in any more data for now.

How to do it...

1. Start a new worksheet and call it **Sales Transactions**.
2. Drag **FullAlternateDateKey** onto the **Columns** shelf.
3. Remove the header by right-clicking on the blue pill and deselecting **Show Header**, as shown in the following screenshot:

Columns		+ YEAR(FullDateAlterna..
Rows		**Filter...**
		Show Quick Filter
		Sort...
	2	Format...
		✔ Show Header
		✔ Include in Tooltip
		Show Missing Values

4. Drag **EnglishProductCategoryName** onto the **Rows** shelf.

5. Drag **SalesAmount** onto the right-hand side of **EnglishProductCategoryName** on the **Rows** shelf. You should get line charts now.

6. To change the lines to gray for all the product categories, drag **EnglishProductCategoryName** onto the **Color** button and click on the right-hand side downward-facing arrow, and then select the **Edit Colors...** option, as in the following screenshot:

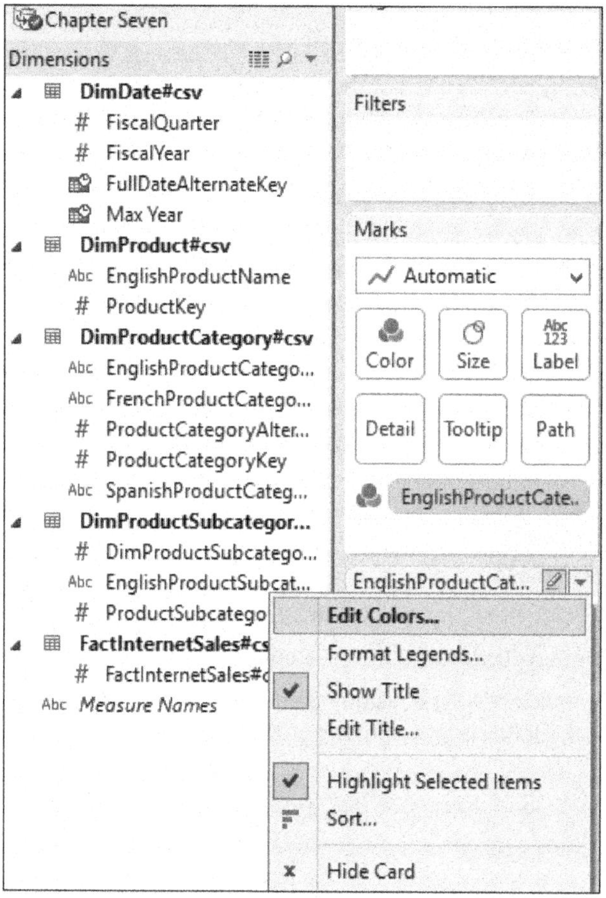

7. Click on each category in turn and select the color to be gray:

8. You can see that **Bikes** has a much higher sales amount than **Accessories** or **Clothing**. The sales amount value for **Bikes** is a behemoth next to the other categories, which unfortunately means that we cannot see the patterns in the data for these categories. To solve this problem, we need to change the axes so that they are synchronized and we can see the patterns. Right-click on the **SalesAmount** *y* axis and choose the option **Edit Axis**.

9. In the **Edit Axis** dialog box that appears, deselect the **Include Zero** checkbox and select the option **Independent axis ranges for each row or column**. Then, remove **SalesAmount** from the **Titles** textbox and deselect **Automatic**. Finally, click on **Apply** and **OK**, as shown in the following screenshot:

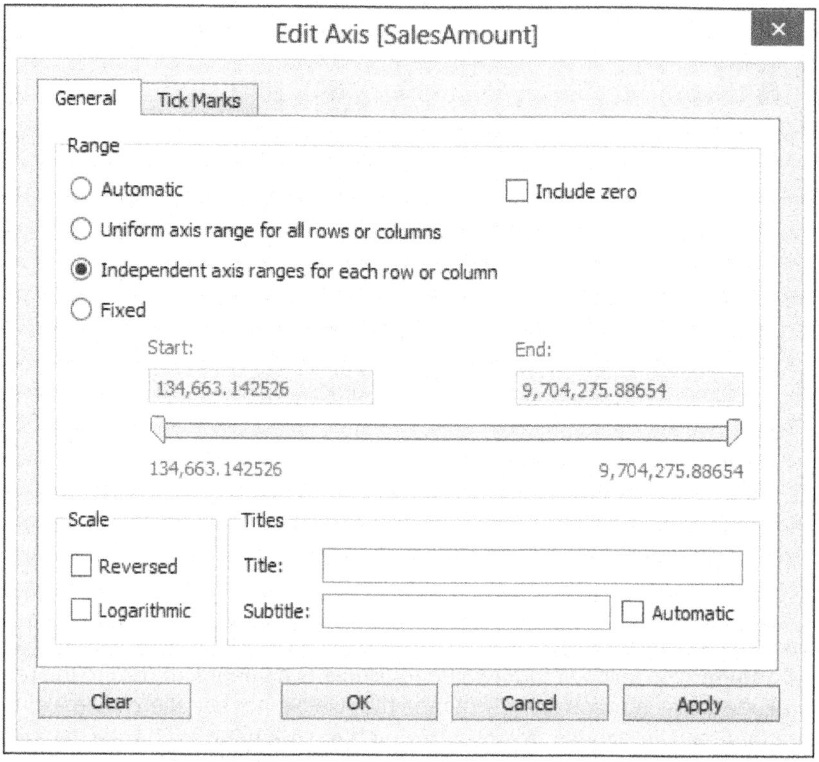

10. Next, click on the **SalesAmount** green pill and uncheck the **Show Header** option.

11. Finally, go to the **Columns** shelf, click on **Year(FullSalesAmount)**, and select **Discrete**.

12. Right-click on **EnglishProductCategoryName** and deselect **Show Header**.

13. Right-click on **SalesAmount** and select **Create Calculated Field**.

14. Next, create a calculated field that calculates whether the latest sales amount is greater than the average amount of sales for each row. In the **Name** field of the **Calculated Field** editor, type Sales Amount Comparison.

15. In the **Text** field of the **Calculated Field** editor, type the following formula and click on **OK**: ZN(SUM([SalesAmount])) - Window_AVG(SUM([SalesAmount])).

16. Let's create another calculated field by right-clicking in the **Measures** field and selecting **Create Calculated Field**. Let's call it **Latest Sales Amount**. The formula should be as follows:

    IF (Year([FullDateAlternateKey])) = Year([Max Year])

    THEN [SalesAmount] END

17. Let's create one more calculated field by right-clicking in the Measures field and selecting **Create Calculated Field**. Let's call it **Diff from All Year's Average**. The formula should be as follows:

    ZN(SUM([Sales Amount])) - Window_AVG(SUM([Sales Amount]))

18. Drag **Latest Sales Amount** to the **Rows** shelf.

19. Click on **Latest Sales Amount** on the **Marks** shelf, and drag **SalesAmountComparison** onto the **Color** button.

20. Let's use color to highlight the result. We will categorize the color into three types: red for below average, gray for close to average sales amount, and blue for greater than the average sales amount. On the **Color** mark for **SalesAmountComparison**, select **Edit Colors...** from the right-hand side downward-facing arrow button.

21. Select **Stepped Color** and type the number 3 to represent three steps. Click on the green box at the left-hand side of the green bar, and a color dialog box will appear. Select blue. Then, select the **Reversed** option and click on **OK**. You can see the result in the following screenshot:

22. Finally, hide the field name for the columns by selecting **FullDateAlternateKey** in the visualization and reselecting **Show Header**.

23. Right-click on **Sum(Latest Sales Amount)** and select **Dual Axis**.

24. Select each *y* axis and deselect **Show Header**.

The result so far should appear as shown in the following screenshot:

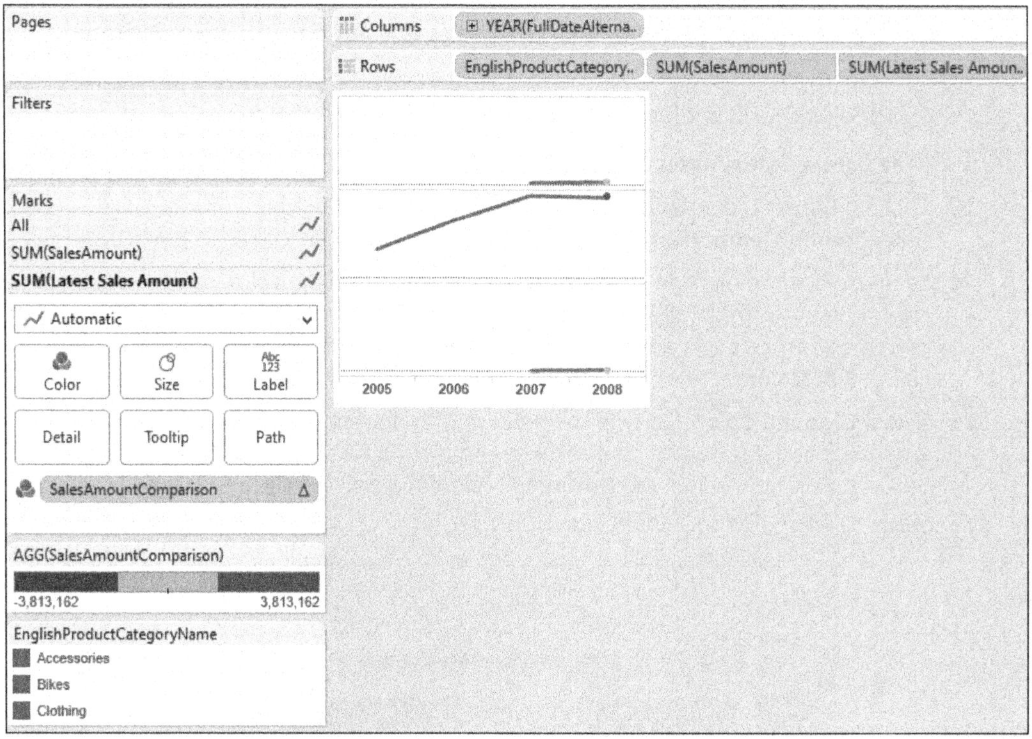

25. Rename the sheet as `Topic 1 Color Sparkline`.

26. Duplicate the sheet by going to the tab name, right-clicking on it, and selecting **Duplicate Sheet**.

27. Rename the sheet `Topic 1 Color Table`.

28. Go to the **Show Me** tab and select the **table** visualization.

29. Drag **EnglishProductCategory** onto the **Rows** shelf.

30. Drag **Year(FullDateAlternateKey)** onto the **Filters** shelf and filter by **Years** so that only data for the year **2008** shows.

31. Drag **Latest Sales Amount** onto the canvas area to show the numbers.

32. On the **Marks** shelf, drag **SalesAmountComparison** onto the **Color** button.

33. Click on the **Color** button and choose the **Edit Colors...** option.

34. In the **Edit Colors** dialog box, choose the **Stepped Colors** option and enter the number 2.

35. Choose the **Reversed** option.

36. Select the left-hand side square box, and in the color dialog box, select gray and click on **OK**.

37. Select the right-hand side square box in the color dialog box, select royal blue, and then click on **OK**. You can see the final settings in the following screenshot:

38. Click on **SUM(SalesAmount)** and sort in descending order.

39. Remove all of the headings for the columns by clicking on each header, and deselecting **Show Header**.

    The resulting visualization should look like the following screenshot:

Pages ▼			Columns
		Rows	EnglishProductCatego..
Filters			
YEAR(FullDateAlternateKey): 2008			
		Bikes	9,162,325
Marks		Accessories	407,050
Abc Automatic ∨		Clothing	201,525

Color   Size   Abc123 Text

Detail   Tooltip

⬢ SalesAmountComparison   Δ
Abc123 SUM(Latest Sales Amount)

AGG(SalesAmountComparison)

-5,905,358   5,905,358

40. Now, let's put them together in a dashboard. To create a new dashboard, right-click on the **Name** tab at the bottom and select **New Dashboard**.

41. On the dashboard sheet, select the **Topic 1 Color Sparkline** and **Topic 1 Color Table** worksheets, and put them next to each other on the canvas.

42. On the dashboard, hide the title for the **Topic 1 Color Sparkline** worksheet by clicking on the downward-facing arrow on the right-hand side and deselecting **Title**.

43. Now, hide the title for the **Topic 1 Color Average** worksheet by clicking on the downward-facing arrow on the right-hand side and deselecting **Title**.

44. Resize the rows on each worksheet so that they match nicely.

45. Navigate to **Format | Shading**.

46. To add banding, go to the sheet tab on the format shading series of options that appear on the left-hand side of the screen. Select **Row Banding** and move the **Band Size** slider until it is halfway along the slider.

47. Navigate to **Format | Lines**. Set each line to **None**.

48. Now click on the right-hand side visualization in the dashboard and then select the **Lines** option from the **Format** menu. In each of the **Rows** options, select **None**.

49. Now go back to the **Format** menu item and select the **Borders** option. On the **Sheet** menu item, select **None** for the **Row Divider** option.

Your completed dashboard should appear as shown in the following screenshot:

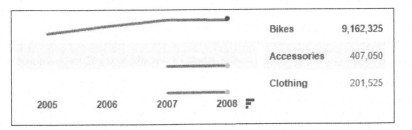

How it works...

Dual axes can be difficult to interpret, particularly if each axis shows different measurements. However, here, dual axes can help us to create a visualization. Using a dual-axis chart here allows us to set the size and color of the circle and the line chart independently.

In this recipe, we used a *ZN* formula. The *ZN* formula is used when you want to replace a zero with null values. We saw the impact of null values in an earlier chapter, and this is one option for us.

There's more...

Tableau has some great functionality, which means that you can have fun with the appearance of sparklines as well as provide more information with them. For example, you could use the **Line End** option for the label and use advanced editing on the text label to format in order to provide more detail for the dashboard users.

Where is the three-dimensional data?

The objective of data visualization is to present data so that it's easier for people to consume, spot trends, and understand the story of the data. There is a debate over the use of three dimensional in charts, and people looking at Tableau may wonder how they can make visualizations that are three dimensional. Three dimensional is not available in Tableau. Three dimensional requires the viewer to spend more time trying to understand the data being presented to them than necessary.

People often consider three dimensional as a way to bring more information into the view. We don't need to use three dimensional to make visualizations beautiful and informative. Beauty can come in the form of simplicity and understanding the data story as easily as possible. Flashy isn't always better, particularly if it misleads the viewer.

If you can't use three dimensional but still want to show different metrics on the visualization, then what are your options? If you want to display a number of variables, use a scatterplot matrix, also known as a splom. This is a grid of scatter charts. What is a scatter chart? Also known as a scatter graph or a scattergram, it is simply a dataset plotted as points on a graph. The x axis represents one variable, and the y axis represents another. We can arrange them in a grid so that the viewer can easily compare along the variable, and vertically between the graphs. We can also enhance the scattergram by adding in trend lines and using color to convey a story.

In this recipe, we will look at creating a scattergram matrix using Tableau and adding in a few reference lines. This is a good option when you are asked to create something to show the relationships between variables. In this recipe, we will create a small dashboard segment that looks at whether the sales differ on a quarterly basis.

Getting ready

For the exercises in this recipe, continue to work on the `Chapter Seven` workbook.

How to do it...

1. Create a new worksheet by clicking on a new tab at the bottom of the canvas. Rename it as `Splom`.

2. Drag **Year(FullYearAlternateDate)** onto the **Columns** shelf.

3. On the **Year(FullYearAlternateDate)** pill, click on the small plus sign on the left-hand side so that you now see the **Quarter(FullYearAlternateDate)** pill.

4. In the **Measures** pane on the left-hand side, rename **Number of Records** to `Number of Sales Transactions`.

5. Drag **Number of Sales Transactions** onto the **Rows** shelf.

6. Change the measure calculation to **Count** by right-clicking on **Number of Sales Transactions**, navigating to **Measure (SUM)**, and selecting the **Count** option.

7. Let's change the visualization to a scattergram by going to the **Marks** shelf and selecting **Shape** from the drop-down list. The chart will now change to a scattergram, as shown in the following screenshot:

Pages	**⫶⫶⫶ Columns**	⊟ YEAR(FullDateAlterna..	⊞ QUARTER(FullDateAlt..
	⫶⫶ Rows	CNT(Number of Sales Tr..	

Filters

FullDateAlternateKey

Marks

x⁺ Shape ▾

Color	Size	Abc 123 Label
Detail	Tooltip	Shape

8. Take the calculation **Diff from All Year's Average** and drag it onto the **Color** button. The color scheme will change to red and green.

9. Click on the **Color** button and select **Edit Color...**.

10. Change the red color to royal blue and click on **OK**.

11. Change the green color to gray and click on **OK**.

12. Next, let's add in a reference line to show the trend lines. To do this, go to the **Analysis** menu item and navigate to **Trend Lines**. Then, choose the option **Show Trend Lines**.

13. The trend lines will appear for each year. Swap it around to show a quarter by dragging **Quarter(FullDateAlternateYear)** onto the **Columns** shelf to the left-hand side of **Year(FullDateAlternateYear)**.

14. Click on one of the reference lines and select the **Format** option. The **Data** pane will now change to the **Format Lines** option pane.

15. For the **Trend Lines** option, click on the drop-down list and select the thinnest line. You can see an example in the following screenshot:

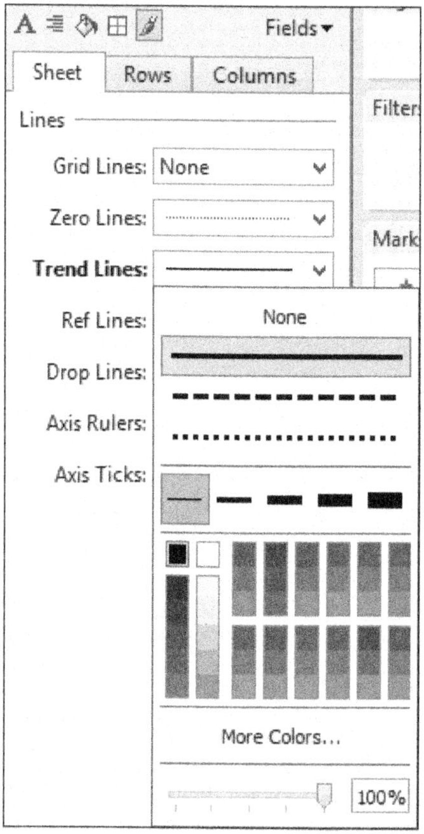

16. Soften the color of the trend line by selecting the light purple color located on the bottom row on the far-right side. You will see the changes made on the trend line.

17. Next, remove the headers in order to make the visualization as compact as possible. Remove the **FullDateAlternateKey** header by right-clicking on it and selecting **Hide Field Names for Columns**.

18. On the *y* axis, right-click and deselect the **Show Header** option.

19. On the *x* axis, right-click and deselect the **Show Header** option.

    The completed visualization now looks like the following screenshot:

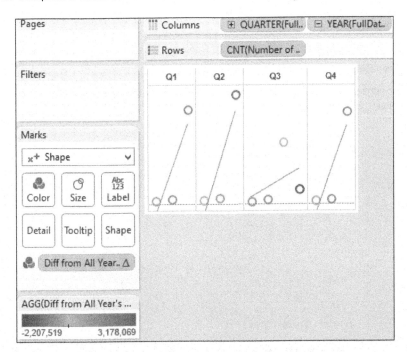

Eating humble pie – Pie charts or not?

Pie charts are probably the most ubiquitous data visualization form. However, their effectiveness is often debated. To summarize, humans are not very good at distinguishing and comparing area or angles. Pie charts use both these mechanisms to convey a message about the data.

People are tempted to use lots of pie charts when visualizing data. Why? Because they like them. However, pie charts take up a lot of space on a page to give one message about the data. It isn't possible, for example, to show timelines very effectively, and they can't be used to convey multidimensional data properly.

In this recipe, we will look at creating a pie chart in Tableau, and then we will take a look at a better way of visualizing the same data. This will help you to understand the debate surrounding the humble pie chart and to see when they are most effectively used.

Getting ready

For the exercises in this recipe, we will build on the existing Chapter Seven dashboard.

How to do it...

1. Duplicate the `Splom` worksheet by right-clicking on the tab and selecting **Duplicate Worksheet**.

2. Rename the duplicated worksheet to `Humble Pie`.

3. On the **Show Me** tab, select the **pie chart** option.

    Your screen will now change to display pie charts. You can see an example in the following screenshot:

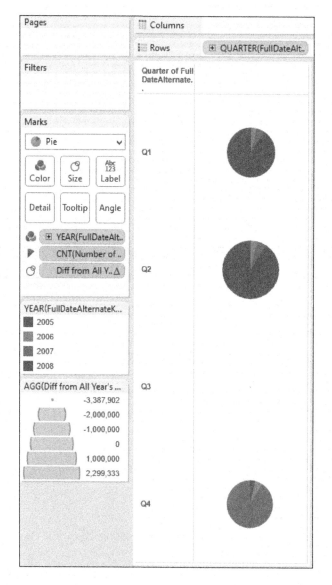

You can see that the pie chart doesn't make any sense. Tableau has tried to display different metrics on the same pie chart, and it does not show any meaningful information.

4. Let's change the pie chart so that it shows one metric only. Remove everything from the canvas in order to start.

5. Drag **Year(FullDateAlternateKey)** onto the **Color** button.

6. Drag **SalesAmount** onto the **Size** button. The data visualization will now look like the following screenshot:

Pages		Columns
		Rows

Filters

Marks

● Pie ⌄

● Color | ☺ Size | Abc 123 Label

Detail | Tooltip | Angle

☻ ⊞ YEAR(FullDateAlt..
▶ SUM(SalesAmou..
☺ SUM(SalesAmou..

YEAR(FullDateAlternateK...
■ 2005
■ 2006
■ 2007
■ 2008

SUM(SalesAmount)
| 29,358,678

7. For some reason, Tableau has put red and green next to each other. Let's change the palette to one that is sensitive to the needs of color-blind people. Go to the **Color** button and click on it, and select **Edit Color...**.

8. In the **Edit Colors** dialog box, choose **Color Blind 10** from the drop-down list, click on **Assign Palette**, and then click on **OK**. Here's a screenshot showing the color settings:

Edit Colors [Year of FullDateAlternateKey]

Select Data Item:
- 2005
- 2006
- 2007
- 2008

Select Color Palette:

Color Blind 10

Assign Palette

Reset   OK   Cancel   Apply

You can see the final pie in the following screenshot:

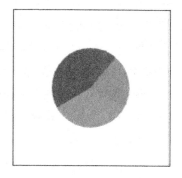

How it works...

Generally speaking, pie charts are to be avoided. Humans are not accurate when they estimate area.

A key part of data analysis is comparison. Pie charts don't allow easy comparison because we find it harder to compare areas, and it is also harder for us to compare slices that are not next to one another.

So when should we use pie charts? They can be used when the area of the pie chart represents a single measure. If there are fewer slices, and the slices represent a percentage of a single measure, then pie charts can be understood easily and quickly. In the previous examples, we used sales amount as a single metric and showed it sliced by different categories. If we used it for multiple categories, then this would be harder to read. As a rule of thumb, no more than five slices is a good guideline.

Pies are useful when we want to put data on a map. Even then, the guidelines on slices should remain the same.

Pies can be nice as a way of filtering dashboards. So, they could filter dashboards by allowing the user to click on a particular slice to filter the whole dashboard. Pies are useful if you are displaying data on a map, as long as there are not too many slices, or you will lose the value of the data visualization.

See also

▶ If you want to know more about the use and abuse of pie charts, there are plenty of resources. Stephen Few's blog, *Perceptual Edge*, is a great place to start. You can view it at `www.perceptualedge.com`.

Sizing to make a data story

It is easy to balance columns in a report, but it is not very easy to lay out a dashboard. The size and location of dashboard elements are critical in helping users to understand the data better. How can you put dashboard elements together to facilitate easy understanding?

One key concept in design is called the golden ratio. It is based on the Fibonacci sequence, which is found in nature all around us and is a familiar concept. The Fibonacci sequence is found in a number of flower petals. You can also find it in art. For example, artists such as Salvador Dali and Le Corbusier have set out their works to approximate the golden ratio in the placement of items within their paintings. The golden ratio itself is 1:1.61, and is represented by the Greek character phi.

By using the golden ratio to design your dashboard, you follow a natural order that is harmonious and familiar. You can use the following diagram to understand how to place dashboard elements:

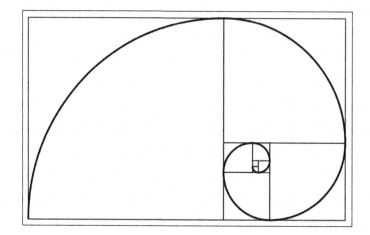

How can this help you to design your dashboard? The golden ratio can be used as a heuristic to help you to tell a story with the data. It can help you to decide what goes where. Here is the preceding design translated into an Excel template, which has been set in blocks. To try things out, you can swap your dashboard components around, and use rectangular blocks to fill out blanks until you have finished with this aspect. The following screenshot depicts this:

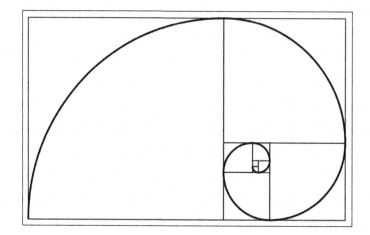

We can use size as a way of determining how the dashboard components are laid out. How can we determine size and positioning? Here are some helpful tips:

- ▶ Prioritize your components in terms of their importance, and then assign them the size.

- ▶ Don't include dashboard components that aren't relevant. We are in the business of making the dashboard clear, not busy!

- ▶ Get your users involved. It is always possible that your prioritization and sizing is not the same as their prioritization. You could generate a series of prototypes of the dashboard. For example, you could paste pictures of your components on the preceding template, make a picture, and then show them the different options. If you want your users to use your dashboard, why not involve them earlier in the process?

In this recipe, we will create a dashboard from the visualizations we created earlier in this chapter. We will look at the different ways in which we can place components on the dashboard, and the tricks to resize things.

Getting ready

For the exercises in this recipe, we will build on the existing `Chapter Seven` dashboard. We don't need to add in any more data for now.

How to do it...

1. On one of the tabs at the bottom, right-click and select the **Create Dashboard** option.

2. Name the new dashboard `Dashboard Sizing`.

3. On the new dashboard, we can treat the visualizations from the first topic as one topic. Therefore, drag **Topic 1 Color Table** onto the left-hand side of the dashboard.

4. Now, drag **Topic 1 Color Sparkline** to the right-hand side of **Topic 1 Color Table**.

5. Drag **Splom** onto the right-hand side of the dashboard.

6. Drag **Box Whiskers** above **Sales Transactions**.

7. Remove the title from **Topic 1 Color Average** by going to the right-hand dropdown list and deselecting **Title**.

8. Remove the title and headers from **Topic 1 Color Sparkline** by going to the right-hand dropdown list and deselecting **Title**.

9. Remove the year from the x axis in **Topic 1 Color Sparkline** by right-clicking on one of the years and deselecting **Show Header**.

10. Insert a title at the top by dragging the text to the top of the dashboard.

11. In the textbox that appears, type `What is my Sales Performance Over Time?`.

12. Change the font to **Segoe UI**.

13. Change the font size to **12**.

14. Let's resize the dashboard by inserting a blank tile underneath the other visualizations. Making it smaller will make it neater! To do this, drag **Blank** to the right-hand side.

Your dashboard will now look like the following screenshot:

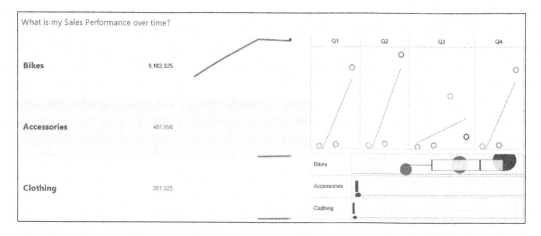

How it works...

In this recipe, we experimented with layout. If we had more product categories, the sparkline would be smaller, there would be more rows, and it would appear much smaller. However, the purpose was to illustrate the importance of sizing. We can see that using the golden ratio as a template is a good starting point, and you can bring the users along with you.

See also

► If you want to know more about dashboard design, Stephen Few's book, *Information Dashboard Design: The Effective Visual Communication of Data*, *O'Reilly Media*, is an excellent read and continuation of this topic.

8
Tell the World! Share Your Dashboards

In this chapter, we will cover the following recipes:

- ▶ Packaging workbooks with data
- ▶ Publishing dashboards to Tableau Server
- ▶ Publishing dashboards to Tableau Public
- ▶ Mobilizing your dashboards
- ▶ Mixing Tableau with SharePoint 2013 Power BI
- ▶ Wrapping up with R – Dashboards as a tool

Introduction

Why is sharing your dashboards important? In today's world, we are simply bombarded with data all the time. Aren't we making problems worse? Are we placing ourselves in a dilemma between two hazards, such as the choice between Scylla and Charybdis? On one side, we have a lot of data. On the other side, we are producing more data to solve the problem of having too much data. Which is the way forward, and why should we share more information?

Dashboarding is the process of data distillation, from the noise to the essence. Dashboarding is about displaying the right data at the right time, to the right people that need it, and in the right format. The right format is the format that people can understand, and dashboarding is one way forward for business questions and business decisions that require distillation.

We can't comprehend the amount of data at the scale and speed that it meets us. It's also hard to sort out the important parts. Dashboarding isn't just a product, it is a result, a solution, whereby we have to distill the data noise to the essential points.

People need the headlines in order to make decisions. These headlines also help them to understand details better. People have to start from somewhere, and giving them broad brushstrokes of the overall picture helps them make a start.

In order to do that, you have to share data. When you start exploring data, you will find that you want to share with people the story that the data tells. Having a passion for data is a wonderful thing!

This chapter will help you share your passion and enthusiasm for data, and show you how to make data-based decisions based on your findings. Be the expert!

Dashboards aren't just about sharing data with colleagues. In this chapter, we will look at publishing data to various outputs in order to meet different needs. We will end by looking at R. Sometimes, you may need to meet with data scientists who will want to analyze the data in depth. For them, R is a useful tool, and it will help them answer their own questions using your dashboard as a starting point.

Packaging workbooks with data

In this recipe, we will look at how we can share our Tableau workbooks, both with and without data. It is possible to share a Tableau workbook by using an extract, which is an internal database that Tableau uses in order to store data for analysis.

Tableau helps you share visualizations with your colleagues. You can share your Tableau workbook as a packaged workbook and send it to anyone. If they have a copy of the free Tableau Reader, they can open and use it straight away as long as you have created an extract. This is excellent, since it means that you can share the workbook with people who have not purchased a copy of Tableau.

Tableau also helps you share visualizations on Tableau Public, a popular free service that allows organizations and bloggers to share information and data freely. Tableau Public is a community offered by Tableau. It would be extremely complicated to transfer data from different networks into a free community service. To make the service perform faster, it is best that the data is stored closer to the Tableau data extract in order to save on network traffic. To do this, you will need to save the data as an extract before publishing data to Tableau Public.

Getting ready

A copy of the Chapter Seven Tableau workbook is required for this recipe.

How to do it...

1. Open a copy of the `Chapter Seven` workbook.

2. Navigate to **File | Save As**.

3. In the drop-down list at the bottom, select **Save as type**, as shown in the following screenshot:

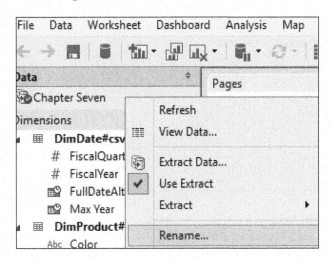

4. Select the **Tableau Packaged Workbook (*.twbx)** option.

5. Click on **Save**.

6. Now, right-click on the data source called **Chapter Seven** and select **Rename...**, as shown in the following screenshot:

7. Rename it to `Chapter Eight` in the **Name:** textbox of the **Rename Connection** dialog box, and then click on **OK**, as shown in the following screenshot:

8. Right-click on the data source **Chapter Eight** and select **Extract Data....**. This will bring up a dialog box, as shown in the following screenshot:

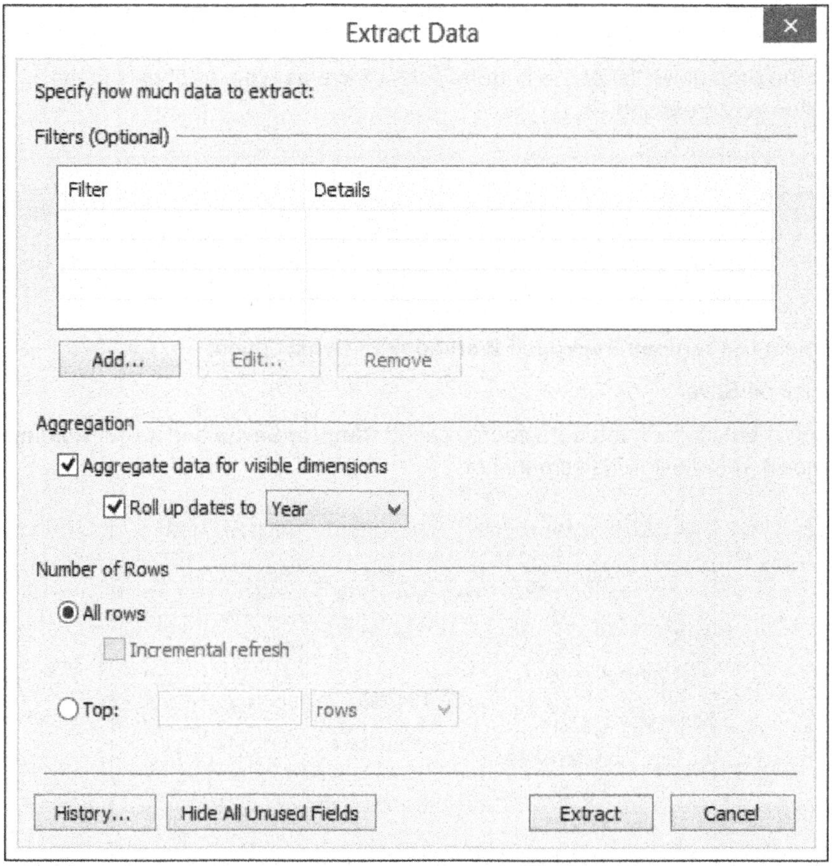

9. In the **Extract Data** dialog box, go to the **Aggregation** section and select the item **Aggregate data for visible dimensions**.

10. Under this item, go to **Roll up dates to** and select **Year**.

11. Click on **Extract**.

12. You will get an information box, as shown in the following screenshot. Click on **OK**:

13. To export the packaged workbook, navigate to **File | Export Packaged Workbook**.
14. Select your destination for the file and click on **Save**.

Your file is now ready to be shared with other people.

How it works...

Why would you want to use an extract? To provide the recipient with the workbook and data, which they can use in offline mode. The extracted data is stored in a **Tableau Data Extract** (**TDE**) file, and is stored on the hard drive of your computer under `\Tableau\Tableau 8.1\ defaults\Datasources`. If you look into this folder, you will also see the sample datasets that are installed when you install Tableau.

Since the data is stored on the hard drive, you can access it quickly. This is very useful for large datasets or those stored in a server across the network. If your Internet connection isn't very good, then you can extract the data to your local disk, and then it is much faster to access the data.

What does the **Aggregate data for visible dimensions** option do? This option aggregates the data using the default aggregation for the measures. Having the data preaggregated in the extract makes it faster to be queried. Remember the mantra Summarize–Zoom and Filter–Drill to Detail? A summary of the data first is very useful. By aggregating data, Tableau is _warmed_ and primed for the data that usually answers the users' first questions, and is therefore faster.

There's more...

If the data is on your hard disk, you will need to think about securing the data. What happens if your laptop gets stolen, for example?

You can work with your IT department to tackle this important question. As a starting point, you could look at encrypting your hard drive with BitLocker and a password as a minimum-security measure.

If data is stored on your laptop, then it is vital to back up your data. For example, you could use a free service such as OneDrive from Microsoft or Dropbox for ease of use, or software such as LogMeIn Backup and Norton Backup.

Publishing dashboards to Tableau Server

You can share your dashboards by publishing them to Tableau Server. In order to help users, you can organize dashboards into projects, tag them, and even choose which worksheets to display and hide.

What is Tableau Server? Tableau Server is where people can share their views about the data within your company. Other people can view your dashboards through a browser, and they don't need to have Tableau installed. You can publish workbooks and data sources to the server, as well as open workbooks and data sources that others have published to the server. However, it is not available to every user. Tableau professional users can publish to Tableau Server as long as they are added as users. They must also be assigned permissions to publish views and data sources using Tableau Professional. If they have the permissions, Tableau Professional users can publish workbooks to a server project, which will also help direct your users toward the relevant workbook quickly.

On the other hand, Tableau personal users can only publish to Tableau Public.

How to do it...

We will use the following steps to publish dashboards to Tableau Server:

1. Open a copy of the `Chapter Eight` workbook.

2. Navigate to **Server | Publish Workbook**.

3. You will now be asked to log in to Tableau Server. You will need the server details, your username, and password. Here is a screenshot of the **Tableau Server Login** dialog box:

4. You will now see the **Publish Workbook to Tableau Server** dialog box, as shown in the following screenshot:

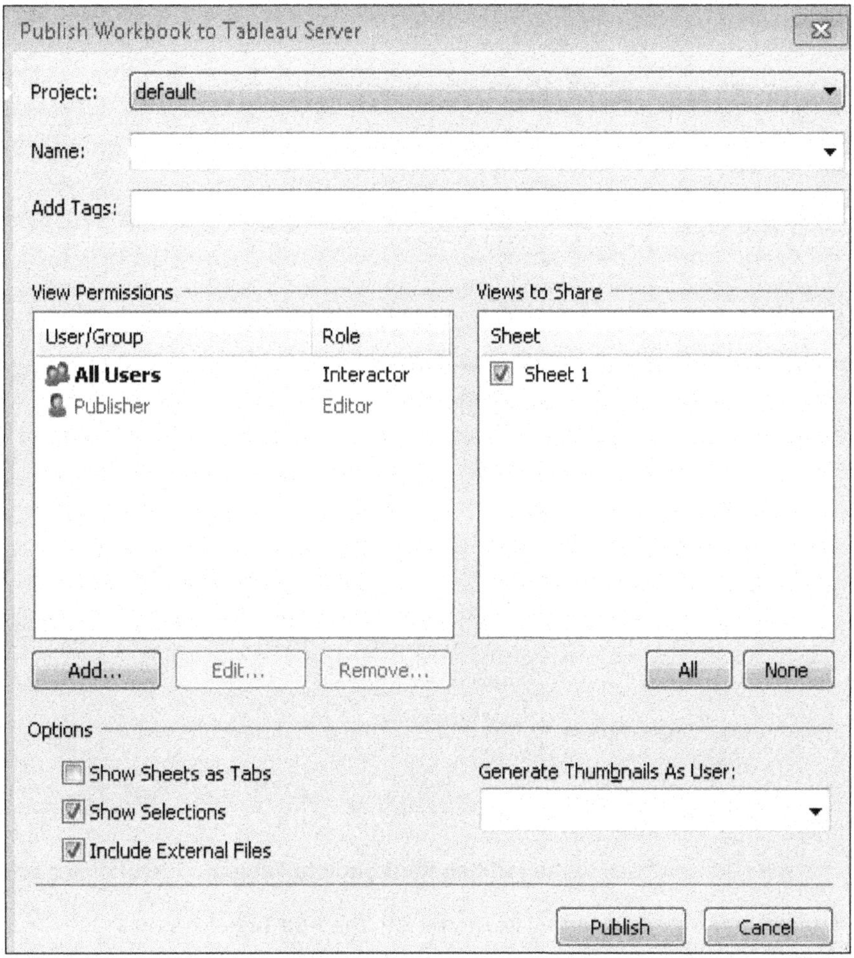

5. In the **Project** drop-down box, select the project you would like to use.
6. In the **Name** textbox, type in `Chapter Eight` for the name of the workbook.

7. Select the **Scheduling and Authentication...** button to permit or deny access to your workbook. To do this, click on the **Add...** button on the left-hand side and you will see the **Add/Edit Permissions** dialog box. For now, we will choose **All Users** and click on **OK**, as shown in the following screenshot:

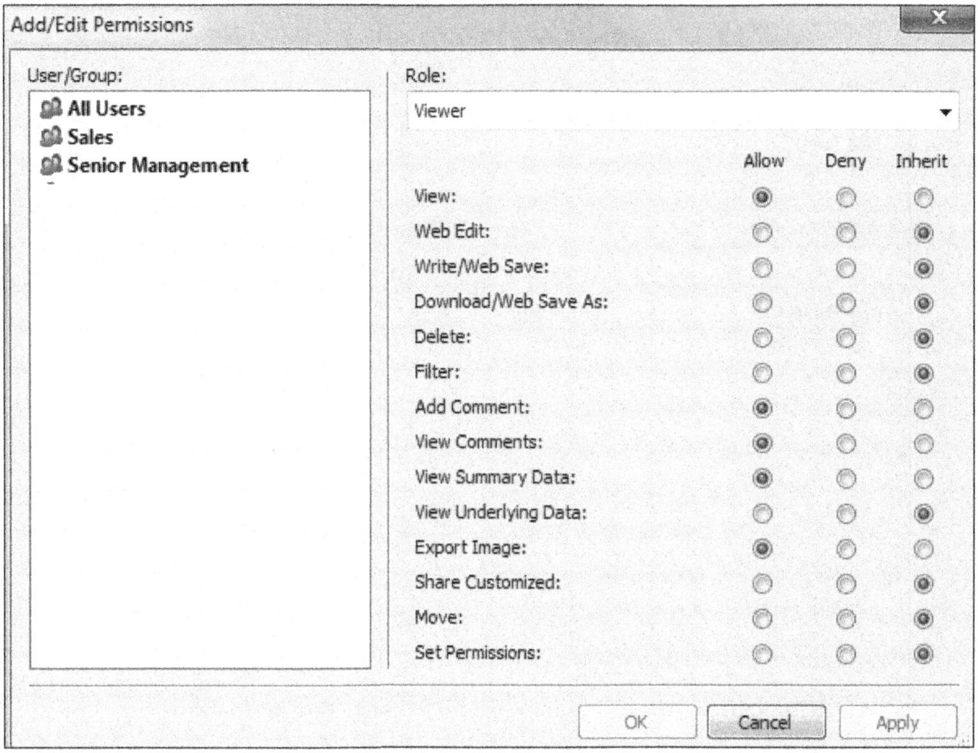

This will take you back to the **Publish Workbook to Tableau Server** dialog box.

8. You can add tags by inserting keywords into the **Add Tags** textbox.

9. Click on **OK** to publish your workbook and view it in Tableau Server.

How it works...

Tableau Server is a corporate tool to share Tableau workbooks. It acts as a central repository to store them.

Tableau Server can also give you a good starting point for sharing workbooks, since you can download someone else's workbook, and use it as a starting point for your own work. Alternatively, you can use the data sources to get a head start with your own work. A centralized repository is useful to facilitate teamwork and collaboration, and Tableau Server is designed for this purpose.

There's more...

A nineteenth-century Jewish folktale tells us about a man who slanders a rabbi. The moral of the story is that gossip is like feathers in the wind; once words are said, it is impossible to take them back or repair all the damage. The same can be said about data; once it is published on the Web, it is cached and written in ink: permanent, eternal, and clear. Before you publish your workbook, make sure that the data can be published and accessed by your stated users.

You might also find it useful to go through a defined checklist with your peers that all of you agree upon before you publish any data. This will help you share the data appropriately.

See also

> ► Tableau offers a range of options to share workbooks on Tableau Server. For more information, please visit `http://onlinehelp.tableausoftware.com/v6.1/pro/online/en-us/i1036445.html`.

Publishing dashboards to Tableau Public

When you publish your dashboard to Tableau Public, the data source(s) must be a Tableau data extract (`.tde`) file. We looked at creating this file in the *Packaging workbooks with data* recipe of this chapter. If you have multiple data connections, then you must repeat this process for each data connection.

In this example, we use small data files. Note, however, that your extract may not include more than 1 million rows when published to Tableau Public.

How to do it...

Perform the following steps to publish dashboards to Tableau Public:

1. Open a copy of the `Chapter Eight` workbook.
2. Navigate to **Server | Tableau Public | Save to Web As...**, as shown in the following screenshot:

Server	Window	Help		
Tableau Public ►		Open from Web...	Ctrl+Shift+O
		Save to Web...	Ctrl+Shift+S
Bik		Save to Web As...	
Ac		Manage Workbooks...	

3. If you do not have an account already, then select the **Register** hyperlink and fill in the resulting form. The following screenshot shows the resulting form:

4. Once you have registered, you can log in. Here's the **Tableau Public Sign In** window:

Tableau Public Sign In   ✕

Logon   +ableau⁺public

Enter your Tableau Public email address and password to log on.

Email: jen.stirrup@copper-blue.com

Password: •••••••

Login   Forgot your password?

No account?   Create one for FREE!

5. You will then get a dialog box named **Save Workbook to the Public Web** with the name of the workbook in the **Name** field. Check the option **Show Sheets as Tabs** and then click on **Save**.

6. The file will start uploading, and you will see a small information box indicating the progress of the upload, as in the following screenshot:

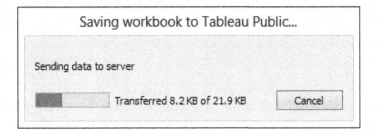

Saving workbook to Tableau Public...

Sending data to server

Transferred 8.2 KB of 21.9 KB   Cancel

You will then see the resulting dashboard as follows:

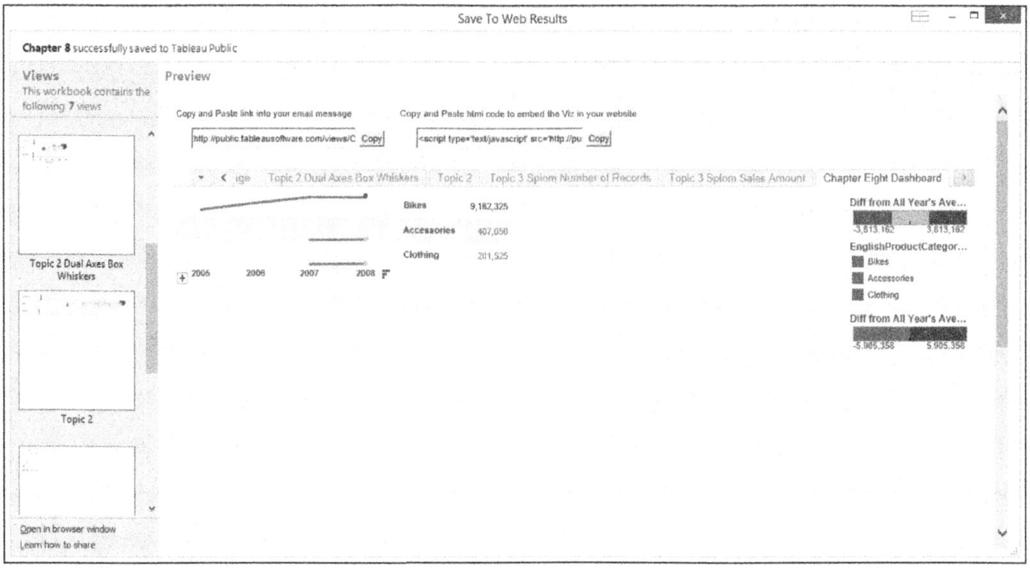

7. At the top of the page, you will see an option to embed the viz into your e-mail or website, as in the following screenshot:

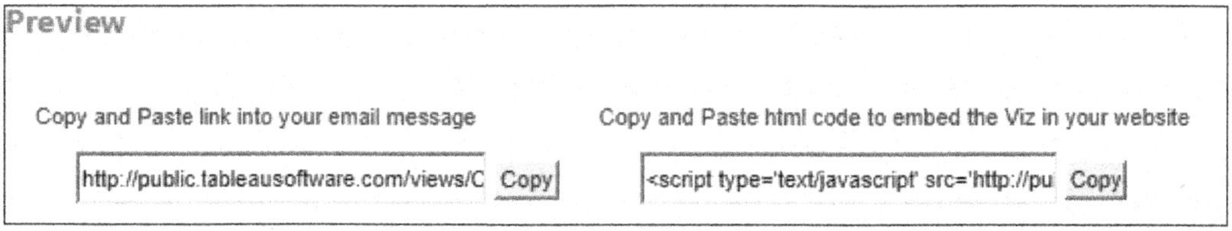

8. At the bottom of the page is the **Share** option. This allows you to control the size of the view and shows the toolbar to adjust size using the display options in the **Share** window.

   You can change the width of the entire dashboard view when viewed in the browser. This option shows the current size by default. You can also change the height of the entire dashboard view when viewed in the browser. This option shows the current size by default.

9. If the **Show Toolbar** option is selected, the toolbar will appear along the bottom of the view.

10. Optionally, use the **URL for RSS links** option to add a URL that will be used as the link for static images in RSS feeds. For example, use this option to specify a destination page for the RSS entry rather than the main page of your blog or website. If you like, you can use this option to add tracking code to monitor traffic coming from your RSS feed.

11. Now you can share your visualization with the world!

How it works...

Tableau Public allows you to share your data visualizations with the world, but why would you want to share them?

In the words of The Guardian, "Data Journalism is the new punk." The central idea is that you can be a data citizen and use data to influence the world around you. You can question authority in an intellectual way, using data as a foundation.

However, data needs to be told in order to be understood, and data visualization is a way in which data citizens can spread the message. Tableau facilitates data citizens by offering Tableau Public, a free facility to spread the love of data. What's not to like?

See also

► If you are interested in reading more about data visualization as the new punk, then please visit `bit.ly/DataJournalismNewPunk` to see the article by The Guardian.

Mobilizing your dashboards

Is mobile business intelligence an even harder subset of business intelligence?

It has been predicted that 77 percent of organizations will be using tablet devices within two years. A recent trend in cutting organizational capital expenditure could mean increased spending on mobile technologies and devices and slightly reduced spending on desktop computers. Furthermore, an emphasis on the reduction of capital expenditure can mean that scalable, *pay as you go* cloud services can replace the on-premise capital outlay that is normally associated with projects. Taken together, these drivers can act as catalysts for the mobilization of business intelligence, which would provide data at the right time, at the right place, and to the right people in the right format.

Mobile business intelligence is more complex than simply making reports smaller to fit a tablet. Data warehouse and business intelligence projects are notoriously difficult to implement, both in terms of delivery and in the resulting user satisfaction. For example, in the UK, the National Computing Centre (2011) study showed that 22 percent of users didn't believe that the business objectives were met by the business intelligence and data warehouse solutions, with a further 53 percent believing that the resulting solution was *average*.

Furthermore, the greatest difficulty among users was that the data was stored in multiple systems and wasn't easy to find; a related difficulty was that information wasn't available quickly enough. It's clear that businesses need to allow critical business information to be more accessible. The tablet device can help the information to be accessible remotely, but it does not solve the fundamental problem of ensuring that the underlying data is correct, integrated, and accessible.

Fostering innovation promotes competitiveness. This realization is apparent in a piece of research by Gartner (2012), which shows that business intelligence is regarded as a key, top-three priority item for **Chief Information Officers** (**CIOs**) in Asia. Furthermore, research by Gartner (2012) shows that business intelligence is, in fact, the number one spending priority among CIOs. When this was translated into monetary terms, market researcher Forrester Research forecasted that the mobile information technology market would be a major area of IT spending in 2014.

Despite this apparent enthusiasm for business intelligence, it is a known fact that business intelligence projects are notoriously difficult to implement. For example, a simple Google search of *why business intelligence fails* produces over 26 million results. A study conducted by the National Computing Centre shows that an astonishing 87 percent of business intelligence projects fail to meet their original objectives.

Mobile business intelligence is about providing business intelligence on any technology, not restricted to any place or time. Platforms for this include smartphones, iPads, and tablets. But mobile business intelligence is not just about providing access to data irrespective of place and time. Speaking broadly, mobile business intelligence provides end users with the capability to access data and make informed decisions anywhere, any time. Physical locations should not restrict executives' abilities to access critical data. Furthermore, they should not have to rely on month- or week-old numbers embedded in emails or presentation reports. The data has to be correct and up to date. Mobile business intelligence appeals to three main groups of people: senior management, sales executives, and service executives. It is also particularly interesting to those who need real-time service alerts and customer data.

Small businesses are using mobile business as an opportunity to use efficiency gains and productivity, and it is often cheaper to buy iPads than it is to purchase a desktop.

Fortunately, Tableau is ahead of the curve in mobile solutions for the masses, having recognized this need for mobile data. Fortunately, we have seen how easy Tableau is to use, and it demonstrably goes to work to deal with the issues that we have discussed here.

In this recipe, we will look at using Tableau Public in order to mobilize data. However, Tableau Server offers an excellent corporate solution, and the reader is advised to refer to the Tableau website for more information.

Getting ready

For the exercises in this recipe, we will continue to use the `Chapter Eight` dashboard. We don't need to add any more data for now.

How to do it...

1. If you have Tableau Server and you are using an iPad, first, download the Tableau mobile app from the iTunes store. If you are using Android, you may retrieve the application from the Android store.

2. Once you have downloaded the application, start the Tableau app on your iPad or Android device, and you will get a login screen.

3. Once you have entered the details for Tableau Server, you will be able to open workbooks as if you were on the desktop.

4. What happens if you don't have Tableau Server or an iPad? If your data is freely available, then you can upload the workbook to Tableau Public.

5. You can then navigate to the workbook URL on Tableau Public and interact with it.

6. On the device, enter the URL `http://bit.ly/TableauPublicGallery`, which will show you the home page on Tableau Public.

7. You will see a link called **GALLERY**. Click on this link.

8. Now, you will see public examples that have been created on Tableau Public.

9. Have fun selecting some of the dashboards on your mobile device, and watch how the page renders the visualization. You can interact with the visualizations too.

How it works...

Tableau Public is publicly available and hosts Tableau workbooks. This service is free. You can also use the examples to inspire your own visualizations.

Companies also have a paid version of Tableau called Tableau Online. This is cloud business intelligence that is hosted by Tableau.

Tableau Server is a corporate version of Tableau, which companies host and support internally. This allows the scale out from Tableau Desktop to an enterprise-wide data visualization solution.

Both Tableau Server and Tableau Public can be accessed on a mobile device. Tableau workbooks are simply served as a website, and they are mobile-enabled. This is extremely useful for people who need their data when they are away from their desks.

There's more...

Despite the demand for mobile business intelligence, there are still issues around its implementation. Mobile business intelligence is a methodology: a design and strategy to make sure that critical data is available in a real time and secure manner. One issue is security, and this affects both internal and external aspects of the enterprise.

Some of the questions around security are fairly obvious. For example, what happens if a mobile device is stolen or not handed back by a retiring employee? Some security implications are less obvious, however. Given that data can be retrieved over any number of a range of mobile devices, security needs to be deployed. While many IT departments provide mobile devices for mobile team members, there are still many team members who use their own mobile devices to access corporate data. Thus, additional security measures need to be taken in order to insulate the source systems against inadvertent behavior by internal team members. This is in addition to the threat from external malicious behavior.

The growing impetus between the demand for mobile and the growth of adoption means that putting cloud and mobile business intelligence together could accelerate the adoption of these individual entities. Organizations could deploy a mobile solution without worrying about the additional cost and management of additional on-premise hardware. Furthermore, they could just send data to the cloud that they need to mobilize. In other words, there would be no need to open up internal source systems to the Internet for mobilization. Instead, the data could be hosted remotely, meaning that there is no need to expose source systems to the Internet for mobilization.

This is why Tableau Public and Tableau Server, combined with Tableau Online, are useful solutions. They offer cloud business intelligence, which means that the management of your business intelligence is relieved from pressure by using the cloud. Take a look at the Tableau website for more information.

How can you create dashboards with mobile devices in mind? Here are some pointers to help you. Remember that people may not have good connectivity. This means that maps can take time to load. Also, the device itself may not be in good condition. Zooming can be problematic for some older devices.

It is important to be aware of cross-browser differences as well as differences in device types. Here, we have just pointed to Tableau Public using a browser on a mobile device.

On a mobile device such as the iPad, Tableau uses Safari by default, but you may also wish to consider Chrome on the iPad as a strong alternative. Chrome doesn't create a new tab for every new dashboard, which allows nice click-throughs. On the other hand, Safari opens up a new tab for every dashboard, and this may be hard to navigate from the user perspective.

See also

- ▶ *Business Intelligence, Mobile and Cloud Top the Technology Priority List for CIOs in Asia: Gartner Executive Programs Survey, Gartner* (2012): http://www.gartner.com/newsroom/id/2159315.

- ▶ *A Better But Still Subpar Global Tech Market In 2014 And 2015, Forrester* (2014): http://www.forrester.com/A+Better+But+Still+Subpar+Global+Tech+Market+In+2014+And+2015/fulltext/-/E-RES104903?intcmp=blog:forrlink.

- ▶ *UK organisations invest in mobility, NCC* (2011): http://www.ncc.co.uk/article/?articleid=16901.

- ▶ *Decline and divide in IT spending, NCC* (2011): http://www.ncc.co.uk/article/?articleid=16860.

- ▶ *Data Warehousing and BI systems let down 22% of users, NCC* (2011): http://www.ncc.co.uk/article/?articleid=16567.

Mixing Tableau with SharePoint 2013 Power BI

Many organizations will already have SharePoint, and a natural question is how to integrate Tableau with the existing infrastructure.

SharePoint could be hosted internally within the organization. However, this business intelligence infrastructure could include Tableau Server too. Therefore, the whole enterprise solution is a jigsaw of different technology services, including Tableau and SharePoint, which enable you to visualize data, share discoveries, and collaborate in intuitive new ways. A solution like this would allow businesses to leverage Excel along with Tableau. It empowers users to use Excel, Tableau, and online collaboration, underpinned with a strong IT infrastructure together in an enterprise solution.

Tableau Server users could have the option to post their dashboards on SharePoint. We will explore this opportunity in this recipe.

Getting ready

For the exercises in this recipe, continue working on the Chapter Eight workbook.

How to do it...

1. Go to the SharePoint page where you would like to embed the Tableau visualization.

2. Click on the **Edit** link at the right-hand side of your SharePoint site.

3. The page will now change to show web parts, as shown in the following screenshot:

BROWSE	PAGE	FORMAT TEXT	INSERT				
			Cut	Body ▼	13px ▼		
Save	Check Out	Paste	Copy Undo	B *I* U̲ abc x₂ x²	🖌 ▾ A ▾ 🖌		
Edit		Clipboard			Font		Paragraph

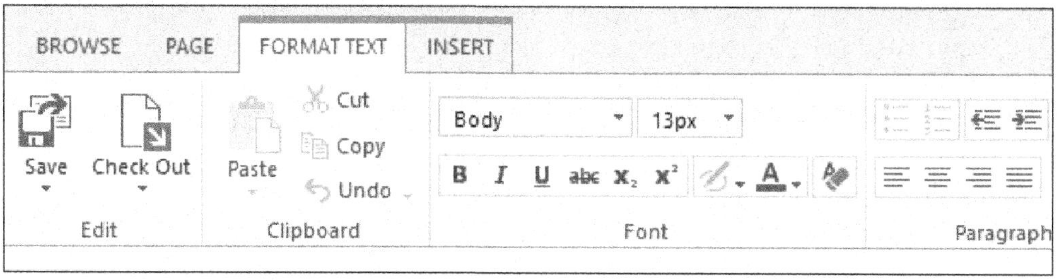

4. Select **Web Part** from the **Insert** menu, as you can see in the following screenshot:

BROWSE	PAGE	FORMAT TEXT	INSERT				
Table ▼	Picture ▼	Video and Audio ▾	Link ▾	Upload File	App Part	Web Part	Embed Code `</>`
Tables	Media		Links		Parts		Embed

Home	**Web Part**
Notebook	Get sta
Documents	Get sta
Site Contents	

Web Part

Pick a web part to insert from the full list of available web parts.
Web parts can display data from other sources, such as list data, search results, forms or another web page.

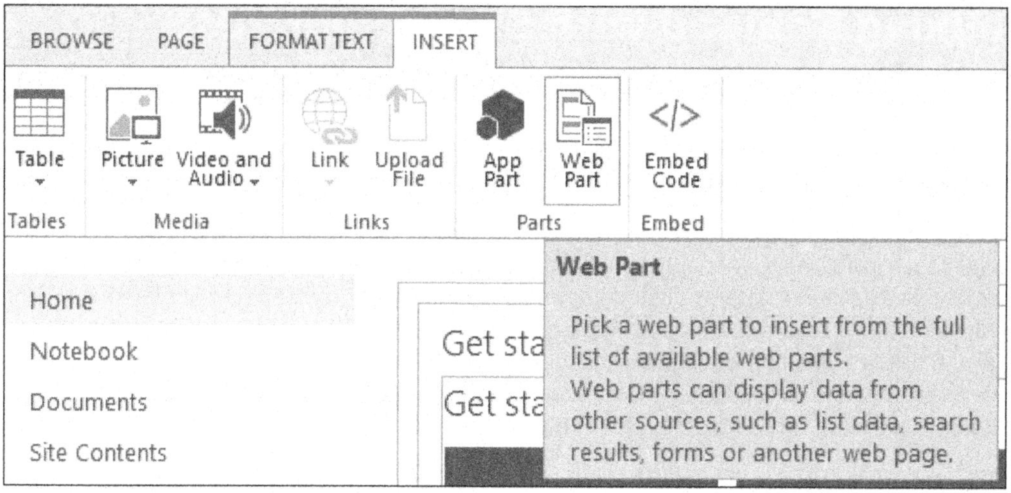

5. Then, select the **Page Viewer** option and click on **Add**, as shown in the following screenshot:

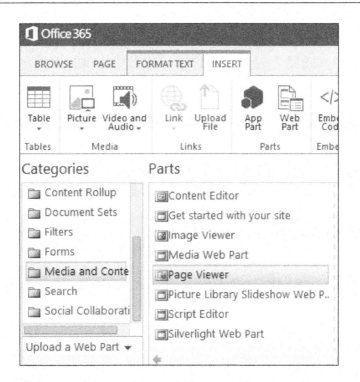

6. Copy the URL for your chosen dashboard in Tableau Server.

7. In the **Page Viewer** edit box, paste the URL for your dashboard in the **Link** field.

8. Click on **OK**.

9. Click on **Save** in order to save your edits to the SharePoint page.

10. You should now be able to see your dashboard in the web page.

How it works...

The **Page Viewer** web part simply renders the page from Tableau Server.

There's more...

It isn't a good idea to mix Tableau and Excel on the same SharePoint page if you are going to allow interactive filters. It can be hard to manage the parameters passing between all the different components. It might also be confusing for the users who think that they are looking at one filtered item, but they are not.

Instead, why not simply set up different pages to show *broad brushstroke* filters? This would be a part of the role of architecting the website. If you have an Excel worksheet and a Tableau worksheet, both filtered to show data for a particular region, then set up a specific SharePoint page that shows both items side by side. In this case, the workbooks will already be prefiltered, and then you will not need to worry too much about organizing all of the parameters for filtering. You then need to set up a SharePoint Links web part with the different links pointing to different sheets. The user will navigate through SharePoint pages, which are prefiltered using the links.

Wrapping up with R – Dashboards as a tool

Why are we wrapping up with R? When you are proudly showing off your data, your audience may include a statistician or a data scientist who wants to take your data away and conduct further analysis. When you are showing off dashboards, it is important to be mindful that you are showing data to an audience with a variety of skills and perspectives. This may include people who need detailed data as well as the business user or strategy decision maker who needs the headline first.

This topic has been included to acknowledge the data scientists and the statisticians in your organization. These individuals may be self-taught or have strong academic backgrounds in this topic. Your dashboards in Tableau can also reach these people, and they can further deepen their investigation by using R.

After all, the dashboard is like a tool for the data scientist as well as the business decision maker. How is your dashboard like a tool? Tableau is fantastic as a prototyping tool, because it can help you create dashboards quickly without well-defined user specifications. This means that your dashboard can grow very organically. Including R allows you to conduct advanced analytics based on your organic dashboards, thereby offering further insights.

Fortunately, Tableau allows you to use R, a functional programming language, plus an environment to study statistics and data science. R has over 5,000 packages in existence, and the range is growing continuously.

This exciting development means that you can use R packages and functions in Tableau's calculated fields, thereby unlocking all of the features of R when creating Tableau charts. For instance, you will be able to use results of R functions to annotate points on a chart, thereby adding context to the data. You can also use the result of R's statistical functions as a source for Tableau charts.

For example, you can color points by cluster using the `k-means` clustering function that is available in R. Since the output of R can be used, business analysts will see the results directly in Tableau without the need to know the R language themselves. This truly unleashes the power of R!

In this recipe, we will look at connecting Tableau to R.

Note that R integration is not supported by Tableau Reader or Tableau Online.

For the exercises in this recipe, we will build on the existing Chapter Eight dashboard in order to access R.

You will also need to have Internet access in order to install R and Rserve. You will also install RStudio, which is a user-friendly way to use R.

Note that this functionality is only available in Version 8.1 or above.

How to do it...

1. Confirm whether you are using a 32-bit or 64-bit system.

2. Your filesystem must allow long file names. To test this, simply create a text file with a long filename.

3. Download R from the R project website at http://www.r-project.org/, making sure you have the correct bitness registry key.

4. The downloaded installation file is called R-3.0.3-win.exe. Double-click on the file, and follow the wizard.

5. When installing on a 64-bit version of Windows, you will be asked whether you want to install the 32- or 64-bit versions of R (the default is to install both).

6. Note that you will be asked to choose a language for installation, and that choice applies to both installation and uninstallation, but not to running R itself.

7. Once R is installed, install RStudio. To do this, go to http://www.rstudio.com/ and click on the **Download now** button.

8. On the next page, you will be given a choice whether to install RStudio Desktop or RStudio Server. Choose **RStudio Desktop**.

9. Look for the heading **Recommended for Your System** and select the link under it. It will be the best RStudio version for your environment.

10. You will get a dialog box asking you whether you want to run or save the .exe file. Click on **Run**.

11. RStudio will now unzip the files and install the program. Success!

12. Once you have installed R, you will need to install Rserve, which is an R package that uses TCP/IP to serve the connection between R and other programs. To do this, open RStudio.

13. In RStudio, click on the **Install Packages** button, as shown in the following screenshot:

Files	Plots	Packages	Help	Viewer	

Install Packages | Check for Updates |

	boot	Bootstrap Functions (originally by Angelo Canty for S)
☐	boot	Bootstrap Functions (originally by Angelo Canty for S)
☐	class	Functions for Classification
☐	cluster	Cluster Analysis Extended Rousseeuw et al.
☐	codetools	Code Analysis Tools for R
☐	compiler	The R Compiler Package
☑	datasets	The R Datasets Package
☐	foreign	Read Data Stored by Minitab, S, SAS, SPSS, Stata, Systat, Weka, dBase, ...
☑	graphics	The R Graphics Package
☑	grDevices	The R Graphics Devices and Support for Colours and Fonts

14. After you have clicked on **Install Packages**, you will get the following dialog box. In the **Packages** textbox, type in `Rserve`, as shown in the following screenshot:

Install Packages

Install from: ⑦ Configuring Repositories

Repository (CRAN, CRANextra) ▼

Packages (separate multiple with space or comma):

Rserve

Install to Library:

C:/Users/Jen/Documents/R/win-library/3.1 [Default] ▼

☑ Install dependencies

Install   Cancel

15. Click on **Install**.

16. When Rserve is successfully installed, the RStudio console will write a message to output its success. The screen will look as follows:

```
> install.packages("Rserve")
Installing package into 'C:/Users/Jen/Documents/R/win-library/3.1'
(as 'lib' is unspecified)
trying URL 'http://cran.rstudio.com/bin/windows/contrib/3.1/Rserve_1.7-3.zip'
Content type 'application/zip' length 713148 bytes (696 Kb)
opened URL
downloaded 696 Kb

package 'Rserve' successfully unpacked and MD5 sums checked

The downloaded binary packages are in
 C:\Users\Jen\AppData\Local\Temp\RtmpgdQJEa\downloaded_packages
```

17. When you look at the **Packages** window in RStudio, you will see that **Rserve** is installed and ticked. Here is a screenshot of the **Packages** window:

Files	Plots	Packages	Help	Viewer

Install Packages | Check for Updates |

☑	datasets	The R Datasets Package
☐	foreign	Read Data Stored by Minitab, S, SAS, SPSS, Stata, Systat, Weka, dBase, ...
☑	graphics	The R Graphics Package
☑	grDevices	The R Graphics Devices and Support for Colours and Fonts
☐	grid	The Grid Graphics Package
☐	KernSmooth	Functions for kernel smoothing for Wand & Jones (1995)
☐	lattice	Lattice Graphics
☐	manipulate	Interactive Plots for RStudio
☐	MASS	Support Functions and Datasets for Venables and Ripley's MASS
☐	Matrix	Sparse and Dense Matrix Classes and Methods
☑	methods	Formal Methods and Classes
☐	mgcv	Mixed GAM Computation Vehicle with GCV/AIC/REML smoothness estimation
☐	nlme	Linear and Nonlinear Mixed Effects Models
☐	nnet	Feed-forward Neural Networks and Multinomial Log-Linear Models
☐	parallel	Support for Parallel computation in R
☐	rpart	Recursive Partitioning and Regression Trees
☑	Rserve	Binary R server
☑	rstudio	Tools and Utilities for RStudio

18. Start Rserve by typing `Rserve()` in the console.

19. Now, open Tableau if it is not already open.

20. Establish a connection to Rserve from Tableau. This is done in Tableau via the **Help** menu item. Then, choose **Settings and Performance**.

21. From this point, select **Manage R Connections...**, as in the following screenshot:

Window	Help		
Abc	Get Help & Support...	F1	
	Watch Training Videos		
	Sample Workbooks	▶	
	Sample Gallery		
	Choose Language	▶	
2008	Settings and Performance	▶	Start Performance Recording
	Manage Product Keys...		✔ Enable Accelerated Graphics
	About Tableau		Manage R Connection...
			Show Messages Again

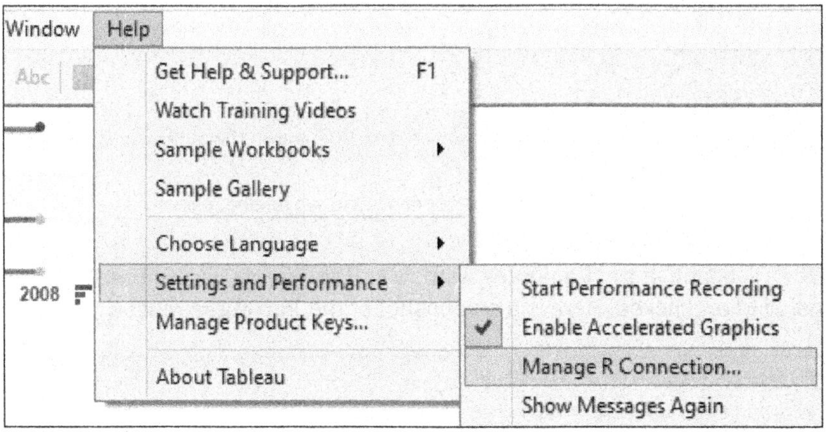

22. You will be asked for connection details, which you can see in the following screenshot:

Rserve Connection ✕

Specify a server name and a port

Server: localhost   Port: 6311

☐ Sign in with a username and password

Username:

Password:

[Test Connection] [OK] [Cancel]

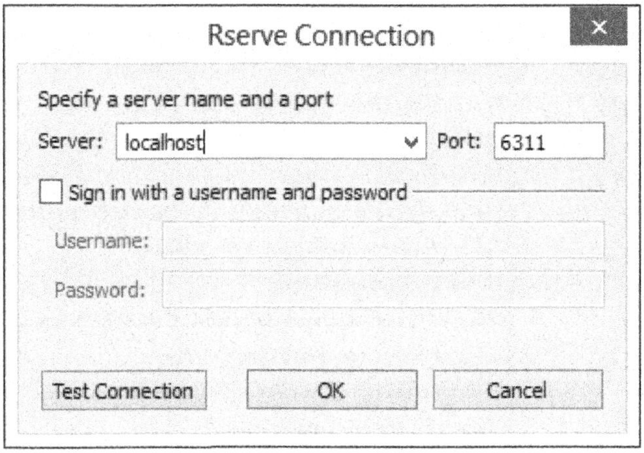

23. Click on **OK**.

24. You have now installed R! For those of you who are new to R, it is worth downloading a sample from the Tableau website, `http://www.tableausoftware.com/about/blog/2013/10/tableau-81-and-r-25327`. This will walk you through the R language.

How it works...

The process starts an R package called Rserve, which uses TCP/IP to serve the connection that allows other programs to use the facilities of R. Rserve has a number of advantages; it is quick because it does not initialize R as part of its startup. It is also cleverly programmed so that each connection has its own working directory, and consequently, each connection does not have an impact on the other connections.

In this recipe, we used RStudio to install Rserve. Tableau offers another way of installing Rserve on their knowledge base, and you can find more information on this at `http://kb.tableausoftware.com/articles/knowledgebase/r-implementation-notes`.

This easy connection brings all of R's data analysis capabilities to Tableau. You can view Tableau as the shop window that makes data visible and accessible to users. R does the hard data analysis behind the scenes.

This means that users can bring the power of R's amazing statistical capabilities to data visualizations in Tableau. Very powerful indeed! Oh, and fun!

There's more...

If you want to know more about R, please visit the R website at `http://www.r-project.org/`. Oh, and be warned; prepare to lose a lot of time totally engrossed in R, Tableau, and data. Data will change your life! Have fun with it, and embrace your inner data love.

See also

- If you want to know more about R, then please look at Bora Beran's blog at `http://boraberan.wordpress.com/` for examples and R's capabilities.
- You could also find some examples on Tableau's solution page at `http://www.tableausoftware.com/solutions/capabilities`.

Index

Thank you for buying
Tableau Dashboard Cookbook

About Packt Publishing

Packt, pronounced 'packed', published its first book, *Mastering phpMyAdmin for Effective MySQL Management*, in April 2004, and subsequently continued to specialize in publishing highly focused books on specific technologies and solutions.

Our books and publications share the experiences of your fellow IT professionals in adapting and customizing today's systems, applications, and frameworks. Our solution-based books give you the knowledge and power to customize the software and technologies you're using to get the job done. Packt books are more specific and less general than the IT books you have seen in the past. Our unique business model allows us to bring you more focused information, giving you more of what you need to know, and less of what you don't.

Packt is a modern yet unique publishing company that focuses on producing quality, cutting-edge books for communities of developers, administrators, and newbies alike. For more information, please visit our website at www.PacktPub.com.

About Packt Enterprise

In 2010, Packt launched two new brands, Packt Enterprise and Packt Open Source, in order to continue its focus on specialization. This book is part of the Packt Enterprise brand, home to books published on enterprise software – software created by major vendors, including (but not limited to) IBM, Microsoft, and Oracle, often for use in other corporations. Its titles will offer information relevant to a range of users of this software, including administrators, developers, architects, and end users.

Writing for Packt

We welcome all inquiries from people who are interested in authoring. Book proposals should be sent to author@packtpub.com. If your book idea is still at an early stage and you would like to discuss it first before writing a formal book proposal, then please contact us; one of our commissioning editors will get in touch with you.

We're not just looking for published authors; if you have strong technical skills but no writing experience, our experienced editors can help you develop a writing career, or simply get some additional reward for your expertise.

Mastering QlikView

ISBN: 978-1-78217-329-8   Paperback: 422 pages

Unleash the power of QlikView and Qlik Sense to make optimum use of data for Business Intelligence

1. Let QlikView help you use Business Intelligence and data more effectively.

2. Learn how to use this leading BI solution to visualize, share and communicate insights.

3. Discover advanced expressions and scripting techniques that will help you get more from QlikView.

Building Interactive Dashboards with Tableau [Video]

ISBN: 978-1-78217-730-2   Duration: 04:31 hours

Create a variety of fully interactive and actionable Tableau dashboards that will inform and impress your audience!

1. Increase your value to an organization by turning existing data into valuable, engaging business intelligence.

2. Master the dashboard planning process by knowing which charts to use and how to create a cohesive flow for your audience.

3. Includes best practices and efficient techniques to walk you through the creation of five progressively engaging dashboards.

Please check **www.PacktPub.com** for information on our titles

CPSIA information can be obtained
at www.ICGtesting.com
Printed in the USA
BVOW04s1420120217
475956BV00003B/40/P